# How
# We
# Write

'*How We Write* is a thoughtful and admirably lucid attempt to explain and demystify the mental processes involved in the activity of writing, using the methods of cognitive psychology, but drawing on other disciplines too. Educators, students, professionals, literary critics, and even creative writers will all find something of interest and practical value in its pages. The discussion of the effects of the computer on the process of writing is particularly shrewd and informative.'

David Lodge

'Mike Sharples pulls back the curtain on writers, revealing the true nature of their work as creative designers.'

Ronald T. Kellogg, *University of Missouri-Rolla*

'Exceptionally clearly structured, and exceptionally well written, thorough and comprehensive. At the core of *How We Write* lies a serious development of the metaphor of 'writing as design' and that gives the book an entirely innovative edge.'

Gunther Kress, *Institute of Education, University of London*

*How We Write* is an accessible guide to the entire writing process, from forming ideas to formatting text. Combining new explanations of creativity with insights into writing as design, it offers a comprehensive account of the mental, physical and social aspects of writing.

*How We Write* explores:

- how children learn to write;
- creativity and idea generation;
- the processes of planning, composing and revising;
- the visual design of text;
- the cultural influences on writing;
- the future of writing and the creation of a global hypertext.

Mike Sharples illustrates the habits, strategies and techniques of successful (and unsuccessful) writers through a wealth of examples.

**Mike Sharples** is Professor of Education Technology at the University of Birmingham. He is the author of *Cognition, Computers and Creative Writing, Computer Supported Collaborative Writing* and (with Thea van der Geest) *The New Writing Environment*.

# How
# We
# Write

Writing as creative design

## Mike Sharples

London and New York

First published 1999
by Routledge
11 New Fetter Lane, London EC4P 4EE

Simultaneously published in the USA and Canada
by Routledge
29 West 35th Street, New York, NY 10001

Typeset in Rotis Sans Serif by Keystroke, Jacaranda Lodge, Wolverhampton
Printed and bound in Great Britain by Redwood Books, Trowbridge, Wiltshire

*British Library Cataloguing in Publication Data*
A catalogue record for this book is available from the British Library

*Library of Congress Cataloguing in Publication Data*
Sharples, Mike, 1952–
   How we write : writing as creative design / Mike Sharples.
      p.    cm.
   ISBN 0–415–18586–6. – ISBN 0–415–18587–4 (pbk.)
      1. English language—Rhetoric—Study and teaching—Theory, etc.
   2. Creative writing—Study and teaching—Theory, etc.   3. Creative
   writing—Psychological aspects.   4. Creative writing—Physiological
   aspects.   5. Creative writing—Social aspects.   6. Authorship.
   I. Title.
   PE1404.S47 1999                                    98–8221
   808'.042'019—dc21                                     CIP

ISBN 0–415–18587–4 (Pbk)
ISBN 0–415–18586–6 (Hbk)

# Contents

# List of figures

## Figures

## Tables

# Preface

Over the past two years I have found an easy way to provoke an animated conversation: I mention that I am writing a book on how we write. People want to know how to teach children to write, how to overcome writer's block, what makes an expert writer and the pleasures or problems of writing with computers.

It is not surprising that people are keen to discover the secrets of creative writing. For most successful authors expertise has been gained the hard way, through a long apprenticeship of writing, being criticised, reflecting and writing again. If the ability to create imaginative and persuasive prose could be packaged up and sold it would offer a direct route to academic success, political influence and commercial gain.

Unfortunately, whatever the authors of 'become a successful writer' guides may suggest, writing does not fit into a neat teachable package. What works for one writer may just stifle another. There is no single best way to write because writing interacts with almost every other mental, physical and social activity. The path to successful writing involves understanding the many different ways that minds engage with the world to create text.

My own interest in writing has been part fascination and part frustration. As a child I was enchanted by the rhythms of language and the patterns that letters made on the page. (One of my earliest memories is of a book to teach reading containing the phrase 'old Lob the farmer' and seeing the large printed words 'old' and 'lob' as if they were pieces of a jigsaw.) But writing never came easily and I still wrestle with words as if they were opponents that must be strangled into submission.

My credentials for producing this book are not that I am a great and natural writer, but that I have been fortunate to work at the University of Sussex as part of a unique team attempting to understand the nature of intelligence and to develop tools to assist learning and mental work. At one point our Collaborative Writing

Research Group contained people with backgrounds in psychology, ethnography, computer science and journalism. Around us were related projects that involved linguists, philosophers and neuro-scientists, sharing their knowledge of how people perceive, learn, think and create.

Our group had a practical aim, to develop tools to assist writers. These tools included computer software (an advanced word processor named the Writer's Assistant) and also conceptual frameworks: ways to help writers understand their own thinking and working. This book's theme of 'writing as creative design' is one such conceptual framework.

Like all academics, writing researchers build up their own forms of understanding and are critical of other perspectives. Social scientists berate cognitive psychologists for not looking beyond the writer's mind and for reducing a complex cultural activity to a set of boxes labelled 'phonological memory', 'encoding mechanism' and so on. Psychologists accuse literary theorists of a lack of rigour and of making an everyday activity unnecessarily complex by using language in deliberately obscure ways, bringing everything into doubt including the very existence of the writer.

In this book I have attempted to do justice to the different perspectives on writing by dividing the book into three main sections: writing in the head, writing with the page and writing in the world. These build on the theoretical frameworks of cognitive psychology, media theory and social constructionism. In some cases I have revisited key aspects of writing, such as genre and the communication between writer and readers, from these different perspectives.

Inevitably, I have had to sacrifice some of the rigour of experimental psychology and the complex arguments of literary theory. I make no apologies for that. There are plenty of worthy books and articles on these topics (and I have included references to my main sources), but precious few that attempt to describe how we write in plain terms.

I have also glossed over some of the important debates. Like a hedge separating the gardens of warring neighbours, writing is a mutual object of dispute seen from many different viewpoints. My own view is that writing is a process of design, a skill that is grounded in the way we use our intelligence to create and share things of meaning in the world.

I owe thanks to the many people who have inspired and informed me. The School of Cognitive and Computing Sciences at the University of Sussex is a stimulating environment in which to think and work. The book grew out of the many discussions of the Collaborative Writing Research Group at the University of Sussex, and it builds on the talk and text of Eevi Beck, Steve Easterbrook, Warren Evans, James Goodlet, Claire O'Malley, Lyn Pemberton, Lydia Plowman, Yvonne Rogers and Charles Wood. The Writing and Computers Association has been an extraordinarily fertile patch of cyberspace, bringing together writers, psychologists, literary theorists and computer scientists in an evolving and illuminating debate. I am grateful to Liz Beaty, Margaret Boden, Ron Kellogg, Gunther Kress and David Lodge for their wise and informed comments on drafts of this book. I should also like to thank Louisa Semelyn and Miranda Filbee at Routledge for the great care that they have taken with the publishing process and for their unfailing helpfulness. Finally, to Liz, Jenny and Evelyn: thank you for being so supportive and for not asking too often when I'm going to be finished.

# Acknowledgements

Acknowledgement is due to copyright holders for their kind permission to include the following material in this book: Figure 1.2 and Figure 6.2 from J.M. Swales and C.B. Feak, *Academic Writing for Graduate Students*, University of Michigan Press, Copyright © 1994 by the University of Michigan; Figure 2.10 from A. Karmiloff-Smith, *Beyond Modularity : A Developmental Perspective on Cognitive Science*, The MIT Press, Copyright © 1992 Massachusetts Institute of Technology; Figure 3.3 reproduced from *Keswick on Derwentwater and the Northern Lakes Maps*, published by Keswick on Derwentwater Publicity Association, 1992; Figure 3.4 (left) from M. Torrance, G. V. Thomas and E. J. Robinson, 'Finding something to write about: strategic and automatic processes in idea generation', in C. M. Levy and W. S. Ransdell (eds) *The Science of Writing: Theories, Methods, Individual Differences and Applications*, Lawrence Erlbaum Associates Inc., Copyright © 1996 Lawrence Erlbaum Associates Inc.; Figure 8.1 adapted from R. Madigan, P. Linton and S. Johnson, 'The paradox of writing apprehension', in C. M. Levy and S. Ransdell (eds) *The Science of Writing: Theories, Methods, Individual Differences and Applications*, Lawrence Erlbaum Associates Inc., Copyright © 1996 Lawrence Erlbaum Associates Inc.; Figure 9.3 from G. Kress and T. van Leeuwen, *Reading Images: The Grammar of Visual Design*, Routledge, Copyright © 1996 Routledge; Figure 9.8 from D.H. Jonassen, *The Technology of Text Principles for Structuring, Designing, and Displaying Text*, Educational Technology Publications Inc., Copyright © 1982 by Educational Technology Publications Inc.; Figure 9.10 reproduced from *The Usborne First Book of Science*, by permission of Usborne Publishing Ltd., 83–85 Saffron Hill, London EC1N 8RT Copyright © 1985 Usborne Publishing Ltd.; Figure 9.11 from A. Wainwright, *A Pictorial Guide to the Lakeland Fells: The Northern Fells*, Michael Joseph Ltd, Copyright © 1992 Michael Joseph Ltd; Figure 11.6 from *Instructional Science*, 2, pp. 119–91, Kluwer Academic Publishers, Copyright © 1973 Kluwer Academic Publishers, Dordrecht.

While every effort has been made to contact owners of copyright material which is reproduced in this book, we have not always been successful. In the event of a copyright query, please contact the publishers.

Part One

# Writing in the head

# Chapter 1

# The nature of writing

The aim of this book is to answer the question 'How do we write?' Writing is a peculiar activity, both easy and difficult. The more you think about how you do it, the more difficult it becomes. Everyday writing tasks, such as composing a shopping list or jotting down a reminder seem to be quite straightforward. You have an idea, you express it as a series of words and you write them down on a piece of paper. It is a natural and effortless process.

Yet we celebrate great writers as national heroes. Shakespeare, Eliot, Austen, Rousseau, Tolstoy, Joyce, Steinbeck, Sartre – they too expressed ideas as words on paper, but somehow they managed to transcend the everyday world and produce works of great insight, elegance and power.

There seems to be an unbridgeable gulf between everyday scribbling and great creative writing. It is not only a matter of having original ideas, though that certainly helps, but of being able to express them in just the right way, to communicate clearly or to excite passion.

Asking authors and poets how they work just widens the gulf. The descriptions you find in books of quotations seem to delight in separating creative writing from the everyday world. Thus, great writing is 'the harmonious unison of man with nature' (Thomas Carlyle), 'the exquisite expression of exquisite impressions' (Joseph Roux) or even 'the achievement of the synthesis of hyacinths and biscuits' (Carl Sandberg).[1]

Even *The Elements of Style*, for many years the handbook of writers and the arbiter of good prose style, has no explanation of the writing process, just questions and mysteries:

> Who can confidently say what ignites a certain combination of words, causing them to explode in the mind?...These are high mysteries.... There is no satisfactory explanation of style, no infallible guide to good writing, no assurance that a person who thinks clearly will be able to write clearly, no key that will unlock the door.[2]

With advice like that, it is no wonder that many would-be creative writers give up after the first few attempts and stick to shopping lists.

Alternatively, we can look inwards and try to analyse our own writing processes. There is no doubt that words well up from somewhere within ourselves and that we can mull them over in our minds, selecting some, rejecting others, before expressing them on paper. But the mental activities that cause particular words to appear in the mind, that allow words to flow smoothly on to paper one moment and then dry up the next, are hidden below consciousness.

So, lacking a coherent account of the writing process, we lapse into metaphors or rules learned at school. I have already called on the familiar hydraulic metaphor in the previous paragraph, through phrases such as 'well up', 'express', 'flow', 'dry up'. Other metaphors for writing include pyrotechnics ('burning with ideas', 'fired the imagination'), exploration ('searching for ideas', 'finding the right phrase') and bodily functions ('inspire', 'writer's block?'). Sigmund Freud, as you might expect, had the last word on metaphors for writing. He argued that since 'writing entails making liquid flow out of a tube on to a piece of white paper', it sometimes 'assumes the significance of copulation'.[3]

There is nothing wrong with metaphors (I shall be relying on them at various points in this book) so long as they are enabling. But a metaphor can too easily become a substitute for understanding. If we were to accept the hydraulic metaphor then we should need to look for ways to 'turn on the flow' when ideas 'dry up' or to 'mop up the overspill' of words that 'gush out' from the 'wellspring of the imagination'. We would soon be so immersed in the metaphor that we could only think through it. Metaphors should be adopted with care, so that they assist in describing writing, but do not act as a barrier to new ways of thinking.

What of the rules for good writing taught at school? The ones I learned have helped me through some tricky moments. They are an odd bunch of edicts: 'a story should have a beginning, a middle and an end', 'put each new idea into a paragraph', 'start each paragraph with a reference back to the preceding one', 'don't end a sentence with a preposition', 'make a plan before you write', 'think about your reader'. Most rules for writing are grounded in common sense and good practice. They can be good companions, always at hand to offer advice when in need, but they don't constitute an explanation of writing, nor a means to understand or develop your own writing abilities. And like most rules of everyday living, they are most useful when learned and then selectively ignored.

This was the extent of our understanding when I first became interested in how to write during the 1970s. There were numerous rules of grammar and style to be learned, a few general principles, some pervading metaphors and many unanswered questions.

Over the past 20 years these questions have begun to be answered and we now have a surprisingly full and consistent account of how people write. It began with the pioneering work of John Hayes and Linda Flower who studied writing as a problem-solving process.[4] They adopted the simple but revealing approach of asking writers to speak aloud while writing, to describe what they were thinking. Through a painstaking analysis of these 'think aloud protocols' they built up a model of the writing process that has inspired a generation of writing researchers. An important contribution of Hayes and Flower was to study writing as it happens.

During the 1980s researchers found new ways to investigate the processes of writing, through analyses of pauses, directed recall (where writers are probed about a writing assignment they have just completed) and collaborative assignments where the writers are observed as they work together. They have built up an account of how we write that describes in detail the main component processes of writing: planning, idea and text generation and revision. This can explain how writers adopt different strategies according to their inclinations and needs. It offers a plausible explanation for problems such as writer's block. And it provides valuable help for teachers and students of writing. The model of writing as problem solving is one important foundation of this book.

But for all its successes, writing as problem solving is just another metaphor. It has borrowed from the language of cognitive psychology, so that some writing researchers talk not about 'exquisite impressions' and 'innermost feeling', but about the 'central executive', 'goals' and 'memory probes'. They show diagrams of the writing process in terms of arrows shunting information between boxes marked 'long-term memory', 'working memory', 'cognitive processes' and 'motivation/affect'. This has the effect of depersonalising the writing process, of making it appear as a self-contained mechanism, within but separate to the person who performs it.

More recently, writing has been analysed as a social and cultural activity. A writer is a member of a community of practice, sharing ideas and techniques with other writers. How we write is shaped by the world in which we live, with cultural differences affecting not just the language we use but also the assumptions we have about how the written text will be understood and used. The study of writing is itself influenced by culture, with some researchers concentrating on the teaching of writing within a multi-cultural society and others concerned more with writing as a professional and business activity.

This book does not reject these models of writing, but aims to incorporate them into a general account, by considering the writer as a creative thinker and a designer of text within a world of social influences and cultural differences. It attempts to resolve some of the paradoxes that face us when we try to understand how we write, such as:

- writing is a demanding mental activity, yet some people appear to write without great effort;
- most writing involves deliberate planning, but it also makes use of chance discovery;
- writing is analytic, requiring evaluation and problem solving, yet it is also a synthetic, productive process;
- a writer needs to work within the constraints of grammar, style and topic, but creative writing involves the breaking of constraint;
- writing is primarily a mental activity, but it relies on physical tools and resources from pens and paper to word processors;
- writing is a solitary task, but a writer is immersed in a world of social and cultural influences.

The book is organised around an account of writing as creative design which I shall sketch out in brief here.

An episode of writing starts not with a single idea or intention, but with a set of external and internal constraints. These are some combination of a given task or assignment (such as the title for a college essay), a collection of resources (for example tables of data about a company's performance that need to be pulled together into a business report), the physical and social setting in which the writer is working (such as in front of a word processor in a newspaper office, or holding a pen and staring at a blank sheet of paper in a classroom), and aspects of the writer's knowledge and experience including knowledge of language and of the writing topic.

Writing is, necessarily, constrained. Without constraint there can be no language or structure, just randomness. So, constraints should not be seen as restrictions on writing, but as means of focusing the writer's attention and channelling mental resources. They are not deterministic, dictating thought in the way that the terrain dictates the path of a ball rolling downhill, nor are they like the rules of writing I listed earlier, guidelines to be picked up or discarded at will. Rather, they are the products of learning, experience and environment working in concert to frame the activity of writing. Constraints on writing can be modified, but to change them a writer needs to understand how they operate, and one skill of a writer lies in applying constraint appropriately. The notion of 'writing as constraint satisfaction' is one of the key themes of the book.

Because an episode of writing begins with a set of constraints rather than a single goal or idea, there is no single starting point. The point when a teacher hands out an assignment to a student might seem to be the obvious start for classroom writing, but it just adds one more constraint. The student may already have been collecting notes and attending classes that form the resources for the writing episode. Similarly, a poet or novelist may spend many months incubating ideas, taking notes and doing research, before starting a recognisable draft. Preparing mentally and physically are normally called pre-writing activities, but they all form an essential part of the writing process.

Constraints act as the tacit knowledge that prompts a writer into selecting a particular word or phrase. As we draft out a text we have no conscious control over the flow of words. The act of transcribing ideas into words ties up mental resources, so that we think with the writing while we are performing it, but we cannot think about the writing (or about anything else) until we pause.

A simple experiment will confirm this. Try to write an easy piece of prose (such as 'what I have done since I woke up this morning') and at the same time recite the nine times table. You will find yourself alternating between writing and reciting; it is not possible to do both at once. Nor is it possible simultaneously to write and think about the text's structure. The only conscious action you can perform while producing text (apart from speaking it aloud) is to stop. If follows, therefore, that a writer in the act has two options: to be carried along by the flow of words, perhaps in some unplanned direction, or to alternate between reflection and writing. Most writers are unable to sustain prolonged creative text production (although, as we shall see later, it appears that a few prolific writers can do so), and so, in the words of Frank Smith,[5] when we write we 'weave in and out of awareness'.

Figure 1.1 shows the cycle of engagement and reflection that forms the cognitive engine of writing. An engaged writer is devoting full mental resources to transforming a chain of associated ideas into written text. At some point the writer will stop and bring the current state of the task into conscious attention, as a mental representation to be explored and transformed.

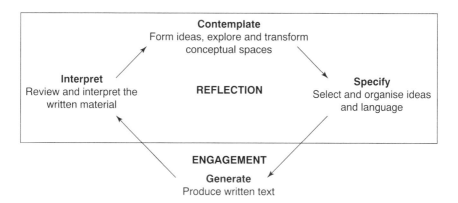

Figure 1.1 The cycle of engagement and reflection in writing

Often this transition comes about because of a breakdown in the flow of ideas into words. It might be due to some outside interruption, a noise or reaching the end of a sheet of paper, or it might be because the mental process falters: the ideas fail to materialise or the words stop in mid-sentence. The result is a period of reflection.

Reflection is an amalgam of mental processes that interact with engaged writing to form the essential activity of composing text. It consists of 'sitting back' and reviewing all or part of the written material, conjuring up memories, forming and transforming ideas, and specifying what new material to create and how to organise it.

At the most general level, the differences between individual writers can be described in terms of where the writer chooses to begin the cycle of engagement and reflection (whether the writer starts with a period of reflection and planning, or with a session of engaged writing) and how it progresses. Each of the core activities – contemplate, specify, generate, interpret – can be carried out in different ways and writers can learn techniques (such as brainstorming and freewriting) to support and extend them.

This is a rather mechanistic account of the writing process. It doesn't capture that agony of waiting for words that refuse to flow, or the delight of conjuring up an unexpected, novel idea. My account of the writing process needs to address the ways by which we create original meaning. How can we summon up a novel idea while writing, seemingly out of nowhere? How does a writer generate original phrases to express well-worn concepts? How have great writers been able to turn a broad topic (such as 'pride and prejudice' or 'the origin of species') into a creative masterpiece?

Fortunately, there is no need to develop a separate theory of creativity in writing. There is much overlap between creativity as part of writing and creative thinking in other areas such as science or music. The underlying mechanisms of creativity – such as daydreaming, forming analogies, mapping and transforming concepts and finding primary generators (key ideas that can drive a generative act) – do not rely on language (although they may involve it) nor are they unique to writing. There have been some recent, and convincing, attempts to explain creativity in psychological terms. Chapter Three shows how these can be applied to creative writing.

For much everyday writing, the account I have sketched out so far is sufficient (though far from complete as yet). A writer generates ideas, creates plans, drafts a text and reviews the work, in a cycle of engagement and reflection. But texts longer than a couple of paragraphs generally conform to an overall structure, a *macro-structure*, that frames the style and content of the text and organises the expectations of the reader. In general, we expect a novel to establish a scene, introduce characters, pose and resolve problems and reach a resolution. A typical

Title

Abstract

Introduction

> The main purpose of the Introduction is to provide the rationale for the paper, moving from general discussion of the topic to the particular question or hypotheses being investigated. A secondary purpose is to attract interest in the topic – and hence readers.

Methods

> The Methods section describes, in various degrees of detail, methodology, materials and procedures.

Results

> In the Results section, the findings are described, accompanied by variable amounts of commentary.

Discussion

> The Discussion section offers an increasingly generalised account of what has been learned in the study. This is usually done through a series of 'points', at least some of which refer back to statements made in the Introduction.

Acknowledgements

References

Figure 1.2 Macro-structure for a prototypical research paper
Source: Swales and Feak, 1994

research paper needs to be written to a tight overall structure (see Figure 1.2),[6] with prescribed sections. Within each section the structure has both an internal coherence and links to other parts of the document (for example, some of the points raised in the Discussion section should refer back to statements made in the Introduction).

A macro-structure is just another kind of constraint, but one that operates at a global level. Writing within a macro-structure is a different kind of activity to recording a chain of associated ideas. Some expert writers have learned the skill of writing to their own familiar macro-structure so well that they can do it largely without deliberation, fitting the words over a well-established framework. But although most people know the structure of a 'thank you' letter, few people can turn out a school essay, a short story, a business report or a technical manual without preparing the structure in advance.

We need to create an explicit framework, at least in part, for each piece of writing. Because of the limitations of short-term memory, we cannot hold both the macro-structure and the emerging text in mind and ensure that both are kept in harmony. Thus, writers have to rely on a variety of means – such as notes, lists, outlines, 'mind maps' and rough drafts – to extend thinking, planning and revising outside their heads. These *external representations* capture some aspect of thinking in a form that can be stored, viewed, considered and manipulated. Once they have been set down on paper, or some other medium such as a computer screen, then external representations become both extensions of thinking and objects in their own right, that can be stored, communicated and manipulated. External representations are the modelling clay of writing. A writer is not only a creative thinker and problem solver, but also a *designer*.

To view writing as a design activity is a great liberation. Writing can be compared to other creative design activities such as architecture and graphic design. Solving problems is one aspect of this broader process. Activities such as sketching and doodling are not distractions from the task of writing, but an integral part of it. A writer need no longer be portrayed as a solitary thinker grappling with ideas, but as a member of a design team situated in a rich environment of colleagues, resources and design tools. Writing as design leads us towards new forms of authoring, such as multimedia design on computer, where text is woven into a rich interaction of form and function.

Even this rough sketch of how we write is enough to resolve the apparent contradictions given at the start of this chapter.

- *Writing is a demanding mental activity, yet some people appear to write without great effort.* Writing involves both engagement and reflection. An engaged writer who has created appropriate constraints can be carried along by the flow of mental association, without deliberative effort.
- *Most writing involves deliberate planning, but it also makes use of chance discovery.* Engaged writing produces texts that become the source material to inspire contemplation and constrain deliberate planning.
- *Writing is analytic, requiring evaluation and problem solving, yet it is also a synthetic, productive process.* Analysis and synthesis are not in opposition, but form part of the productive cycle of text design.
- *A writer needs to work within the constraints of grammar, style and topic, but creative writing involves the breaking of constraint.* Constraints serve a dual purpose. They act as a tacit frame for mental activities, but an experienced writer is also able to represent constraints as explicit structures, either mental or external, to be explored and transformed. These transformations break out of the original framework, and in so doing create a new (and perhaps more productive or original) set of constraints.
- *Writing is primarily a mental activity, but it relies on physical tools and resources from pens and paper to word processors.* It is not possible to write a long piece entirely in the head and so a writer needs to develop macro-structures and create drafts in some external form. Viewing writing as design emphasises the rich interactions between the mind and the external world.

- *Writing is a solitary task, but a writer is immersed in a world of social and cultural influences.* Writing is both solitary and collaborative, in that a writer often works alone, but with a language that has evolved in society, drawing on the ideas and texts of others. Writing as design is interpretive – the writer creates new meanings out of the particular set of resources and skills that form the context of writing. These give each writer and each text a distinctive personal style.

The remainder of the book fills out the account of writing as creative design. It addresses further questions such as: How do children develop the ability to write creatively? What are the individual differences between writers? How do the writing processes of skilled and unskilled writers differ? What can writers learn from other areas of design? How does a writer fit into the wider culture of textual and visual design?

Chapter Two looks at children's development of writing abilities and how children gain a mastery over one of the most difficult mental activities. In Chapter Three we explore theories of creativity and show how these can be used to understand the mystery of creative writing. Chapter Four introduces writing as design, by studying how designers think and showing how writers can learn techniques from designers. Chapters Five, Six and Seven consider writing in detail through the activities of planning, drafting and revising. Chapter Eight focuses on the individual writer and considers the approaches, strategies, techniques and habits that make each writer different. Chapter Nine looks at the visual space a writer creates, and at writing as visual design. Chapter Ten views the writer within a world of social influences and cultural differences. Chapter Eleven discusses the methods and practices of collaborative writing. The final chapter speculates on the future of writing, such as on-line conferencing and text virtual reality, with writing becoming part of a global process of multimedia design and interactive communication.

The book draws from a variety of sources, including experiments with writers, text linguistics, the psychology of cognitive development, and observations of writing in context. Although these provide a foundation, I shall try to cut down on the more technical language and present the account in a direct and straightforward way. Inevitably, this means I skate over much of the theory and tend to choose arguments that support the 'big picture' rather than detailing the opposing views and supporting evidence.

I deliberately do not make a distinction between literary composition and humdrum scribbling. Instead I shall argue that the general mental processes are the same in both cases. The difference lies in how the writer is able to harness experience, imagery, thought and language to creative effect, and for what purpose.

I have also not divided the book according to genres (such as the novel, the text-book, the student essay) nor by the status of the writer (learner, student, everyday writer, professional writer). These divisions are secondary to the continuous process of becoming a writer. People are not born great writers, nor is there a magic transformation from novice writer to acclaimed author. Writing is a craft that needs to be learned and can lead on to particular specialisms such as academic, business or novel writing. Those who develop the skills of creative writing do so gradually, by reflecting on their experiences of reading and writing and by learning the styles, strategies and techniques of written communication. Even the most talented writers need many years of practice to become experts.[7]

The purpose of this book is to describe how we write, rather than to teach composition. But an important part of developing the skill of writing lies in being able to understand the way we write, and how to alter it to suit the different audiences and demands of writing. When we learn to write we become locked into a particular set of strategies for coping with the mental demands of composition. Our own way of writing becomes so familiar that it is difficult to appreciate how anyone could write otherwise. It is only by understanding how other people write, and the writing process in general, that we can learn to control and extend our own writing abilities.

# Chapter 2
# Becoming a writer

Writing develops out of talking. By the time children learn to write, around the age of six or seven, they have acquired most of the adult forms of grammar. But written language is not just speech written down. A child needs to learn not only the conventions of spelling and punctuation, but also ways of organising text at sentence level and above. How does a child learn to become a writer? What are the influences of talk on writing? How does teaching affect this process?

We cannot study children's thinking directly. Asking children to describe their thoughts while writing, as Hayes and Flower did with adults, is decidedly unrewarding. Children talk, or they write, but they don't talk about what they are thinking. Instead we have to examine children's written and spoken language. These are the fossil traces of their mental processes and, as with studying rock fossils, we need to collect together various types of evidence, at various ages, in order to form a plausible account of how children develop their writing abilities. The evidence comes from recordings and transcriptions of children talking, from their written work at different ages, and from the games they play with language. (The account of how written language develops out of talk is based on *Learning to Write* by Gunther Kress.)[1]

Young children are immersed in a world of language. They learn how use language appropriately in different contexts. The ways they talk with friends are very different to how they speak to a teacher or parent. The language between children is concerned with negotiating, confirming and denying, establishing who is in command and what are the rules of their games. Through play, they are also creating imaginary worlds where they can try out adult activities and phrasings. The dialogue in Figure 2.1 is between two seven-year-old children who have just begun to play a game with dolls, winching them up into the loft of a doll's house for a party.

---

*Elaine:* They've come to the party too, haven't they?

*Lucy:* No, not all of them are grown ups. Most of them are children. Including him.

*Elaine:* Including what?

*Lucy:* Him. He's a child.

*Elaine:* No he isn't. He's a big grown-up.

*Lucy:* But he isn't going to the party.

*Elaine:* No, because he's too old.

*Lucy:* OK.

*Elaine:* Everything's going OK.

*Lucy:* Should be pull . . . oops! [*Giggles*]

*Elaine:* He's saying, 'My darling, I want you to snog me.'

*Lucy:* He gets up and then. He gets up and says, 'Now, you kids. Now what are you kids playing at?' And he gets hooked in the back. [*Giggles*]

---

Figure 2.1 Extract of a dialogue between two seven-year-old children

A conversation between children and adults is characterised by the child making requests or looking for confirmation and the adult prescribing what the child should do, or attempting to support the child's understanding. Figure 2.2 shows a conversation involving the same two children, at the end of their play session when Lucy's father has arrived to collect her.

Through conversations like these, children learn to use language in context. A context of language use that is particularly important to developing writing abilities is the 'story time'. This might take place in the classroom or at bedtime. It generally involves a single adult speaker, one or more children as listeners and a book. The language used in these contexts is special to the child. Stories include phrases not

---

*Elaine:*  Next Thursday can I go round to Lucy's?

*E's mother:*  Oh dear. Well we'll have to wait and see.

*L's father:*  Have to see how Rachel feels.

*Elaine:*  If it's OK will you phone me up?

*L's father:*  Or get Lucy to write you a note.

*E's mother:*  That's a good idea. Yes.

---

Figure 2.2 Extract of a dialogue between two seven-year-old children and their parents

found in conversation, such as 'once upon a time', they grip the emotions through exciting and fantastic events and the problems they pose generally resolve into a firm conclusion.

Another context for language that leads to writing comes when the child recounts an event, such as an incident that happened at school. Here, the storytelling rôles are reversed. The child is the teller and one or more adults are the (relatively) silent listeners. What is missing from these, compared with book stories, is the fantasy element. A child who starts to bring in absurd events will usually be told sharply to 'stop telling stories'.

Thus, by the time children begin to write, they have not only acquired a good vocabulary and repertoire of language styles and structures, but can also draw on some basic genres, such as the 'book story' and the 'recounted event'. In the classroom, children will also be learning other genres, with their specialised terms and structures, such as 'describing what you've seen' or 'acting out a drama'. These are the linguistic resources needed for adult writing.

---

Paradoxically, the most difficult form of language for children to turn into writing is conversation, because to do so they would have to act out two or more respondents, taking their turns at contributing. Children can, however, draw on 'partner-free' language from the recounted event and the book story. Of these, the easiest to apply is the recounted event, because the child has already acted as language producer. But now the child is being encouraged to 'tell a story'. The child may well mix in the vocabulary of adult storytelling (for example, by beginning with 'once upon a time' or ending with 'the end') and include elements of imagination and fantasy.

Figure 2.3 shows a story written by a seven-year-old child that exemplifies this 'recounted event' form of writing. There are clear differences between this child's story and one that would be written by a competent adult writer, not just in its limited vocabulary and errors of spelling. The story is essentially an 'acting out onto paper' of an imagined sequence of events. But the child has not been fully able to judge what the reader needs to know to follow the story. The use of the definite article 'the' in 'the rabbit' implies that the reader has already been introduced to the rabbit. As adult readers we can, of course, infer that the rabbit was bought at the

---

one day in the street a sale was on and a little girl was gowing to school and hur mum said take this dinner munny but she knew that it was to much and she spent sume of it. Wen she got to school the teacher said where have you been the girl said nowhere sorry. at home time she took the toy rabbit home and her mum said go to bed. The End.

---

Figure 2.3 'Recounted event' story written by a seven-year-old child

sale; the point is the child, by using the definite article, is assuming that we know what she knows.

The explanation for why young children's writing makes assumptions about what the reader knows may be psychological: the child cannot see the text from the viewpoint of an imagined reader. But studies[2] have shown that children before the age of seven are able to imagine the world from the perspective of other people. A more likely explanation is that the child was fully engaged in writing the story, applying her mental resources to acting out an imagined sequence of events, and sometimes failed to describe in full the mental scene.

The structure of the story in Figure 2.3 suggests engaged writing, with the child imagining an event, composing a short segment that captures it in writing and then replying to the question 'what next?' with another event. I am not suggesting that the child consciously forms the 'what next?' question in her mind, but rather that the writing continues *as if* it had been asked. Thus, the text is arranged around a series of written events, coordinated by adjacency or by the simple connectives 'and' and 'but'. The same story is shown in Figure 2.4, marked up with dividing lines between the events.

---

one day in the street a sale was on || and a little girl was gowing to school || and hur mum said take this dinner munny || but she knew that it was to much || and she spent sume of it. || Wen she got to school the teacher said where have you been || the girl said nowhere sorry. || at home time she took the toy rabbit home || and her mum said go to bed. || The End

---

Figure 2.4  The 'recounted event' story marked up to show divisions between events

The exceptions to this strategy are at the start of the sentences. The child does not use sentences as grammatical structures, but rather as an adult might use paragraphs, to encapsulate complete scenes: the street sale, the school, back home. The opening phrase for each sentence is a marker that establishes the setting for the new scene. In each case, the language structure of the opening phrase is more complex, with inversion ('one day in the street a sale was on'), a subordinate clause ('when she got to school') and a prepositional phrase ('at home time'), each of which breaks up the narrative flow. It seems that the child is beginning to integrate the chain of events that flow from a 'what next?' strategy with the language of the storybook. The use of 'The End' to close the story is the most obvious import from storytelling.

If, by the age of seven, a child is beginning to employ adult forms of language and is able to write to a 'storybook' genre, then is there any fundamental difference between child and adult writing? Is learning to write just a matter of gaining a

There are vans of all shapes and sizes selling ice-cream, hotdogs and hot drinks. There are queues around all the big mechanical objects which you can ride one. Around the side of the field there are stalls and shooting galleries. There is a mini zoo with all different animals of different sizes. There is a band playing all sorts of tunes, there is a bingo stand where you can always hear someone calling 'house'. There is a ghost train on which young and old people are on and seem to be enjoying there selves.

Figure 2.5 'What's next to?' structure from a story by an 11-year-old child

richer vocabulary and a wider range of language forms and genres: the Description, the Lab Report, the Argumentative Essay and so on?

Although seven-year-old children are beginning to adopt mature forms of language, often successfully, in their writing, they are stuck in a developmental rut. The problem lies with the 'what next?' strategy of writing. It is well suited to writing narrative story texts and it can be adapted with little difficulty to simple descriptive writing, as in Figure 2.5, by substituting 'what's next to?' for 'what next?'. But as a writing strategy it is not sufficient to deal with texts of a more complex structure, such as argumentation, where ideas need to be coordinated and themes developed above the level of the sentence.

A child cannot easily develop the 'what next?' strategy into a more mature composing process because she is caught up in engaged writing, thinking with the text rather than about it. When she pauses, the child's thinking is focused on the imagined world. Only when the child is able to stop and reflect on her own mental processes can she break out of the 'what next?' trap and progress towards more mature forms of writing. This can be a long and difficult period of writing development, and one that schooling may hinder rather than help if it focuses on the written product rather than the writing process and on giving overall grades rather than rewarding breakthroughs.

The evidence from studies in the United States and Europe is that the period from age 10 to 14 is crucial to children's development of writing abilities. It will take some space to investigate this, because it involves an interaction between children's thinking, writing and general language abilities, but it forms the gateway to my account of how we write. To illustrate children's writing during this period, read the two texts in Figure 2.6 before you read on. Try and decide which piece was written by an 11-year-old child, and which by an adult, and then think about how you came to that decision.

The texts are on the same theme: a description of a fairground. They are both approximately the same length and neither of them contains gross errors of grammar, punctuation or spelling. Yet the first is clearly written by a child (Anne,

*Text 1*

I am standing near the Surfer, watching all of the people paying, then climbing into the empty cars, then it starting up and everybody screaming and the loud music, children eating toffee apples and Candy Floss holding flags and balloons. It is getting late the children leave and only adults are left to spend money.

The ghost train goes in and you hear screaming, then out comes frightened passengers. Only a few people remain now, the screams die down, the shows pack away, only a few people remain, walking through the quiet empty shows that will be alive once more.

I remembered the penny arcade, the children shouting, winning money losing money, I remembered how the people screamed on the big wheel which they would do again the next day.

*Text 2*

The long tunnel under the parade was the noisiest, lowest cheapest section of Brighton's amusements. Children rushed past them in paper sailor-caps marked 'I'm no Angel'; a ghost train rattled by carrying courting couples into a squealing and shrieking darkness. All the way along the landward side of the tunnel were the amusements; on the other little shops: Magpie Ices, Photoweigh, Shellfish, Rocko. The shelves rose to the ceiling: little doors let you into the obscurity behind, and on the sea side were no doors at all, no windows, nothing but shelf after shelf from the pebbles to the roof: a breakwater of Brighton rock facing the sea. The lights were always on in the tunnel; the air was warm and thick and poisoned with human breath.

Figure 2.6 Two texts on a Fairground theme

aged 11) and the second by a skilled adult writer (the extract is from *Brighton Rock* by Graham Greene). What does the first text contain that identifies it as a piece of child's prose? What does this tell us about the writing processes and abilities of children around this age? How can a child develop writing abilities to match those of an accomplished adult? And what of less able adult writers – are their writing strategies similar to those of an expert writer, perhaps lacking in style and polish, or are they closer to those of an 11-year-old child?

An obvious difference between the two passages is in the use of punctuation. Graham Greene commands the full range of punctuation, whereas Anne has not yet moved beyond the comma and period. But turn Greene's colons and semi-colons into commas, and it is much harder to detect differences of style and language between the two extracts.

We might use terms like 'vigour' and 'sensitivity' to describe Greene's prose, or suggest that he 'successfully evokes the childhood memories of the reader'. But this relies on the skill of a reader to interpret the author's style and intentions, then package the assessment as a critique. Since it incorporates the experience of the reader, interpretative analysis may be a useful method of literary criticism, but it is a poor means to understand the writer's thinking.

Another method is to identify differences in the vocabulary and linguistic structures between the two texts. Many linguistic indices have been devised, but they all follow the same approach, which is to identify and count aspects of the text, such as sentence length or proportion of subordinate clauses, that indicate its readability. More complex language makes texts harder to read. These indices can be useful as general measures of readability, and some teachers and researchers have been tempted to use them as measures of writing development. Unfortunately, they just don't work.

One of the most sophisticated of the indices combines ten measures of grammatical complexity into a single score of 'syntactic density'. A related score of 'vocabulary intensity' measures the diversity and level of vocabulary, word building, and the use of multi-syllable words.[3] Applied to the two extracts above, the 'syntactic density' measure gives the Greene extract a score of 2.93, which puts it amongst writing by children of grade level four (age nine to ten), and gives Anne a score of 2.61, or grade level three (age eight to nine). The vocabulary intensity scores for the two extracts are identical, equivalent to writing at the seventh grade (age 12 to 13). On another, more widely used, readability measure Anne's text comes out as the more complex, with a grade level of 10 or 11, compared with Greene's writing at between grade six and nine. But this should be no surprise. A readability measure is no more or less than a measure of how difficult the text is to read; it says nothing about the ability or maturity of the writer.

---

Attempts to explain the difference between the writing of an older child and an adult by comparing the surface forms of language are doomed to failure. The essential difference lies not in the vocabulary nor the grammar, but in the mind that produced it; in particular, the ability of adults to reflect on their own writing processes. To understand the writing abilities of children and adults we need to look closely at the concurrent development of language and thought.

At a very early age children are able not just to understand language, but to make judgements about it. In an experiment[4] three children all aged two and a half were asked to judge spoken sentences as 'good' or 'silly'. Some of the examples were correct English, such as 'Bring me a ball' and for others the speakers reversed the order of the noun and verb: 'Ball me a bring' or 'Ball bring'. All three children responded with 'silly' more often to the reversed sentences than the correct ones.

By the age of eight, children have moved beyond making judgements of right and wrong and can discuss abnormal language by offering their own examples to correct it. Here, the experimenter is asking an eight-year-old child to comment on the correctness of sentences:

*Experimenter:*  How about this one . . . 'boy is at the door'?
*Child:*   . . . if his name is Boy . . . the kid is named John see . . . John is at the door . . . or a boy is at the door . . . or he's knocking at the door.

What is remarkable about this is that the child is not concerned with whether the sentence matches reality (is there really a boy at the door?) but is commenting on its structure. He has understood the meaning expressed by the grammatically incorrect sentence, has given an ingenious suggestion of when it might be correct ('if his name is Boy'), and has produced three sentences that express similar meaning with different structure.

By age 11, children can play similar games with written language. As part of a study into how children explore language and develop their writing abilities,[5] I gave 11-year-old children an illustration and a story (part of which is shown in Figure 2.7) and asked them to choose, from lists of alternatives, the words most appropriate to the story.

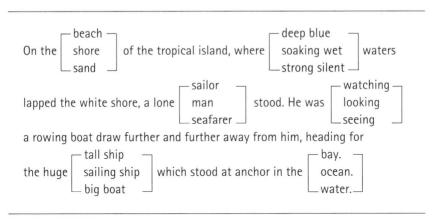

Figure 2.7  Part of a language test for 11-year-old children

The children worked in pairs and talked about their choices. They were able to give good accounts of their reasoning, in terms of specific examples.

*Child A:*  I chose 'water' not 'ocean' because 'ocean' means it's too far out to anchor.
*Child B:*  'Seafarer' is better than 'sailor' because it's old-fashioned and the picture's of an old-fashioned boat.

A child does not need any special cognitive abilities or teaching to be able to think and talk about language. Normal children, in stimulating surroundings, begin commenting on the language of others from around age three onwards. As they mature, they become able first to judge the correctness of spoken language, then to comment on it by example, and then to do the same for written language. Language games such as 'I spy' are part of growing up. However, there is a significant hurdle on a child's route to mature writing: the ability to monitor and control one's own language production.

Below are some examples taken from four adults who were asked to talk about their thoughts while writing. The task is deliberately similar to one that a teacher might give a child: Write a short story with the title 'A Night at Luigi's'. As they wrote the adults described:

- *their general composing strategies:* 'So first of all you need to set the background';
- *the setting and plan for the story:* 'Luigi's will be an Italian restaurant', 'He's going to spend the night at Luigi's without this person turning up';
- *revisions to the plan:* 'I'll change the restaurant . . . er, club to restaurant';
- *the text as it is being written:* 'I ate with gusto . . . er, great pleasure' (simultaneously writing 'I ate with great pleasure');
- *the relation of the text to the plan:* 'I'm carrying on with the dialogue now because it's going to develop the plot';
- *their attitude to the writing:* 'This story's coming alive';
- *writing problems:* 'I'm stuck . . . because I'm coming to a sequence that I don't know whether I should continue or not'.

When children are asked to carry out the same process, of describing their thinking while they plan and write a story, there is a clear difference of age. While children aged 12 to 14 make all the types of comment shown above, the comments of younger children are almost all restricted to reciting the text being written, or to indicating problems.

Between the ages of about 10 and 14[6] children are developing the ability to articulate their thoughts while they write. If they can *talk* about what they are thinking, it suggests that they are also *thinking* about their thinking. In other words, around this age children are moving from engaged writing to a mixture of engagement and reflection.

Evidence to support this claim comes from a number of sources: studies of children's writing activities; investigations of children's thinking; and assessments of children's written products. Taken together, the studies suggest that children's meta-cognition (thinking about thinking) is not only of interest to researchers, it is the key to a child's progression to adult writing.

The first strand of evidence comes from studies of children's writing activities by Carl Bereiter and Marlene Scardamalia.[7] They investigated the ways that children write, by a variety of experimental methods. They compared the products of children who wrote under different conditions, such as being given familiar and unfamiliar essay topics. They analysed the style and structure of children's texts, looking for clues to the child's mental development. They looked at children's processes of writing by prompting them to think aloud and by asking them how they had carried out a recent piece of composition. And they studied what happened when adults intervene in the process by, for example, offering general hints when the child stops writing.

One of their main findings was that writers employ two general strategies of writing, which they termed *knowledge telling* and *knowledge transforming*. Knowledge telling is the 'what next?' process that we have already encountered. Working within a broad set of constraints (such as the topic of an essay) the writer generates language that expresses a single initial concept or event, transcribes it onto paper, and then uses that concept as a cue to probe long-term memory for other associated ideas. The writer retrieves a further idea, writes it down, and carries on in the same manner until the ideas stop flowing or the text reaches something recognised as a conclusion.

This is the only writing strategy that a younger child can command, but it should not be seen as necessarily unsuccessful or immature. It works well for many traditional classroom writing topics, such as 'What I did on my holiday', or 'The nature walk' or 'How we baked a cake'. The child can readily integrate events from her own experience with episodes from story books or her imagination, by stringing them together one after another while keeping within the general constraints. Since it is similar to recounting an event through talk it does not demand new powers of reasoning, so the child can concentrate on the flow of ideas and language.

Nor is this strategy of writing by knowledge telling restricted to children. Adults often employ it for more informal or expressionistic writing, or for first drafts. They set some general constraints – topic, audience, purpose, style – and then summon up a stream of ideas which they express in words, each sentence leading the train of thought on to the next.

When it is well constrained and controlled, knowledge telling can produce sustained imaginative writing. It is particularly suited to popular fiction, where the writer can create an imagined world and then recount events within it. Isaac Asimov describes this as the story 'writing itself':

> What I do is think up a nice, snappy ending, figure out where I ought to start, and then make it up as I go along. . . . Generally on page *x* I haven't the faintest idea of what will be ten pages later on.[8]

The problem with knowledge telling is that it entices children up a developmental cul-de-sac. For the strategy to work, each idea must act as a cue to the next one. The writer holds the idea in working (short-term) memory while writing it down. Then as soon as this is finished, while it is still current in working memory, the writer must summon up a related idea to replace it. The writer's mind is entirely devoted to creating and transcribing a chain of associations; there is no space for reflection.

Reflection means halting, and for young children this causes difficulties. The child needs to abandon the current idea and then later take it up again, either by remembering the previous context, or by re-reading and re-interpreting the text. For an adult this may seem straightforward, but a child has to decipher shaky handwriting and poor spelling, and work out which series of words correspond to the last complete idea. As Bereiter and Scardamalia found from their studies, children often find it hard to re-start writing once they have stopped.

But without reflection there is no way of continually monitoring progress, to ensure that the text fits a structure and moves towards a conclusion. Isaac Asimov may have been able to reach a 'nice, snappy ending' but many children cannot. Often they stop writing when they have run out of ideas rather than have closed the text.

The other strategy, knowledge transforming, begins with a set of constraints as for knowledge telling, but instead of these being tacit, hidden knowledge, the writer forms some of them into explicit mental spaces. Bereiter and Scardamalia describe knowledge transforming as a mental dialogue between content and rhetoric. (It is tempting to think of these as voices in the mind, like Good and Bad Conscience, but it would be better to regard them as frameworks for thinking.) The content space contains the writer's beliefs about the writing topic, and the rhetorical space holds knowledge about the text, such as its style, structure, purpose and audience.

The writing progresses by the writer attending to some aspects of the current constraints as problems to be solved. The problem might concern the writing task, such as how to structure an essay on 'Should drugs be legalised?' This is a rhetorical problem and it might lead the writer to organise the text in terms of the differing effects of hard and soft drugs. This now becomes an issue of content, as the writer considers examples of hard and soft drugs. Difficulties with distinguishing their effects may cause the writer to consider a different structure for the essay, a rhetorical problem. The writing comes from expressing and resolving these mental problems, with ideas being fashioned for meaning and for textual form by the interplay between mental spaces.

Few younger writers attempt a knowledge transforming strategy, and when they do it is usually unsuccessful. Figure 2.8 is a story by an 11-year-old child. Its structure is very different to the children's texts shown so far. It is based around a series of interlocking problems and their solutions. The hijackers need fuel to take off, so they threaten to shoot the pilot unless the police give them the fuel. They don't get it, so they shoot the pilot. Now there is nobody to fly the plane, so they trade passengers for a new pilot.

This is a promising plot, but many of the crucial pieces are missing. The text is so compressed, almost telegraphic, that any attempt to reconstruct its under-lying structure must involve guesswork. Figure 2.9 gives some indication of its

I was on a plane flight 504 to Spain when we stopped to re fuel. Three men and a woman hi-jacked us and made the captain fly the plane to Egypt. We stayd at Cairo airport for six days we didn't have mach to eat because the hi-jackers were mean and nasty. At one time they held the captain at gun point he said he would kill him if they didnt get some petrol but the police said no. They shoit him and they said will you give us some petrol the said yes but how would you drive the plane. So they said some peopl for a captain they said the police said no we want twenty people. I was one of the twenty that got free.

Figure 2.8 Story by an 11-year-old child showing an immature knowledge telling strategy

complexity. It shows my reconstruction of the conceptual structure of the last three sentences, with the solid line boxes representing text present in the story and dotted boxes being my inferences as to the remaining parts of the child's problem–solution schemas. The diagram suggests that the child has struggled to develop a mental plot, and has only been able to translate a fraction of it onto paper.

The main implication of knowledge transforming for a child's development of writing is that it demands reflection. In order to write successfully using a knowledge transforming strategy, a child must bring into mind the overall plans and constraints along with the current state of the task, pose and solve mental problems and explore beliefs.

This brings us to the second strand of evidence that children progress from engaged writing to a mixture of engagement and reflection. The psychologist Annette Karmiloff-Smith has built up a detailed and convincing explanation of how meta-cognition occurs – how we come to think about our thinking. She has based it on a synthesis of experiment and theory across a range of skills including music, drawing, mathematics, science and language. To do justice to her aim of 'taking development seriously' would take up many pages, so I can only sketch an outline of her theory here.[9]

Children develop new skills, such as playing the piano, or performing arithmetic, by interacting with the world around them. They learn as a result of direct teaching, rehearsal, play and chance encounter or usually some combination of these. Over time, they extend their mental and physical abilities until the performance becomes automatic. Instead of picking out a tune note by note, the child can play a piano piece as a whole. Instead of labouring over each pair of numbers, the child can add and subtract across multiple columns. They perform the skill as a holistic procedure, apparently without conscious deliberation and without being able to describe their reasoning after the event.

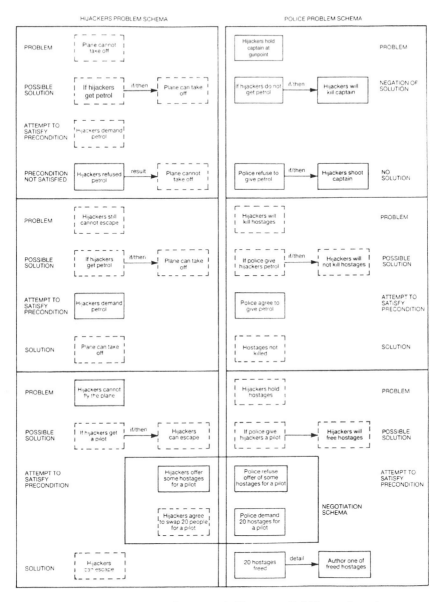

Figure 2.9  Map of the structure of the story in Figure 2.8. Solid boxes show the concepts that appear in the text; dashed boxes show concepts that can be inferred from the story structure

Source: Sharples, 1985

The results can be impressive. Children, and adults, can perform many skilled tasks – such as typing, playing a musical instrument or reading – more successfully without the interference of a conscious mind. But this form of mastery carries the penalty of inflexibility: the processes are isolated from each other and cannot easily adapt to changing circumstances. This may be an advantage for some activities (where we interact with a machine, such as touch typing, or follow a symbol system, such as reading), but performing inflexibly without conscious thought makes us ill-suited to situations that require creativity and an ability to adapt to a changing world. So, evolution has provided humans with the ability to break out of this cognitive trap by capturing the performance of a skill in a conscious, explicit form.

A child spontaneously acquires the ability to reflect on performance, as a result of having mastered a skill sufficiently to perform it as an automated whole. The first phase is to control the skill (though not necessarily consciously), well enough to be able to combine different types of performance and to insert procedures from one performance into another. Then comes the ability to make conscious decisions about how to accomplish the task, and to talk about a performance as an abstract entity.

An example from Karmiloff-Smith's work will make this clearer. She studied children aged five to eleven doing simple everyday drawings such as of a person or a house. First she asked them to draw a normal one, then she gave them the instruction to draw a house or a man 'that doesn't exist'. The aim was to find out what happens when children break an automated procedure. Children as young as four know how to draw houses and people, having practised many times until it becomes easy and automatic. Asking them to draw one that 'doesn't exist' forces them to modify this routine performance.

Karmiloff-Smith found that children of all ages managed the task. The young children and the older ones could change the shape of all or part of the drawing. They could also leave out elements, drawing a man with one leg or a house with no door. But very few children below the age of eight added an extra element of the same type, such as an extra arm or leg on the man. Nor were younger children likely to change the position or orientation of elements (a head sticking out of the side of a body), or to insert an element from a different category of drawing (a house with wings). Children aged eight to ten were able to make all these types of alteration. Figure 2.10 shows examples of drawings from children at different ages.

In order to test whether the young children were simply less imaginative than the older ones, Karmiloff-Smith asked another group of five-year-olds to draw 'a house with wings' and 'a man with two heads'. To the experimenters' surprise, they could in general draw the flying house without problem, and all but one began the man by drawing two heads – but then went on, slowly and with difficulty, to draw two bodies, one for each head, with separate pairs of arms and legs. Often they were unhappy with the result and kept trying again.

The reason why younger children can draw houses with wings but not a man with two heads seems to be that the first task can be done by drawing a complete house and then adding on the wings. But drawing a two-headed man means breaking into the 'draw a man' routine (which usually starts at the head) so as to place two heads on the same body. Eight-year-old children can do this without difficulty, but the skill is just not available to most five-year-olds.

Changes to shapes of elements.
Left: child, age 4 years, 11 months.
Right: child, age 8 years, 6 months.

Deletions. Left: child, age 5 years, 3
months. Right: child, age 9 years.

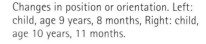

Insertions of elements from same
category. Left: child, age 8 years, 7
months. Right: child, age 9 years, 6
months.

Changes in position or orientation. Left:
child, age 9 years, 8 months, Right: child,
age 10 years, 11 months.

Insertions of elements from other
categories. Left: child, age 8 years,
3 months. Right: child, age 10 years,
9 months.

Figure 2.10  Examples of children's drawings of things that 'don't exist'
Source: Karmiloff-Smith, 1992

Karmiloff-Smith's experiments have clear implications for writing development. The
age at which children become able to control and vary a skill varies with the task
and environment. Eight-year-old children who can insert and transform elements
from drawings do not generally have such control over their writing. The reason
appears to be that children learn to draw earlier than they learn to write. Evidence
from a variety of tasks suggests it takes children roughly five years of regular
practice to achieve a basic automated mastery of a complex skill, so if they learn to
write at about age six we would expect the transition to reflective, controlled
writing to begin around age 11.

*Adventure While Travelling*

I ran out the door an over to my friend's house. I got through the window and past there gaurd dog. Then I ran up stairs to wake my friend, then I woke him. Then we ran to his shed and got our flying suacer that we made, then me and him, took of. Then we destroyed the martians space ship and the in the end we killed the martians. That was the end of the close encounter. Then the day after the martian's invaded earth. They killed humans and destroyed houses and buildings. Me and my friend thought and though day after night how to kill them. Then we got a chemistry set and made a bacteria. Then they came to Britain and destroyed London and all the big citie's, Then the came to Edinburgh. We let the bacteria out of the tube. It killed all the martians and we never heard of them again.

*Extract from* An Island Adventure

I then started to make my way through the jungle. After, about two hours walking I came to the end of the jungle, and there I was at the foot of a hill. I said to myself 'I have to climb that hill to see if theres any remains from the wreckage of my boat'. I started my long journey up the hill at last. I climbed for about 1 hour and I had only got half way up. I looked straight up above me and there I saw some vultures tearing up some kind of carcass. I scrambled to where the vultures were eating and frightened them away. The remains looked like the arms and legs of a man. I looked under the bushes and there I saw what looked to me like a human skull with some rotting flesh on it. I thought the Island might have been inhabited but the thought faded away quite quickly. After that I climbed to the top and took a look out to sea in the distance I saw tiny black dots come towards the shore. There was native looking people in them. After about half-an-hour, they landed on the shore. It looked like they were lighting a fire and chanting something. Then suddenly I saw them killing a native man with a club. After they had killed him a few of the native men started cutting him up. They must be cannibals I said to myself.

Figure 2.11 Stories written by the same child, age 11, at the start and end of a nine-month scheme to develop his written language

I have already described the first phase of writing development, which involves children gradually improving their performance at knowledge telling. Children between the ages of about seven and ten can write with increasing fluency, but they cannot easily take command of the process. Then, around age 11, they begin to experiment with their writing process, trying out new styles and combining different genres, such as inserting elements of dialogue into a story. Later, they develop the ability to discuss their own thinking and writing in the abstract, and can articulate their plans and decisions.

Sometimes the development of self-reflection in writing can happen rapidly and reveal itself through an obvious improvement in the style and structure of the written product. Figure 2.11 shows two stories written by an average-ability 11-year-old child. He wrote them nine months apart, under classroom test conditions with similar set topics: 'An Adventure while Travelling' and 'An Island Adventure'. During the intervening nine months he had taken part in a teaching scheme[10] designed to help him to understand and develop his writing abilities.

The first story is a typical 'what next?' narrative, the product of knowledge telling. Figure 2.12 shows its structure. There is no evidence of planning or forethought. The martians are killed half way through the story, but he has continued with a second similar episode, presumably to fill up the remaining classroom time.

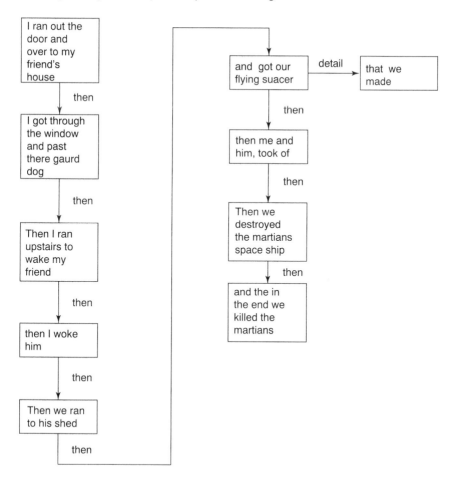

Figure 2.12  The 'what next?' structure of the Adventure While Travelling text in Figure 2.11

The second, *Island Adventure*, is also arranged around a linear narrative, but he has inserted into it sections of reflective commentary ('I said to myself . . . '; 'I thought the Island might have been inhabited') and description (of the carcass and the natives). The gradual development of the theme and the relevance of the actions to the plot suggest that he has built the story to a plan: climbing the hill fulfils the aim of looking for wreckage, and it also provides a vantage point for observing the natives. At sentence level he has attempted to break out of the 'subject predicate' sentence structure ('After, about two hours walking I came to the end of the jungle'; 'there I was at the foot of a hill').

This child has made a clear developmental change towards being able to plan and reflect on his writing abilities. In this case the result is a well-crafted story. But Karmiloff-Smith offers an interesting observation on the consequences of developmental change. Sometimes gaining the ability to reflect on one's performance results in a drop in the quality of the product. There may be a number of causes for this phenomenon. The child may be taking up valuable mental space by reflecting on a performance as it happens, disrupting the flow of ideas. Or the child may be trying to grasp and apply poorly understood, part-baked theories about how to perform.

---

The third piece of evidence for an important developmental change in children's writing comes from assessments of children's texts. Does writing fit the pattern observed by Karmiloff-Smith for other skills, with children's compositions getting worse as they begin to reflect on their performance? The answer is 'yes'. A number of researchers have found independently, and often to their surprise, that children do not progress smoothly in their writing. Harpin studied 290 children over two years and concluded that 'some children appear to advance very little over considerable periods of time. Others appear to mark time for months and then accelerate with startling rapidity to overhaul their peers.'[11] Some of the researchers we encountered earlier have found the same phenomenon. Kidder, who developed one of the linguistic indices discussed at the start of the chapter, measured the quality of texts from children aged six to 13. She found that both sentence structure and vocabulary declined around age 10 to 11. Bereiter and Scardamalia also noted that 'our most successful experiments so far in affecting children's composing processes have not led to discernible overall improvements, as judged by impressionistic rating'.

The implications for the teaching of writing are disturbing: help children to become more mature, reflective writers and the quality of their compositions may well go down. Consider this from the child's perspective. Around the age of 11 a child begins, spontaneously, to think about how she writes. But whenever she does so, this disrupts the flow of her ideas into text. She is also discovering that written language is complex, containing patterns and structures that she barely begins to understand. The harder she tries to make sense of her composing process, the worse the outcome as judged by teachers.

'It was Thursday the 19th, Bengiman Briggs, had just woke up from a rough night at sea, and found that he had been maroonded on an island, Wich island, what island, he did not know.' I dont know were to start its all so strange one thing it looks like a deserted island ('but he was wrong') ill go for a swim its to late now for building a shelter. Splash splash splash. Oh its lovly ('10 minutes later quite far away from the shore') ahhahhahh a whale splash splash splash _____ splash knife splodge well at least I will have meat for weeks. I better find a bed for the night ill try this path im comeing to forest this should be good for shelter, at last ('it was right at the side of the forest where he found a nice place to sleep').

Figure 2.13 Extract from *An Island Adventure* story written by an 11-year-old

Figure 2.13 shows a story written by another child who had taken part in the scheme to develop writing abilities. Over the nine months of the scheme she had, according to her school teacher, become dramatically addicted to reading and she had begun to explore new styles and structures of writing. The story is written at the end of this period. It was assessed by two teachers, one of whom gave it an average score, and the other a very low grade. The assessment is understandable – her spelling and punctuation are poor, and there is little overall structure to the text.

What neither of the teachers knew, though, was that this was her first attempt to combine third-person commentary from a narrator with a first-person evocation of the thoughts of a story character. Her ability to integrate the two viewpoints represented a breakthrough to more reflective writing. The message for teaching is that if we want to encourage children's development of writing abilities we need to take account not only of what children do *better* from day to day, task to task, but also what they do *differently*.

Faced with the evident failure of her best efforts, an intelligent child may well ask herself, 'Why bother? Why try to think about how I write?' But, as we have seen, the child has no choice in the matter. Re-describing one's own performance as conscious thought happens spontaneously once a skill becomes automatic. What we as parents and educators can do is to help learners to recognise this and use it to their advantage. Otherwise the failures may be repeated into adulthood.

Self-reflection can lead to the bottom of a U-shaped learning curve, but it may not be sufficient to carry one up the other side. Immature writing strategies can survive well beyond childhood. Some years ago I carried out a small comparison of inexperienced and experienced adult writers.[12] I set them all the task of writing, in 30 minutes, a short story on the topic of 'A Night at Luigi's' and I recorded their verbal reports as they wrote. The writers were all mature students studying for a psychology degree, and so were practised in thinking about their thinking.

The non-expert writers were well aware that they should plan and control their writing. But they could not apply this abstract knowledge about how they *ought* to write to the practical task. Their difficulties began with devising a story plan. They knew that a plan was needed, but could not produce one to suit the task:

> I haven't inspired myself by setting the scene enough to come up with a story.

So they fell back on a knowledge telling strategy, imagining the scene at Luigi's and acting it out onto paper:

> Now I'm going to go, so to speak, through the door of Luigi's Restaurant and see if having something to eat brings anything to mind.

The one structure that they did impose on the text was to increase the tempo, the same strategy as used by the 11-year-old child for the first story in Figure 2.11. It had the effect, as it did for the 11-year-old, of producing an escalating spiral of events, becoming more frantic as the writers tried to fill up the time they still had available:

> I'm trying to extend the incident now to fill in the time. Got to extend the incident itself so I need to bring more people into it.

The resulting stories were similar to those of 10- to 11-year-old children – bizarre chains of events (knife fights, restaurant burned down) lacking pace or plot. After the event, the writers were well aware of their failure to control the writing as they performed it:

> Well first I thought of a basic structure in my head. Going to a restaurant. Getting some food. Food leading to some sort of problem, ending in mayhem, was the basic structure. Right at the beginning. But then there was how to get from step to step, as we went along.

To become a skilled writer in whatever area – fiction, journalism, technical documentation – requires more than maturity of thought and a command of language. The writer must be able to summon up mental schemas to frame and propel the activity. Just as an expert musician can play scales, chords and melodies from memory, as an architect knows standard forms and properties of materials, and as a chess player can recognise and respond to over 20,000 chess positions, so a skilled writer gains a tacit knowledge of language, style and structure.

An academic writer has schemas to cover the writing of reports, grant proposals, summaries and research papers, at all levels from the overall form of the text to the structure of a single sentence. An author of fiction acquires a different set of schemas, for setting scenes, introducing characters, maintaining suspense and so on. Some can be learned explicitly, from an academic supervisor or from books on techniques for writers, but mostly they are acquired through the apprenticeship of extensive reading and writing for different purposes and audiences.

Musicians, chess players and architects must also serve long apprenticeships, but they generally have the benefits of belonging to a group where they can compare and discuss their performance, and they can call on a specialised language to describe the structure of a musical performance, a chess game or an architectural design. Adult writers generally have no such support system. They usually work alone, and have no language with which to describe to themselves the process of writing and the structure of texts, beyond a poorly remembered and largely inappropriate knowledge of school grammar. Writers can of course read other books and review their own drafts, but most texts, like most buildings, hide their construction. A writer is like a musician with a collection of recordings but no musical scores, or a chess player competing against himself, or an architect with buildings to view but no plans or drawings to reveal their design.

Some college-level books offer helpful and often well-founded advice for aspiring writers and for teachers of English and composition, but they generally focus only on the written product – appropriate language and style – and ignore the writing process. A notable exception is *Writing: Teachers and Children at Work* by Donald Graves.[13] Written to help teachers understand children's writing, it portrays writing as a craft, a process of shaping material towards an end. In a series of case studies of classroom practice, Graves shows how teachers can guide children's writing, by conferring with children, showing them how rehearsal and revision form part of writing, examining and explaining how adults write, supporting the growth of new writing styles and giving children's writing a purpose by publishing it between hard covers. Helping children to write for audiences outside the classroom contributes strongly to their development as writers. A publication by a child is both a record of achievement and an enfranchisement. It demonstrates that authorship is not just the preserve of celebrities and scholars, that a child can hope to cross the bridge to adult writing.

I worked with six children on the writing scheme from which I have drawn examples in this chapter. Four of the children made good progress. They enjoyed playing with language and discovering new ways of writing. The other two, both boys, were hopeless. They refused to join in the language games. They had no appreciation of words as objects to be explored and revised. They seemed incapable of doing more than scribbling a few words in atrocious handwriting. Then I noticed an announcement in the local newspaper for children to write about their sporting heroes. Taking a risk out of desperation, I told the boys that the newspaper wanted to hear from them as football fans and that I would help them to get their writing published. They each wrote a couple of sentences about their local team, laboriously re-typed them into a word processor, printed out the results and put them in an

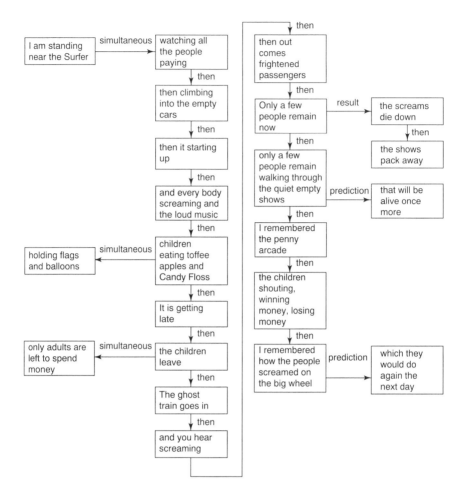

Figure 2.14 Map of the structure of Anne's text

envelope for posting. The following week their work appeared in the newspaper and they became the envy of their classmates. In a report at the end of the project, their class teacher noted that both boys had subsequently sent off several other pieces of writing, to newspapers and a children's television programme.

To return to the two texts at the beginning of the chapter, what distinguishes Graham Greene's piece from Anne's, apart from the central metaphor of 'a breakwater of Brighton rock', is its structural complexity. Anne's extract has a core of linear narrative, a 'what next?' chain of events, linked by the passage of time. Figure 2.14 shows a diagram of Anne's story structure. She describes some simultaneous events, but from a fixed perspective: the view from the Surfer. Her conclusion is structurally more complex, indicating some reflective maturity, shown by the predictive clauses 'that will be alive once more' and 'which they would do again next day'.

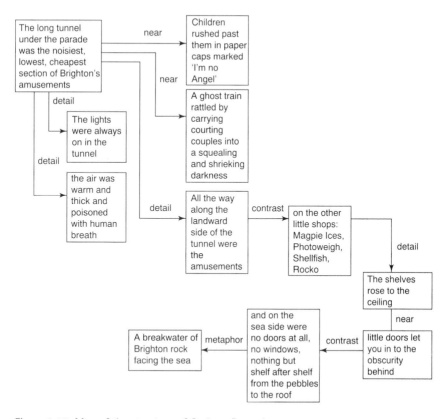

Figure 2.15  Map of the structure of Graham Greene's text

The structure of the Greene extract (Figure 2.15) is not based around a linear narrative, but instead shows a progressive zooming of viewpoint from the tunnel to shelves with sticks of rock. It sets up two contrasting descriptions at different levels of detail – of the landward side of the tunnel contrasted with the seaward side; and the landward side of the shops matched against the seaward side. Its oppositions of amusement and commerce, of light and dark, can be read as a metaphor for Brighton and for the book itself. It concludes by binding together the description of the scene with two statements, about the perpetual light and the stale air of the tunnel.

The labels 'knowledge telling' and 'knowledge transforming' mark out the two broad types of mental activity involved in generating material for writing. They capture an important distinction between producing ideas by following chains of mental association, and setting up mental spaces that can be explored and transformed. Knowledge transforming is a deliberate, conscious activity. Children need to progress to a reflective awareness of their own thought and language before they can begin take control of writing and begin to mould their own distinctive styles and schemas.

But we have not yet reached the essence of creative writing. What is creativity? The phrase 'creative writing' is steeped in the romantic idea of the lone writer with mysterious powers of imagination, summoning up great ideas and powerful metaphors from the dark subconscious. Chapter Three draws on recent research that attempts to demystify, but not devalue, creativity. Creativity is not a power held by a few gifted individuals, but is an everyday activity.

# Chapter 3

# **Constraint and creativity**

Great writers appear to have a talent for natural inventiveness that sets them apart from everyday scribblers and makes their creativeness seem mysterious and forever out of reach. The word 'creativity' carries the resonance of fertile minds conjuring up lasting and inspiring works. Accounts of creativity that have been handed down by biographers and have become part of our shared mythology are about sudden inspiration or raw, untutored genius. Coleridge's vision of Kubla Khan appeared in a dream; Einstein worked out the special theory of relativity without advanced training while working as a patent clerk third class.

Let me try and demolish these barriers to understanding. Creativity is an everyday activity. As with any human performance there is a spectrum of ability and the existence of a few great creative minds does not make creativity unreachable, any more than seeing a great unicyclist at a circus turns riding a bicycle into an unattainable task. Great creativity is usually the product of a long apprenticeship and considerable effort. Stories of inspiration appearing from nowhere do not stand up to scrutiny.

Take Coleridge, for example. He and his fellow Romantic poets celebrated the unconscious mind as a source of creativity, but he also wrote that in some poems 'every line, every phrase, may pass the ordeal of deliberation and deliberate choice' and that it was 'arduous work'.[1] As we shall see later, the popular account of the poem 'Kubla Khan' appearing to him in a dream is more myth than magic. Ideas are not formed in a void – they come from the mind and surrounding resources of the writer.

This is not to say that through hard slog anyone can become a creative genius. Some people do occasionally show the ability to experience problems and their solutions in genuinely novel ways, but this is as much a product of their habits and upbringing as innate genius. Einstein had been encouraged to study algebra and geometry from the age of eight and he took great delight in solving mathematical problems, often set for him by his uncle.[2] The German scientific education emphasised the importance of visual thinking in the sciences, and at the age of 15 Einstein attended a school founded by an educational reformer who emphasised the power of visual imagery and of turning everyday intuitions into clear ideas. It was in this environment that Einstein first posed himself the 'thought experiment' of what it might be like to ride alongside a lightwave that led to the Special Theory of Relativity.

This chapter examines the process of creativity in writing, and if I should make it appear somewhat mundane, then I would argue that this is a great deal more helpful to an aspiring writer than making it out to be precious and inaccessible. Coleridge and Einstein were undoubtedly great and inventive thinkers and their achievements shine across the generations, but the methods they used to gain insight and original ideas – such as dream-like reveries and visual imagery – can be analysed and taught.

To explain how creativity occurs, we need first to make an important distinction between originality, appropriateness and creativity.

All writing is original (except for simply copying out an existing text) in that it generates text that has never been composed before. This is because language is itself a generative rule-governed system. By following the rules of language we can produce endless well-formed sentences, most of which have never previously been expressed. 'Good grammar' is not the only form of rule-governed language; street slang, technical jargon and newspaper headlines are just as 'regular' as standard English. To illustrate this, Figure 3.1 shows a set of rules to produce tabloid newspaper headlines such as PLUCKY GRANNY FREED BY COP. Just these twelve rules are sufficient to generate over 100,000 different headlines.

To play at being a headline writer, write down the word 'headline' on a blank sheet of paper. Find the rule in Figure 3.1 with the word 'headline' on the left side of the arrow (it is the first one in the list). Choose at random from one of the phrases (separated by vertical lines) at the right side of the rule. Let's say you choose 'actor affected BY actor'. Write that phrase down underneath 'headline'. Then, for each of the new words shown in lower case in turn, find a rule with that word on the left-hand side. Follow that rule to choose one of the phrases from its right-hand side, and substitute the phrase for the word. Carry on like this until you get a complete headline of upper case words. Thus, one run through might generate:

headline
actor affected BY actor

| | |
|---|---|
| *headline* → | *item verb* AFTER *situation* \| *actor affected* BY *actor* \| *actor type* \| *modifier event – puller !* \| *actor affected* IN *situation* |
| *actor* → | *adjective person* \| *person* |
| *situation* → | *modifier event – puller !* \| *modifier event* \| *modifier type* \| *modifier event type* |
| *person* → | COP \| SOAP STAR \| BABY \| GRANNY \| RAIDER \| DON \| COUPLE \| ROCK STAR |
| *affected* → | CHARGED \| SAVED \| FOUND \| FREED \| HUNTED \| BITTEN |
| *adjective* → | PLUCKY \| MASKED \| HAVE-A-GO \| BATTLING \| DRUNKEN \| LOONY \| GORGEOUS |
| *modifier* → | TERRORIST \| MOTORWAY \| SUPERMARKET \| NIGHTCLUB \| VICE DEN \| AIRPORT \| HOTEL |
| *event* → | RESCUE \| RAID \| KIDNAP \| POISONING \| ROMP \| DISASTER \| CRACKDOWN \| SCANDAL \| BLAZE \| MURDER |
| *type* → | POSER \| HOAX \| MYSTERY \| SHOCK \| ALERT \| DANGER \| WARNING \| HORROR \| DRAMA |
| *item* → | AXE \| BODY \| LOOT \| DRUGS \| CLUE |
| *verb* → | SOUGHT \| UNCOVERED \| HIDDEN \| REVEALED \| DISCOVERED \| EXPOSED \| FOUND |
| *puller* → | EXCLUSIVE \| SCOOP \| LATEST |

Figure 3.1 Rules for generating tabloid headlines

    adjective person affected BY actor
    PLUCKY person affected BY actor
    PLUCKY GRANNY affected BY actor
    PLUCKY GRANNY FREED BY actor
    PLUCKY GRANNY FREED BY COP

The process is purely mechanical and by choosing right-hand sides of rules at random you can generate headline after headline, such as:

    SOAP STAR HELD IN VICE DEN RAID – EXCLUSIVE !
    MASKED RAIDER BITTEN BY HAVE-A-GO GRANNY
    BODY FOUND AFTER HOTEL FIRE DRAMA

Sometimes they will be bizarre

    MASKED BABY SAVED IN NIGHT CLUB POSER

| | |
|---|---|
| *story* → | INITIAL-SITUATION *active-event* FINAL-SITUATION |
| *active-event* → | *complication action-sequence* |
| *complication* → | MOTIVATING-MOTIF* MOTIVATION |
| *action-sequence* → | *plan qualification action* RESOLUTION |
| *action*→ | ACTION* *story action* \| ACTION* |
| *plan*→ | INFORMING-ACT* PLAN-PROPER |
| *qualification* → | QUALIFYING-ACT* QUALIFICATION-PROPER |

**Figure 3.2 Rules for generating story structures**
Source: Pemberton, 1987

but no more so than ones that have actually appeared in newspapers, such as the classic FREDDY STARR ATE MY HAMSTER. The results will mostly be original (in that they have never appeared in print before) and they all conform to the peculiar conventions of tabloid headline writing.

Tabloid headlines are a restricted (some might say stunted) form of language and we would need a different and far larger set of rules to generate even the simplest sentences in a child's story. But linguists have devised rules to cover standard English and many of its spoken and written variants. The regularity of language does not stop at the sentence. Figure 3.2 shows a set of rules to generate story structures. It works in just the same way as the headline generator, starting from the initial 'story' rule (if an element is followed by an asterisk it means 'choose one or more').

Instead of producing a series of words it generates outlines for stories, such as

INITIAL-SITUATION MOTIVATING-MOTIF MOTIVATION INFORMING-ACT
PLAN-PROPER QUALIFYING-ACT QUALIFICATION-PROPER ACTION ACTION
RESOLUTION

where each item in the outline is a story element that could be turned into a series of sentences (by a further set of rules). Lyn Pemberton[3] devised the rules to cover a wide range of story types from medieval epic tales to detective stories. They are based on the insight that such stories can be described in terms of a movement from a lack of something (in a detective story it is usually a lack of a suspect) to a situation where that lack is either resolved or repeated.

Thus, there is no mystery behind originality. It comes directly from the generative regularity of language itself, which humans acquire, employ to speak and write, and communicate to the next generation of language users. (There *is* a mystery as to how we learn such a complex system as language, but that is a separate issue.[4]) None of this implies that we hold complete, orderly sets of grammar rules in our heads, merely that language is a generative system and that we exploit it to produce original stories and sentences.

Children learn to speak by being immersed in a world of verbal communication, and perhaps also by having a brain that is adapted to learning and using language. Their talk can be both original and grammatical because they have acquired language that is structured so as to generate novel and regular utterances. As they learn to write, children transfer this linguistic productivity over to their written work.

This may explain originality at the sentence level, but what about story structures? We do not spend our childhood uttering medieval epic tales, nor does anyone suggest that we have an innate ability to generate detective stories. It does, however, seem plausible that we acquire the basic story-level structures by abstracting them from the repeated experience of telling and being told stories. We can call on a partial story grammar, in the form of mental schemas rather like some of Pemberton's rules, but in our own terms. Most adults know, in some sense, that a story generally contains an initial situation, active events and a final situation, even if they do not use these exact terms to themselves. And they know that in many cases the central 'action' section is formed from some complication (a problem to be solved; a need to be fulfilled) followed by actions to resolve it. So, even though no story writer will be driven by the exact mental equivalent of Pemberton's rules, as they write they can call on mental schemas with similar characteristics.

You may well have noticed the gaping hole in my argument so far. The language rules generate headlines, sentences or stories, but most of the results will be useless. A tabloid journalist who sat around generating headline after headline at random until one happened to fit the news story would soon be out of a job.[5] Originality in writing is necessary, but not sufficient. The content and style must also be appropriate to the writer's audience and purpose. What is it that distinguishes originality from appropriateness?

We arrive at appropriateness by imposing constraint. Constraints allow us to control the multitude of possibilities that thought and language offer. There are so many ideas that we might have, and so many possible ways of expressing them, that we have to impose constraint to avoid thinking and writing gibberish. Constraint is not a barrier to creative thinking, but the context within which creativity can occur.

Constraints are both external and internal. The external constraints include the writing task, the audience, the tools available for writing and the surrounding world of human and physical resources. The internal, mental constraints are of two general types: content (what to write, including the facts and experiences we are able to summon up) and rhetoric (how to write it, including style and structure, to fit the audience and purpose).

The process of forming and working within constraints is carried out below consciousness by even the youngest writer. We cannot help fitting text into patterns. Ideally, we should be able to apply just sufficient constraint to be able to generate only the most suitable thoughts and ways of expressing them in words. But this rarely happens, so writers are continually juggling mental constraint. Too much self-imposed constraint and the flow of ideas dries up and language becomes clichéd; too little and the ideas rush in an uncontrollable flood.

I am going to call on a metaphor to explain how we generate appropriate ideas within a framework of constraint. In Chapter One I warned against relying on metaphors to explain writing, so I shall use this one with caution. But it is helpful because it gives a graphic illustration of current theories of idea generation, and by pushing the metaphor we can extend these theories to cover creative thinking and writing.

Imagine you want to make a journey from a start point, such as the town of Cockermouth, following some general constraints, such as 'travel east by a scenic route'. Figure 3.3 shows a route map of the area.

You identify Cockermouth on the map (at the top left) and then search the map for a nearby location. Possible routes spread out from the start in all directions, but the general constraints suggest a route eastwards and towards hills (marked by triangles on the map). Thus, you might set off along the minor road to Castle Inn. At Castle Inn you assess the current position, decide that it fits the constraints (scenic and heading east) and record it. You then select the next road that fits the constraints, east towards Bassenthwaite. At this point both constraints cannot be satisfied so you have to temporarily set one aside and so head south, not east, past the hills.

This process, of following trails of association guided by constraints, forms the standard explanation of how we generate ideas for writing. The map is an analogy of long-term memory (LTM). Each town or village on the map indicates a mental concept and the roads stand for associations between concepts.[6]

The way we generate ideas is to start by identifying an initial topic, such as the title for an essay. The topic and the writing situation, along with our own knowledge and experience, form the constraints. We start by using the topic to probe long-term memory. This activates related concepts which the subconscious mind filters according to the current constraints. The most appropriate concepts are retrieved into conscious attention as an idea and framed as language. The writer consciously evaluates the idea and if it is acceptable writes it down. The new idea stays in working memory long enough to activate another probe of long-term memory. This retrieves a further related idea, and so on. Figure 3.4 shows a comparison between idea generating and route following.

This idea generating process is exactly the knowledge telling process that we met in Chapter Two (the diagram at the left of figure 3.4 is a simplification of one Bereiter and Scardamalia used to illustrate knowledge telling).[7] By enacting the process shown in the diagram we produce a chain of related ideas typical of 'what next?' writing.

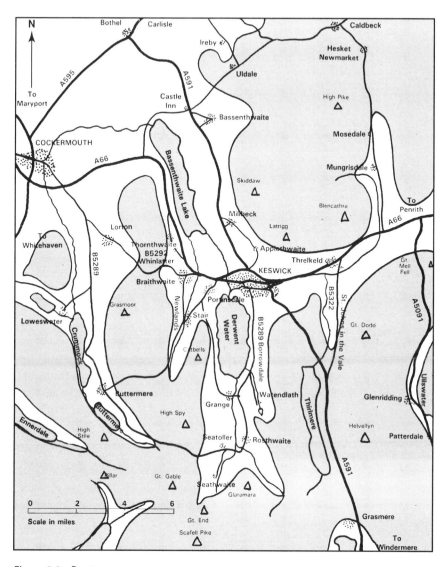

Figure 3.3 Route map
*Source*: Keswick on Derwentwater Publicity Association, 1992

If we take the route following analogy a little further it reveals some other characteristics of knowledge telling. The process depends crucially on setting just sufficient constraints to guide the journey. Impose too many and you quickly reach an impasse (like the traveller at Bassenthwaite with no route east). A mental impasse is one cause of writer's block, when the words refuse to flow. The way out is either to back up to a previous point or to relax some of the constraints. Both of these are classic techniques for overcoming writer's block.

If too few constraints are imposed then the journey wanders around the starting point, or the traveller chooses a few landmarks to visit but cannot find the way from

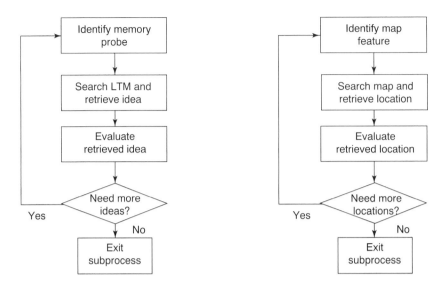

Figure 3.4 Comparison of Idea Generating and Route Following processes

one to another. This is just the experience that the non-expert writer described in Chapter Two, using his own route analogy:

> Well first I thought of a basic structure in my head. Going to a restaurant. Getting some food. Food leading to some sort of problem, ending in mayhem, was the basic structure. Right at the beginning. But then there was how to get from step to step, as we went along.

To be successful, knowledge telling needs to be guided by appropriate general constraints that can apply throughout the task to narrow down the possibilities at each step (such as 'go east', 'take scenic routes'; or for writing, 'follow the set topic', 'use concrete examples'). It also helps to follow familiar routes, which in idea generation means calling on stored mental schemas.

A schema is a cluster of related concepts and constraints that frame thinking and acting. We get through everyday life by applying repeated schemas rather than treating each situation as a new problem to be solved. A familiar situation triggers a mental schema, which provokes a decision or action. In writing, we work to schemas when we call on a cliché or use a well-worn metaphor, or write to a standard structure such as 'the company report'. Employing schemas means trading off an easy, undemanding mental journey against the possibility of making discoveries *en route*.

The basic knowledge telling process, as I have described it, is too limited. Travellers would be foolish to plan a route step by step unless they didn't much care where they were going, were more interested in the landmarks than the route, or lacked a good map. The same is true of writing: writers tend to use knowledge telling when exploring ideas or (as with children) they cannot read their mental maps.

If knowledge telling is analogous to following a mental route map, then the equivalent of knowledge transforming is to see one's mental map *as a map*, and to deliberately construct, explore and transform *conceptual spaces*. (Margaret Boden developed a detailed analysis of creativity as mapping, exploring and transforming conceptual spaces in her book *The Creative Mind: Myths and Mechanisms.*[8]) A conceptual space is a set of related concepts relevant to some purpose. It differs from a schema in that it is accessible to conscious inspection; a conceptual space can be deliberately invoked to solve problems and explore possibilities.

This notion of describing problems and solutions as wholistic entities was first developed by the Gestalt school of psychology. Gestaltists saw thinking as grasping the structural properties of a complete situation, rather than reasoning about its elements. Thus, an experienced chess player does not consider each possible move, but visualises the chess board as an entity (a *Gestalt*) and perceives patterns of strategy. A conceptual space forms a *Gestalt* of concepts for creative thinking.

For example, consider the map in Figure 3.3. If we wanted to travel east from Cockermouth as quickly as possible then we would choose a route of main roads avoiding town centres (such as following the A66 and taking a detour round Keswick). In planning the route, we view the map as a *Gestalt* and ignore the detail to focus on the main roads and towns. We construct and explore a simplification of the map relevant to our purpose.

Bereiter and Scardamalia[9] describe writers as creating two conceptual spaces – one appropriate to the content of the writing task and one for the rhetoric – but it is more likely that a mature writer can summon up many conceptual spaces during the task at different levels of detail (rather like a driver with maps for different parts of a journey: a general atlas, city plans, route maps etc.). Thus, to write on the title 'Should murderers be given the death penalty?', the writer may call on conceptual spaces to evaluate different forms of crime and punishment, to contemplate different argument structures or to compare the topic with related ones such as euthanasia.

Thinking within a conceptual space eases the task of writing by restricting the search through long-term memory for appropriate ideas and appropriate language to express each idea. This can stifle imagination if it consists of over-familiar concepts and schemas. For example, the word 'restaurant' summons up a predict-able set of events (arrive at a restaurant, sit down, order a meal, order the wine, eat the meal, pay, leave) that would form a tedious story. But conceptual spaces, even predictable ones, also provide the source material for creativity.

By representing a tangled web of associated concepts as an organised conceptual space, a writer gains a mental structure that can be systematically explored and transformed. The simplest kind of exploration is to take a predictable space and to play 'what if' by applying simple operations to elements of it such as 'delete', 'repeat', 'negate', 'substitute' and 'reverse the order'.

Now let's say Luigi runs the restaurant and, er, he wants to create an image of, er, a good image, so he wants the customers, he wants them to come back, he wants them to talk about Luigi's, so how would he do that? OK. Now let's say somebody orders wine and, er, he tastes it. OK. So, if the wine's not good they send it back. So that's no story in there. But there is a story if the wine is good and it goes back. Would be even more of a study, story, if Luigi tastes it himself and takes it back. OK. I think we've got a story.

Figure 3.5 Verbal report from an expert writer

Take the standard restaurant scenario. What would happen if: too many visitors arrived at once ('repeat'); or if they did not or could not sit down ('negate'); or if the wine arrived after they had eaten the meal ('reverse the order'); or if they could not pay the bill ('negate')? Operators like 'negate' and 'repeat' are quite general. They form the basic tools for mental problem solving and skill development in many areas, not just writing. They can be applied to any elements of any conceptual space.

What evidence do we have that writers use these techniques in practice? Figure 3.5 is part of a verbal report from an experienced short story writer. He took part in the same study as the inexperienced writers described in Chapter Two and was set the same task, to write on the topic of 'A Night at Luigi's'.

The writer begins by setting general constraints (Luigi runs a restaurant, and he wants to create a good image). He then invokes the conceptual space of ordering wine at a typical restaurant: order wine; waiter brings wine to the table; customer tastes the wine; if the wine is bad the customer sends it back; otherwise customer drinks wine. He considers the main decision made by the customer ('if the wine's not good they send it back'). Realising that this would not make an interesting story, he tries a negation operator ('if the wine is good and it goes back'), and then a substitution ('Luigi tastes it himself and takes it back'). He ends up with a plot (which he then turns into a draft story) about a restaurant owner who impresses his customers by publicly tasting and rejecting his own wine.

Another productive technique is to exaggerate or overemphasise parts of a conceptual space, pushing at its boundaries. Thus, we might imagine a gigantic restaurant (perhaps in a shopping mall), or a greatly extended meal (the movie La Grande Bouffe), or a manic waiter (Manuel, in the TV series Fawlty Towers), or a restaurant in outer space (Douglas Adams' The Restaurant at the End of the Universe). It is not just event spaces that can be exaggerated, but also literary forms, settings and language itself.

Exaggeration of conceptual spaces is a technique used by every great comic writer through the ages. Shakespeare took the language of officialdom to the extreme in the pompous pronouncements of Malvolio in *Twelfth Night*; Laurence Sterne, in *Tristram Shandy*, mocked the conventions of narrative form through exuberant digressions; Matt Groening exaggerates every dysfunctional quirk of a typical American family in *The Simpsons*.

Conceptual spaces can also be transformed and merged. The psychiatrist Albert Rothenberg[10] carried out numerous interviews with creative people and found evidence of general creative processes, such as 'Janusian thinking' and 'homospatial thinking'. Janusian thinking is the simultaneous conceptualisation of opposites, for example portraying love and hatred as aspects of the same emotion. Homospatial thinking is actively conceiving two or more discrete entities occupying the same space. Thus, a great achievement of Jane Austen was to combine convention and passion, pride and prejudice, within the Regency family. Or to give a less exalted example, George Lucas merged the genres of the Western and the World War II fighter pilot movie into *Star Wars*.

Mapping, exploration and transformation of conceptual spaces is not just the preserve of novelists and movie directors. It can be applied to everyday non-fiction writing, from changing the ingredients of a recipe to writing a company report in the form of an open letter to shareholders. The challenge is, first, to become aware of one's own conceptual spaces and, second, to see how to transform these mental structures whose fixed form we have come to take for granted. In short we can distinguish appropriateness from creativity in that creativity involves setting appropriate constraints to invoke conceptual spaces relevant to the task and then exploring and transforming them to create products that the writer *could not have imagined previously*.

---

This is a part, but not the whole, of creativity. Thinking has another dimension separate to the distinction between knowledge telling and knowledge transforming: that of levels of consciousness. At one end is *high focus* thinking.[11] At its most explicit, a writer might deliberately create a conceptual space as a mental problem to be solved. At the other extreme is *low focus* thinking, characteristic of daydreaming, where entire conceptual spaces and episodes from memory are blended and linked by a common flow of emotion or sensory experience. A whiff of perfume, a feeling of loss, a recollection of the taste of sherbet might open a flood of undifferentiated impressions. Rather than being two separate modes of thought, they form a continuous spectrum, so that a person might emerge from a daydream of low focus thinking into a more controlled bout of analytic thought, abstracting common features from the experiences to produce new ideas.

To return to the map analogy, low focus thinking is like putting your eyes out of focus so that the detail of the map blurs and you see only the main areas – the lakes, the valleys, the hills – and then taking some aspect of this *Gestalt* (such as the map's division into three regions of hills surrounding a central lake) as the basis for planning a journey.

High and low focus thinking both contribute to creativity. One way in which they can combine and support each other is through the deliberate summoning of an emotional experience in the mind, until it wells up and drives composition. The emotion acts both as a generator and a filter of thought, prompting and fusing ideas that have in the past been associated with that same mood. The poet Wordsworth (who gave a remarkably perceptive account of how he thought and wrote) described the process as 'emotion recollected in tranquillity':

> the emotion is contemplated till, by a species of reaction, the tranquillity gradually disappears, and an emotion, kindred to that which was before the subject of contemplation, is gradually produced, and does itself actually exist in the mind. In this mood successful composition generally begins, and in a mood similar to this it is carried on.[12]

Wordsworth used this method not only to re-create recent experience (such as his sudden encounter with a field of daffodils) but also to summon up particular memories from his childhood. He called them 'spots in time' and described them as not only 'links with a past self, but [as] sources of adult confidence and creativity'.[13] In his notebooks he followed each recollection of childhood memories with a commentary describing their connection with his current self. By this repeated process of evoking childhood experience and linking it to reflective commentary, Wordsworth wrote his long autobiographical poem, *The Prelude*.

The wholesale transformation and combination of conceptual spaces by low focus thinking can result in the most commonplace and the greatest creative acts – commonplace because it occurs in dreaming, and great because these dreams occasionally produce analogies that can be captured by an aware mind and applied to solve a fundamental problem. Analogical thinking has been much studied as a source of creativity and it would be too great a diversion to discuss it here. But it is worth noting that analogies are born of ambiguity in language and image. Words with multiple meanings allow puns; visual illusions enable familiar shapes to be seen in unexpected ways. By showing children the richness of language and imagery – telling jokes based on puns, making pictures by collage – we are laying the foundations of creative analogy.

Knowledge telling and knowledge transforming are the fundamental processes of idea generation for writing, and the spectrum from high to low focus thinking covers the states of mind in which these processes occur. We can see how these fit together in Table 3.1.

*Table 3.1* Dimensions of creative thinking

|  | Knowledge Telling | Knowledge Transforming |
|---|---|---|
| High Focus | Associational Thinking | Problem Solving |
| Low Focus | Idea Flowing | Daydreaming |

High focus knowledge-telling is typified by the technique of brainstorming, where one or more people agree on a topic and then call out words or phrases associated with it as rapidly as possible. Usually a separate person writes them down as they are called out. The aim is to generate new ways of understanding or exploring a topic through the train of connected ideas. It can be harder to work this technique alone, because there is nobody else to respond with another perspective, but a good approach is to set down the topic at the top of a large sheet of lined paper and then write one idea related to the topic per line, deliberately suppressing any temptation to evaluate the idea or turn it into prose.

Idea flowing is that rare and usually enjoyable state when a writer is fully engaged with the task and ideas flow effortlessly onto paper either as notes or as a draft text. Time flies by and the writer loses track of the surrounding world. Because the activity is only barely moderated by the conscious mind it can be difficult to induce, but it is most likely to happen when the writer is motivated by the writing itself, rather than some external reward, and when the difficulty of the task matches the writer's knowledge and ability.[14]

High focus knowledge transforming is when the writer treats the task as a problem solving activity, setting explicit goals and searching for solutions to the puzzle of fitting together content and rhetoric into a meaningful, appropriate and well-structured text. Academic and technical writers are more likely than novelists to use problem solving as a general method, but most writers call on high focus knowledge transforming at some point to address particular problems such as how to present an argument or express a complex cluster of ideas.

Low focus knowledge transforming is Wordsworth's 'emotion recollected in tranquillity': picturing an experience as an entity to be moulded and polished. This can include invoking more than one conceptual space and thinking by analogy, envisioning commonalities and differences.

All of these activities are aspects of creativity. When a writer just sits and thinks there are no barriers between creative reverie and concentrated problem solving. Indeed, all these processes combine and augment each other. High focus contemplation summons up emotions that can provoke a flow of ideas; the experiences and insights produced by dreamlike thinking become the raw material for reflective analysis.

Traditionally, the teaching of writing has concentrated on just one of these four creative processes – writing through high focus problem solving – with students typically taught to plan and pre-structure their thinking. In recent years, some teachers of writing have encouraged a knowledge telling approach, particularly as a way of getting started. Peter Elbow[15] asks students to abandon the deep-seated notion that they have to plan ahead, and instead encourages them to start by writing anything – nonsense, or the same word over and over if necessary – until the ideas begin to flow. Unfortunately, the classroom – noisy, uncomfortable, regulated

– is just the wrong environment to promote that feeling of timeless euphoria needed for idea flowing.

The aspect of creativity that is most difficult to comprehend, let alone explain, is the claims by some people that a complete composition has appeared to them in a dream. A letter attributed to Mozart describes this experience:

> provided I am not disturbed, my subject enlarges itself, becomes methodized and defined, and the whole, though it can be long, stands almost complete and finished in my mind, so that I can survey it, like a fine picture or a beautiful statue, at a glance. Nor do I hear in my imagination the parts successively, but I hear them, as it were, all at once. What a delight this is I cannot tell![16]

Coleridge describes (in third person) the origination of 'Kubla Khan' in very similar terms:

> The Author continued for about three hours in a profound sleep, at least of the external senses during which time he has the most vivid confidence, that he could not have composed less than from two to three hundred lines; if that indeed can be called composition in which all the images rose up as *things* with a parallel production of the correspondent expressions, without any sensation of consciousness of effort. On awakening he appeared to himself to have a distinct recollection of the whole, and taking his pen, and paper, instantly and eagerly wrote down the lines that are here preserved.[17]

The similarity of the two accounts is more than superficial, and may give some clues to this type of creativity. First, there are doubts as to the reliability of both accounts. Mozart's letter is widely believed by musicologists to be a forgery,[18] and as Boden tactfully points out, literary historians have found that 'Coleridge was not over-scrupulous about getting his checkable facts right.'[19] So, there is a lack of hard evidence that complete works can arise unbidden in the minds of musicians or writers. But it may well be the case that Mozart, Coleridge and others could perceive a composition as a *Gestalt*. Far from being rare, the perception of serial events as a composite whole is the basis for everyday perception. Our eyes continually move around a scene, yet we perceive the scene as a single image. Seeing is a natural and essential activity, and this may be the next clue: the musician or writer is so practised that composing becomes natural and essential.

The evidence from studies of experts in fields involving visual imagery is that by repeated practice they turn the experience of performing repeated activities into visual patterns. A novice chess player considers possible moves, but a chess expert sees the board as a pattern of strategies. A novice radiologist laboriously scans an X-ray for indications of disease, but an expert can diagnose the image as a whole in under two seconds. This fits with another similarity of the two accounts (in so far as they can be believed): they both describe their *Gestalt* composition in visual terms, as 'a fine picture' and 'all the images'. Perhaps, some musicians and writers can gain the ability to summon up musical or textual schemas as visual images.

If we call, yet again, on the map analogy, it may be like living for so many years in a city, and making so many journeys through it, that you gain a good mental city map, so that if you need to devise a new journey you can see it as a line on the mental map, rather than a progression through the streets. Thus, a possible explanation for Coleridge's vision is that the powerful mental images surrounding the 'stately pleasure dome' (assisted by 'two grains of Opium, taken to check a dysentery') evoked a visual schema for a poem, into which fragments of the vision of Kubla Khan were fused to form a simultaneous picture and poem. Instead of creating the poem in sequence he could 'look down' on the framework of a composition and see it fill with 'correspondent expressions'. This is speculation, but the importance of visual imagery is a recurring theme in self-accounts of creativity and needs to be examined further, by looking at how diagrams, pictures and other *external representations* form an integral part of the writing process.

---

So far I have described creativity as a mental process, occurring entirely inside the head, with the writer's only contact with the outside world being to record the ideas expressed as language onto paper or screen. Great creativity, as we have seen, can sometimes come through the involuntary detachment of dream sleep, or the self-imposed isolation of daydreaming, or the netherworld of drug-induced hallucination. All these have been well used, and abused, by writers in search of inspiration. But they are inherently time-consuming and difficult to achieve in the everyday world. They also hit the barrier of a writer's working memory.

The scenes that dance in the mind during sleep disappear as soon as the writer awakes; for most people daydreams can only capture, at best, one or two ideas at a time; drug-taking is both expensive and inadvisable in an office environment. Sleeping, daydreaming and drug-taking are inefficient ways to deal with the demands of time-pressured, structured writing.

The only way to perform complex knowledge manipulation with a limited short-term memory is to capture ideas on paper (or some other external medium such as a tape recorder or computer screen) not only as a finished product, but also in the form of *external representations* that stand in place of mental structures. So long as ideas and drafts are locked in a writer's mind then modifying and developing them will overload working memory. By externalising them, the writer can explore different ways of structuring the content, apply systematic transformations, re-represent them as diagrams or formulae, share them with others, and return to them at a later date.

To take our account of writing further we need to look beyond writing in the mind to examine the rôle of external plans and drafts, and to consider how a writer can manipulate these through the processes of planning and revising.

This is the place to dispose of the road map analogy. It has been useful in illustrating aspects of conceptual spaces, but a conceptual space should not be seen as a neat printed mental map, laid out for us to use with clear landmarks and connections. Rather, we have partial access to frustratingly incoherent, labile mixtures of language and visual imagery. The order we impose on them comes not through detached introspection, but from our interaction with an external world of orderly and ordering artefacts.

Part Two

# Writing with the page

# Chapter 4
# Writing as design

Many writers have, at some point, dallied with the idea of composing by dictating into a tape recorder. It can seem an ideal way to write. You switch on the recorder, lie back with your eyes closed, and start speaking. As the words emerge from your lips they are captured on the machine. Later you or, if you are particularly fortunate, your secretary can type them up. Some highly successful authors have worked this way (in earlier times they did it by dictating to a furiously scribbling amanuensis), including Milton, Goethe, Walter Scott, Edgar Wallace, Paul Gallico, Barbara Cartland, Henry James, James Thurber and Eugene Ionesco.[1]

For most writers, however, dictation doesn't appear to work. It can help the writing of young (grade one and two) children and students with learning disabilities. But a series of studies comparing dictation with handwriting and typing, for business and student writing, have shown that the method of production has no effect on the quality of the finished text.[2] And with dictation there is the added penalty of having to type up the spoken words, or wait while someone else does it.

Why should a method of writing that appears so attractive be so unsuccessful? A clue comes from a further study that looked at the interaction between the type of text and the method of writing.[3] Expository (argumentative) essays composed by dictation were less coherent than narrative essays produced by either dictation or handwriting. It appears that dictation may work for narrative writing, where writers (like the romantic novelist Barbara Cartland) can act out a story by a process of knowledge telling and recital, and perhaps for some poetry or highly personal 'stream of consciousness' prose, but not for the type of composing that involves high focus thinking and problem solving. Unfortunately, that covers most of business, academic and student writing.

Writing by dictation is like walking in the dark. Seeing and interacting with the environment guides a writer just as it does a walker. In walking, the environment is fixed by the surrounding terrain. In writing, the environment must be built, in part, by the writer.

The writing environment is a rich and complex mixture of books, files, notes, drafts and tools for writing. A writer employs *writing implements* such as pencils, pens, erasers, word processors and dictating machines to create, erase or modify marks on *media*, such as sheets of paper, file cards, computer displays and audiotapes. The marks act as signifiers, to form an inter-related system of *external representations* that can convey meaning to the writer and others. A writer also calls on external *resources* such as reference books and colleagues for information and support.

The environment surrounding a writer is not inert, the passive receiver of marks. It actively conditions the way we write, by supporting (or 'affording') some activities and restricting others. To understand the interaction between writers and their environment we need to look not at the material properties of writing implements, media, representations and resources, but how they are *used*.

A pencil is a pencil not because it is a thin stick of graphite in a sheath of wood, but because it can be employed in a particular way as a writing implement. When we write with a pencil it is no longer a separate object, but a conduit for ideas. If you observe someone in the act of writing you may ponder on the properties of the pencil and how the writer holds it, but for the person engaged in writing the pencil does not exist as a separate entity.

What to an outsider may look like a highly unsavoury writing implement, a chewed ball-point pen, or a stub of a pencil, may be just the right tool for expressing a writer's mood or intentions. Steinbeck revealed: 'For years I have looked for the perfect pencil. I have found very good ones, but never the perfect one. And all the time it was not the pencils but me. A pencil that is right some days is no good another day.'[4] The same is true of any other writing implement. Rudyard Kipling, for instance, used only the blackest ink and refused to write literature with a pencil because that was the implement he used for reporting. There is no ideal tool for writing, just the one most suited to the writer and the current situation.

Writing media can also be experienced in very different ways, depending on the situation. Some writers like the crisp purity of a sheet of white paper. Others prefer to write in a familiar well-thumbed notebook. Alexandre Dumas used blue paper for novels, pink for journalism and yellow for poetry.[5] These are not trivial obsessions. For many writers, their environment is fragile. If everything 'feels right' then they can concentrate on the flow of ideas into text. Any disturbance draws their attention away from the act of writing. Although the way writers experience different implements and media can be highly personal it is possible to analyse the effects by considering what activities they afford and restrict.

A dictating machine or tape recorder, as we have seen, allows the words to flow freely but provides no means of viewing the text as a whole, nor of seeing the words as they emerge.

Typewriters have a single purpose, to record the flow of words. They are suited to writing that is rapid and conversational. As Marshall McLuhan put it:

> The rhythm of typing favours short, concise sentences, sentences with oral form. The typewriter makes you more conscious of the acoustic qualities of words, since the words themselves are produced in a background of sound. There's a tendency to say words to the typewriter.[6]

Typewritten text is separated from the writer. It appears, by the magic of the mechanism, in neat letterforms on the page. Some writers are inspired by seeing their efforts presented in an elegant typefont. For others typewritten text seems remote, with a finality that discourages revision.

The pen or pencil is the most intimate of writing implements. It is always ready to hand. The writer carves out each word on the page and the style of the handwriting indicates the speed and care of the writer. The hand moves steadily onwards, offering a more continuous engagement than the staccato rhythm of the type-writer. Pen and paper are also highly adaptable. They can accommodate many types of writing, from a hurried scribble to a carefully crafted manuscript. Margin notes, annotations, lists, diagrams, deletions and revisions can all be set down together on the page as a permanent reminder of the writer's activity.

What neither the typewriter nor the pen provides is the means for text to be easily revised. The writer fixes an impression on the page. Paper is flexible (literally and metaphorically) but the marks on paper are hard to move or delete. By contrast the computer word processor allows words to be shifted or revised at will. In Daniel Chandler's evocative phrase, 'Words are no longer carved in stone, they dance in light.' However, with a word processor, the writer's view of the text is restricted to a small window on a large document, making it difficult to gain a good 'sense of the text'.[7]

Table 4.1 maps five common writing media – computer screen, sheets of paper, file cards, dictating machine, sticky notelets, white board – against their properties as supports for writing. A tick shows that the medium demonstrates the property in normal usage (whiteboards, for example, could be made portable, but normally are not), and a question mark indicates that it could provide some support. The properties are:

*Entire document.* An entire document of medium length can be held on the medium.
*Usable in end product.* The material can be used directly in the final document, without the need for transcribing or rewriting.
*Portable.* The material is easy to carry around.

*Overview.* The writer can rapidly gain an overview of a large document

*Allows reordering.* The items can be easily reordered.

*Allows non-linear organisation.* Items can be grouped spatially, or by means of explicit links, into networks, tree structures, tables, and so on.

*Permanent.* The material can be kept permanently available, for re-use in other documents.

*Allows annotations.* The items can be annotated with memo notes, highlights, and so on.

*Copyable.* All or part of the material can easily be copied.

*Indexable.* Items can be accessed rapidly by means of an index created on the same medium.

*Re-representable.* One type of representational structure can be transformed automatically into another type, for example a document can be presented as an outline.

The table shows that sheets of paper, file cards and the computer screen all score well in their support for writing. Paper has the benefit of providing an overview of the text (for example by laying the sheets side by side). File cards can be laid out in non-linear organisations. A computer gives the ability to change representations. Conversely, no single medium is ideal for writing. Each writing medium supports some activities while impeding others. A writer who reaches for a sheet of paper or switches on a word processor is making an important decision, often unconsciously, about how to write.

*Table 4.1* Writing media and their properties

|  | Computer screen | Sheets of paper | File cards | Tape recorder | Sticky notelets | White board |
|---|---|---|---|---|---|---|
| Entire document | ✓ | ✓ | ? | ✓ |  |  |
| Usable in end product | ✓ | ? |  |  |  |  |
| Portable | ? | ✓ | ✓ | ✓ | ✓ |  |
| Overview |  | ✓ | ? |  |  | ✓ |
| Reordering | ✓ |  | ✓ |  | ✓ | ✓ |
| Non-linear organisation | ? | ? | ✓ |  | ✓ | ✓ |
| Permanent | ✓ | ✓ | ✓ | ✓ | ? |  |
| Annotations | ? | ✓ | ✓ |  | ✓ | ✓ |
| Copyable | ✓ | ✓ | ? | ? | ? |  |
| Indexable | ✓ | ✓ | ✓ | ? |  |  |
| Re-representable | ✓ |  |  |  |  |  |

Although it performs other duties, such as something to chew, twirl, tap or scratch your head with, the prime function of a writing implement is to make marks on some external medium (invisible marks in the case of a tape recorder). And the prime function of a writing medium is to be a holder of external representations.

The term 'external representations' refers to everything that a writer produces outside the head as part of a writing task, including notes, doodles, sketches, outlines, tables, spreadsheets, diagrams, draft text and annotations. External representations are not simply thoughts made concrete. They have their own intrinsic properties.

The words of a text form a *linear* order. A list also has a linear order, with the items consisting of notes rather than fully-formed text. An outline for a text indicates a *hierarchy*, of headings and sub-headings. A concept map shows a *network* of interlinked items. A table shows *systematic relationships*. Each type of structure makes some operations easy and restricts others. For example, it is easy to reorder elements in a list, but harder to show cross references. Making links between elements in a network is simple, but arranging them into a linear order is harder.

By externalising thoughts as written language, we can record them, transmit them and present them for copying and publication. Although external representations can be described in abstract terms (such as the number of items they contain, their order or their meaning) they can only be preserved and communicated across time and space by being made concrete.

Here is a central dilemma of writing. Ideas and spoken words are ephemeral. As soon as they are expressed they begin to fade in the minds of listeners. To preserve them, words and ideas need to be recorded on some medium: paper, audiotape, computer. Once captured, however, they ossify. An idea written down becomes dissociated from the mind that produced it. Words on paper cannot answer questions or engage in conversation, and the further removed they are from the situation in which they were written, the more they hide their provenance. Writing, then, is a continual struggle to find ways of keeping alive one's ideas and intentions, while also preserving them in a form that allows them to be stored, copied and communicated to a distant audience.

Over many centuries writers have devised ways to communicate the vibrancy of meaning to an audience through inert media. Poetry and playscripts, illuminated manuscripts and illustrations are all ways that writers have found of exploiting a combination of external representations and media to create new forms of expression.

So far, we have the classic image of a lone writer sitting in front of a sheet of paper or a word processor screen struggling to communicate to a distant audience. Although some writing is lonely and difficult, most is quite mundane, fairly easy and carried out as a part of everyday life. Even the most solitary of writers relies on resources such as a dictionary and thesaurus. We continually reshape the ideas and words of others for our own needs. If it is done deliberately and extensively then it becomes unacceptable copying and plagiarism, but we cannot help reusing the imagery, ideas and expressions of others. Even the most original of writers cannot avoid the occasional cliché, and none of us can escape the meanings and influences of the world around. Later chapters will explore writing in the world, but for the moment consider how that most elementary of writing activities, making a shopping list, is shaped by the writer's surroundings.

In making a shopping list we generally start with a broad goal: to write out a list of items to buy. We pick up a pen or pencil and find a piece of paper large enough to hold the list, but small enough to fit easily in the pocket. Then we might wander round the kitchen looking for items of food that have run short and need to be replaced. We write down the items that we need in an order that is prompted by discovering spaces in the cupboards. Or we might think ahead and group them in a way that would assist the shopping trip. Each item in the list is written in a way that enables us to read and understand it some minutes or hours later, but it need not be understandable by anyone else. Even this simple and relatively effortless writing task involves choosing a writing implement and medium, simultaneously writing and interacting with the environment of the kitchen, and creating an external representation with an order of items and style of writing that assists the shopping.

Writing is 'a conscious and creative communication with materials to achieve a human effect'. This phrase comes not from an account of the writing process, but from a book on design, as a definition of the design process. The only alteration I would make to it is to add 'and through' before 'materials': Writing (and design in general) is a conscious and creative communication *with* and *through* materials to achieve a human effect.

Bryan Lawson, in his influential book on *How Designers Think*,[8] lists the essential qualities of design. All of them apply equally to writing:

• *Design problems are open-ended and cannot be fully specified.* They are not like the classic problem-solving processes studied by cognitive psychologists, such as chess or the Tower of Hanoi, with a fixed goal and a sequence of problem states, each of which can be evaluated in terms of its nearness to the goal. The goals of design emerge or are clarified during the activity. We can fix a single main goal of a writing task only in the broadest of terms (such as 'to write a book on How We Write', or 'to write an essay on The Origins of the Second World War'). At the level most immediately helpful to the writer, that of providing a guide to action, the goals are vague, multifarious and continually changing. (If I think about my own goals at this moment, they include: to characterise writing as design; to explain writing goals; to write in an engaging style; to provide examples; to use standard English; to express my current ideas; to write the next word.) The number of goals a designer may have are uncountably large, as are the number of actions that could be performed at any point.

- *The design process is endless.* A designer is faced with an inexhaustible number of possible solutions, and when to end the design process is a matter of judgement. It follows that a designer is rarely pleased with the product, but stops when it no longer seems worth the effort of trying to improve its quality, or when halted by some external factor such as running out of time and resources. What a designer intends can never be rendered exactly. The more original the message, the more a designer has a feeling of having inadequately expressed it. 'That is why it is dangerous to let an author correct his own proofs; he always wants to rewrite the book.'[9]

- *There is no infallibly correct process of design.* There are many different and equally successful approaches, and good designers are able to control and vary their strategies according to the task. It follows, too, that there is no single way to teach or learn design. Along the way, this book will suggest useful techniques for writing, such as notes networking, freewriting and writing to macro-structures, but their usefulness always depends on the writer's situation, purpose and audience.

- *The process involves finding as well as solving problems.* The design process does not consist of a neat sequence of steps leading up to a finished product, and much of a designer's time is spent in identifying and refining the problem. In Lawson's words, 'It is central to modern thinking about design that problems and solutions are seen as emerging together rather than one following logically upon another.'[10] This mirrors modern thinking about writing, beginning with the insight of Flower and Hayes that 'the act of writing is best described as the act of juggling a number of simultaneous constraints. This is in contrast to seeing it as a series of discrete stages or steps that add up to a finished product.'[11]

- *Design inevitably involves subjective value judgement.* A designer asks questions that are value-laden and produces products that can only be judged by a subjective assessment of quality.

- *Design is a prescriptive activity.* Unlike the process of scientific discovery, where the aim is to describe the world, design is concerned with what might, could and should be. It prescribes and creates the future, and so demands ethical scrutiny.[12]

- *Designers work in the context of a need for action.* Design is a process that will result in some change to the environment. The environmental impact of writing is normally less than that of engineering or architecture, because writing changes the landscape of thought. We can easily produce cases (such as *The Communist Manifesto*) where texts have incited great actions, but this hides the fact that all writing produces an effect on the reader (such as informing or persuading), and all writing can act as the inspiration and source material for further writing activity.

Given that writing is a design activity, at least in so far as it fits the essential properties of design set out by Lawson, this raises the question 'What can writers learn from designers?' The most obvious lesson is that texts, and other external representations, are artefacts that can be shaped and revised. However, there are also some particular aspects of design that can inform writing. Two important ones are *primary generators* and *design languages*.

A *primary generator* is a powerful but easily stated idea that a designer summons up early in the task to prompt and guide the activity. The term is due to Darke,[13] who interviewed British architects about their intentions when designing local authority housing. She found that the architects tended to latch onto an idea or aspect of the problem very early in the design process. It might be to create a mews-like street, or to build around an open space, or to keep the roofs level despite undulating ground. The idea narrows down the set of possible solutions and acts as a framework around which to create the design. The architects then typically create some rough designs to express the essence of the primary generator and then explore them to see what other ideas they evoke.

Some novelists have described their initial process of forming ideas in very similar terms. Faulkner[14] talks of a story coming to him in a 'single idea or mental picture'. After that, the writing of the story is 'simply a matter of working up to that moment, to explain why it happened or what caused it to follow'. Gabriel García Márquez describes a similar process in creating the tone of 'magical realism' for *One Hundred Years of Solitude*:

> I had an idea of what I wanted to do, but there was something missing and I was not sure what it was until one day I discovered the right tone – the tone that I eventually used in *One Hundred Years of Solitude*. It was based on the way my grandmother used to tell her stories. She told things that sounded supernatural and fantastic, but she told them with complete naturalness. When I finally discovered the tone I had to use, I sat down for eighteen months and worked every day.[15]

It is not just great writers that can benefit from a primary generator, nor does it need months of waiting for inspiration. The essay topic that a teacher gives to a writing class can also act as a primary generator. A good topic, such as 'A Night at Luigi's', has resonances that provoke questions in the writer's mind. Who is Luigi? What kind of a place does he own? What happens there at night? Unfortunately, all too many essay topics close off idea generation, either because they summon up mundane events with little scope for imagination ('What I did on my holidays') or because they are beyond what the writer might know or could easily find out ('Why do some children take drugs?').

To be effective, a primary generator should provoke rather than answer questions. It should be within the scope of what a person already knows or can learn with the assistance of a teacher or colleague.[16] And it should be relevant to the writer's needs and interests.

A writer can call on any of the techniques of creativity discussed in Chapter Three – such as brainstorming, exploring and extending conceptual spaces, Janusian thinking, or homospatial thinking – to summon up a primary generator. For academic writers, a primary generator may come in the form of a research question or a thesis proposal. These early ideas can influence both the writing and the research process. In academic texts the writer often states the primary generator explicitly in the introduction or title. For this book it is 'writing as creative design'. I had intended for some years to produce a book on the psychology of writing, but I couldn't find a way to express my understanding that writing occurs in the world, not just the head. Also, some years ago when I was carrying out research into cognition and writing, a colleague had made the telling comment that I could not hope to provide a complete account of writing unless I could explain creativity. After some years of writing worthy but piecemeal academic articles, I read two books that resonated with my views of how people write. *The Creative Mind*, by Margaret Boden, offers a compelling explanation of creativity. Although it draws on studies of great writers, artists and scientists, it presents the creative process in a way that includes everyday thinking. Bryan Lawson's *How Designers Think* discusses the psychology of design through techniques and examples that apply just as well to writers as to architects. The books prompted me to think about whether their accounts are comprehensive and appropriate to writing and that formed the primary generator for this book: can writing be described in terms of creativity and design?

As their work progresses, designers gain further insight into the problem and this may lead them to reject or modify the primary generator. A primary generator can sometimes block design by raising unanswerable questions, or monumental practical problems (such as John Utzon's outstanding but almost unworkable design for the Sydney Opera House), but if the designer succeeds in overcoming such difficulties and the ideas and questions were novel, we are quite likely to recognise this as an act of creativity.

---

Another practical lesson that writers can learn from designers is the power of a design language. The term 'design language' can be interpreted in different ways, but I use it here to describe the terminology, or meta-language, that writers use to talk to themselves and others about the process of writing and the properties of texts. A design language is a code shared by designers.

Design languages are in part explicit and conventionalised and in part the abstracted experience of groups of practitioners. Typically[17] they consist of:

- *Collections of elements*: terms for the basic elements of design such as shapes, styles, actions, techniques and metaphors;
- *Sets of organising principles*: descriptions of how the elements might be composed to build up things that have meaning;
- *Collections of qualifying situations*: examples of how elements and principles of composition might change based on the context.

To take an everyday example from another area of design, there are many ways to talk about doors. We can discuss their properties ('the red door', 'this door is difficult to open') through an everyday language of design and function. This serves our needs as users of doors, but it covers only a fraction of the ways to talk about their form and function. Carpenters need to discuss the material required to construct doors, architects refer to them as parts of a particular type of building (Neo-Georgian, Palladian). Ergonomists, concerned with human factors such as ease of use, talk about the 'affordance' of a door (a door with a flat plate at shoulder level affords pushing, a round doorknob affords turning). As users of products we only tend to notice the design language when it fails to meet our needs or expectations: a Georgian door that looks out of place on a modern house, a featureless door that doesn't indicate where it should be pushed.

The same is true of writing. What makes design languages for writing special is that they employ the same medium as the product itself: we use words to write and also to describe how we write. Compare that with an architect who produces plans on paper for buildings in brick or concrete. Writers can intermingle text and meta-text (is this making sense?) and create texts that refer to their own construction, as I have done when I describe how I write this book. An experienced author can create layers of self-reference that reveal the text as an artefact and cause readers to reflect on how and why it was designed.

There are many ways to describe texts and how they are produced, from the everyday language of readers ('boring', 'unputdownable') to the intricacies of linguistics and literary criticism. Generally, we appreciate a text because it hides its design. We prefer holiday novels that allow us to engage with their content rather than study their structure. We only usually become aware of the language of text design when the text fails us, through poor grammar or style, or when the text is written to confront readers and their expectations.

An important difference between texts and most other artefacts is that texts are sometimes designed to be *deliberately* difficult. For writers, knowing and using a design language is both a means of hiding the design of a text from the reader (to make it easier to read) and of manipulating a text to show its design and so subvert the cosy complicity of writer and reader.

What comprises a design language for writing? The main requirement is that it should match the cycle of reflection and engagement (see Figure 1.1), helping a writer to interpret, contemplate and specify writing as it progresses. It should also allow writers to communicate their intentions and strategies, and to store them for later use. Every writer has a personal design language, in terms of collections of written plans and notes, methods for organising them into file systems and databases, and various notations such as outlines or idea maps. But students are generally not taught an explicit design language for writing at school or college, so they acquire one piecemeal, picking up techniques and organising principles from books and colleagues.

The first and greatest design language for writing is classical rhetoric. In recent times the term 'rhetoric' has become debased, called on to deride overstuffed speeches, or to describe intricate figures of speech such as *metalepsis* and *diaphora* that sound like obscure liver complaints. But rhetoric was devised to meet a very practical need.

In Athens from the fifth century BC crimes were tried by citizens' juries. There were no lawyers or public prosecutors; the plaintiff and defendant each had to argue the case in person through a single set speech. For an Athenian citizen, the ability to compose clear and well-argued speeches was a valuable insurance policy. Professional speech-makers offered assistance and training, and their remit widened over the years to advising on how to compose orations to suit any occasion, from a wedding speech to an address to the emperor. They devised rhetoric as a comprehensive language for talking about the parts of a speech and the processes of composition. Tysias, one of the earliest rhetoriticians, defined rhetoric as the *demiurgos* (artificer, or designer) of persuasion. Quintilian, the greatest of the Roman teachers of oratory, called rhetoric the 'science of speaking well'.

In describing the process of composition, classical rhetoric made a clear distinction between *inventio* (invention and idea generation), *dispositio* (the arrangement of ideas for presentation) and *elocutio* (their expression in an appropriate style of language). The division between the invention and the disposition of ideas has become blurred in modern teaching of writing, being lumped together under the heading of 'planning', but the Greeks were wise to keep them separate, at least for the purpose of teaching. The arrangement of ideas in a person's mind, or in a written plan, is not necessarily the best one for presenting to an audience. By separating *inventio* and *dispositio*, planning the content and planning the presentation, rhetoric stresses the need to consider the effect of different arrangements on the reader.

Central to *inventio* and *dispositio* is the need to uncover and to present the *staseis* or 'basic issues'. In legal arguments these often arise as questions from the central conflict of opinion: 'you did it', 'I didn't', 'did he do it?' Some modern forms of writing and speaking still centre on a single stasis: the academic paper addressing a central research question, the detective story leading the reader towards 'who did it', the newspaper leader article, the formal debate.

Coverage of *inventio* included very practical advice on types of reasoning and how to construct arguments. Quintilian, for example, discusses reasoning by analogy. The best analogies are between 'things nearly equal', such as a comparison of two political situations or similar events ('someone who has accepted money to sit on a jury is also likely to take money to give false witness'). Avoid analogies between very different things, especially if they hinge on the meaning of a single word such as 'liberal'. Quintilian gives a rather coy example of a false analogy: 'We praise someone who is liberal with their money, so we should do the same for someone who is liberal with their embraces.'

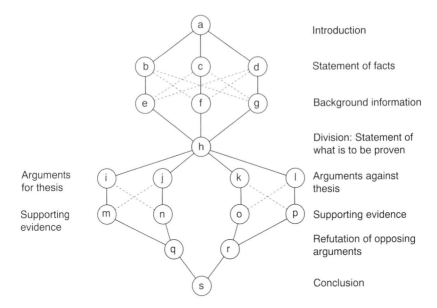

Introduction

Statement of facts

Background information

Division: Statement of what is to be proven

Arguments for thesis

Arguments against thesis

Supporting evidence

Supporting evidence

Refutation of opposing arguments

Conclusion

Figure 4.1 Prototypical argument structure (presenting both sides of an argument)

*Dispositio* involves bringing the ideas together in a coherent form, to stress the central issue and to produce the best effect on the reader. Even the most interesting of material will remain in a confused heap until *dispositio* orders and inter-relates it. The great limitation of classical rhetoric was that it was restricted almost entirely to one genre, the argument. But that genre was worked over in great detail. Aristotle and other Greek rhetoriticians laid down a basic structure for an argument that still serves as a useful template. It is essentially the one illustrated in Figure 4.1. The anonymous textbook *Rhetorica ad Caius Herennium* defined it thus:

> The Introduction is the beginning of the discourse, and by it the hearer's mind is prepared for attention. The Narration or Statement of Facts sets forth the events that have occurred or might have occurred. By means of the Division we make clear what matters are agreed upon and what contested, and announce what points we intend to take up. Proof is the presentation of our arguments, together with their corroboration. Refutation is the destruction of our adversaries' arguments. The Conclusion is the end of the discourse, framed in accordance with the principles of the art.

*Elocutio*, the third stage of composition, is what we have now come to associate with rhetoric. Through *elocutio*, or communication of ideas to an audience, the orator can call on a wide variety of rhetorical figures and tropes, starting (alphabetically) with *adynaton* (the impossibility of expressing oneself adequately on the topic) and ending with *zeugma* (where one verb serves two or more clauses).

If all this seems as relevant to twentieth-century communication as a papyrus scroll, then consider the text in Figure 4.2. It is from the start of a user guide for a personal computer.[18] The entire extract is structured for rhetorical effect. It begins with a classic encomium or bestowing of praise ('Congratulations on the purchase of your new Macintosh'). Having thus softened the reader, it launches into a string of *hyperbole*, or exaggeration of scale, to describe the qualities of the Macintosh ('highest performance', 'real ease of use') ending in *anaphora*, where the same word is repeated at the beginning of a sequence of clauses ('it's also easy to set up, easy to use, and easy to expand). After *hyperbole* comes *prosopopeia*, another of the 'grand figures' of persuasive rhetoric. *Prosopopeia* is the attribution of human qualities to an inanimate object, in this case the user manual which will 'guide you through the setup procedure, tell you how to expand your Macintosh, and provide many tips on using your new system'.

---

### Welcome to Macintosh

Congratulations on the purchase of your new Macintosh. Your computer is designed to give you the highest performance combined with real ease of use. It's also easy to set up and easy to expand. This book guides you through the setup procedure, tells you how to expand your Macintosh, and provides many tips on using your new system.

Your Macintosh computer is powered by the new **PowerPC** micro-processor (or "chip"). This microprocessor was designed by Apple Computer, Inc., Motorola, Inc., and IBM Corporation. The **PowerPC** microprocessor uses Reduced Instruction Set Computing (RISC) technology to deliver very high performance at the lowest possible cost. The **PowerPC** RISC microprocessor represents the state of the art in microprocessor design.

Your new Macintosh will run almost all of your existing Macintosh software, but for best performance and greatest speed, look for the new software programs designed especially for computers that contain the **PowerPC** microprocessor. You'll find **PowerPC** microprocessor-compatible programs at any software store that carries products for the Macintosh computer.

---

Figure 4.2  Extract from the start of a computer user guide

The next paragraph is arranged in threes for rhetorical effect. The key word 'PowerPC' is stated three times. The second sentence names three companies. The microprocessor is described through three superlatives: 'very high performance', 'lowest possible cost', 'state of the art'.

Fortunately for the computer user, the entire manual is not a demonstration of the rhetorician's art. The remainder is written in a different style, as a straightforward *narratio*, or statement of facts.

The final stages of classical composition, *memoria* and *pronuntiatio*, memorising the speech and delivering it, were essential in the days when orators were expected to deliver extended speeches from memory. Nowadays, these functions have been largely overtaken by the technology of print and publishing. The advice is still pertinent, however, to anyone delivering a speech in public. Techniques such as remembering items by associating them with a physical space (such as imagining items in a list as objects found on a mental journey) form the basis of present-day 'improve your memory' books. Regarding delivery, Quintilian's statement of the need to consider the effect of a composition on its audience applies equally to writing:

> For the nature of the speech that we have composed in our minds is not so important as the manner in which we produce it, since the emotion of each member of our audience will depend on the impression made upon his hearing.[19]

Other design languages for writing are not nearly so well elaborated as rhetoric. This is not surprising given their 2000-year handicap, but they do have the advantage of embracing new genres, of incorporating modern theories of psychology and of paying more heed to the problems and context of the individual writer. The most comprehensive design languages for writing come from modern literary criticism and from cognitive psychology. Unlike rhetoric, neither were developed explicitly to help composition, but writers can call on their structures and terms to describe the writing process. I shall give just a brief outline of the approaches here, as I have called on the terminology and general approaches of literary criticism and cognitive psychology throughout the book.

The modern structural approach to literary criticism began with the Russian formalists of the early twentieth century. They claimed that culture had become so familiar that it had sunk below consciousness. As we become accustomed to events, however strange they may initially have been, they cease to provoke sensation. The rôle of art is to 'defamiliarise', to question the ordinary and to confront expectations. As Shklovsky put it, 'art exists that one may recover the sensation of life, it exists to make one feel things, to make the stone *stony*'.[20]

Literature can defamiliarise by making the ordinary difficult and by using the rhythm and imagery of language to describe an object or event as if it were seen for the first time. Because both text and meta-text are expressed through written language a writer can play tricks with words to reveal and defamiliarise language itself. The formalists were interested in *how* a story is told, in the writer's use of literary conventions and the structure of language.

This interest in language structure paved the way for *semiotics*, the study of signs. The essence of semiotics is that language is an arbitrary association of word and meaning. There is nothing essentially 'cat-like' about the word 'cat'. It is a concocted set of letters used to denote a type of animal. Ferdinand de Saussure, the originator of semiotics, described language as a system composed of *signifiers* (actual written or spoken words) and *signified* (the meanings associated with the words). Because there is no logical or innate link between the words and their meaning, he argued, the only way we can make sense of language as a system is not by hunting for the meaning of words, but by studying the web of structural associations within and beyond a text. Story grammars, macro-structures and rhetorical devices are all tools with which to explore the system of language.

Saussure turned literary criticism from a craft into a science. Later semioticians such as Barthes developed a science of criticism and poetics which aimed to reveal the structure and elements of text. Narratives, Barthes proposed, depend on essential elements, or *functions*, around which the plot revolves: general functions, such as a murder in a detective story, or specific ones such as the meeting between the young orphan Pip and the escaped convict Magwitch at the beginning of Dicken's *Great Expectations* (which leads later to the revelation that Magwitch is Pip's benefactor).[21]

Types of function include *cardinal functions* (elements that are essential to the plot), *catalysers* (elements that prepare the reader for the cardinal functions) and *indices* (elements that give the reader a sense of the place or time, such as descriptions of fashions in clothing or entertainment). Some novels are structured mainly around indices (such as James Joyce's *Ulysses*, or the works of Virginia Woolf); others, such as spy stories or detective novels, are often based on a cardinal function. Many novelists plan their work in terms of cardinal functions, and these can be seen as one kind of primary generator.

Barthes and the later semioticians not only analysed the structure of texts, but also went well beyond the individual text to look at the ways in which the mass culture of advertising, media such as television and fashion provide a grand interlinked system of signs. The work of structuralists such as Barthes, Lévi-Strauss, Derrida and Eco spawned a generation of authors who played with the traditional form of novels, providing alternate endings (such as John Fowles' *The French Lieutenant's Woman*) or wholesale reconstructions (such as hypertext novels with multiple paths, that can only be read on computer).

The implications of Saussure's insight – that there is no essential, fixed link between language and meaning – go way beyond experiments with the structure of novels. Jacques Derrida was not the first, but he was certainly the most influential person to point out that if words have no fixed meaning, then there is no 'authorial voice' behind a text, no authentic meaning to be discovered by close reading.

It follows from this that language is determined by culture. If something seems obvious in a text it is because our implicit cultural assumptions make it so. In another culture, with another set of guiding assumptions, the same words may be a source of unending questions and problems. The great English novels of George Eliot, Jane Austen and the Brontë sisters, for example, portrayed a view of the essential stability of society, with its all-pervading rituals and social stratifications, that seemed quite natural and quintessentially English to readers of the time. Nowadays, these same novels can be seen as the product (all the more powerful for being unstated) of a time when Britain was an imperial power, confident in its institutions, and literature served to reinforce the prejudices of a divided society.

The language of literary criticism that began with the scientific vocabulary of 'sign' and 'signifier' has, over the decades, taken on terms from sociology, anthropology and psychotherapy. They can seem as arcane and remote as the tropes of classical rhetoric. The essential message, however, can be easily stated, but its implications are profound and are still being explored by writers and literary theorists: structuralism tells us that the link between words and their meaning is arbitrary; post-structuralism adds that this arbitrary link is culturally determined and ever-changing. We shall return to this issue later, in Chapter Ten.

During the same period that literary theorists were building the edifice of semiotics, psychologists were engaged in a smaller-scale project, to describe the cognitive processes of writing. They began with a similar interest to the Russian formalists, to explain *how* a text is written. However, whereas the formalists concerned themselves with the structure of the finished text, cognitive psychologists studied the mental processes of writers.

The earliest, and by far the most influential, studies of writers at work were under-taken by John Hayes and Linda Flower. They asked writers to talk as they wrote, about what they were thinking. Through a close analysis of these verbal *protocols* Hayes and Flower attempted to uncover the writers' plans, goals and methods. This general approach, of *protocol analysis*, was adapted from studies of human problem solving, and it is based on the assumption that writing is, primarily, a problem-solving activity. Writers have *goals* they wish to achieve (such as to write a story on a given topic), they form *plans* that indicate how to achieve the goal and then enact the plan through a variety of *methods* (such as generating ideas).

Hayes and Flower drew on the protocols to devise a general model of the writing process. It identified three main mental processes: planning (including generating information relevant to the task, organising information and setting goals), translation[22] (turning plans and ideas into text to meet the goals), and reviewing (which combines evaluating the text and editing either the text itself or the ideas and goals). Interactions between these processes can begin to explain the activities and verbal protocols of writers, and the model offers a plausible explanation for problems such as writer's block and for differences between expert and inexpert writers.

The picture that has emerged from early cognitive studies of the writing process is of a complex and demanding activity, involving the writer in satisfying multiple constraints. Constraints are both helpful, cutting down a writer's search of memory, and demanding:

> It is no wonder that many people find writing difficult. It is the very nature of the beast to impose a large set of converging but potentially contradictory constraints on the writer. Furthermore, to be efficient the writer should attend to all these constraints at once ... Unfortunately, this ideal rarely occurs because of the limited number of items our short term memory or conscious attention can handle.[23]

More recent accounts, including John Hayes' revised model of writing and the later work of Linda Flower, have moved beyond an examination of mental processes to consider the writer as a member of a community of practice. These studies have included investigations of authors' orientations to writing, the use of external representations to structure the task and share understanding, the characteristics of different writing tools and media, and the social, organisational and cultural context in which writing occurs. Despite very different methodologies, ranging from ethnography to experimental psychology, these studies have revealed a surprisingly consistent picture of the activity of writing.

There is no point in describing the work in detail, because I have referred to it throughout this book, along with some of the terminology of cognitive psychology. Where I take issue with the early cognitive studies of writing is that they saw writing as primarily a problem-solving activity and this coloured the way they described it. Hayes and Flower borrowed freely from the language of problem solving, with terms like *subprocesses*, *problem spaces* and *task execution*. This type of language tends to depersonalise writing: it is something that could equally well be performed by a disembodied mind, or a suitably programmed computer. Writing as design involves problem solving, when the writer sets goals, makes plans and satisfies constraints, but these processes support the broader purpose of writing which is to communicate with and through the text to achieve a human effect.

In this book I have deliberately not stuck with one terminology, because none captures writing as a cognitive process, a creative act and a cultural activity. Instead, the book attempts to convey a design language for writing that combines the most useful parts of rhetoric, literary theory and cognitive psychology.

---

It is now time to revisit the diagram of the writing process from Chapter One to take account of writing as design. The diagram in Figure 1.1 shows composing as a cycle of contemplating ideas, specifying plans and intentions, composing text and interpreting the text, leading to further ideas and continued composition. Figure 4.3 shows an extended version that captures writing as design.

The diagram shows planning and revising as distinct activities within the overall writing process. As with composing, they both involve a cycle of reflection and engagement. A writer forms a plan, specifies its content and structure, and

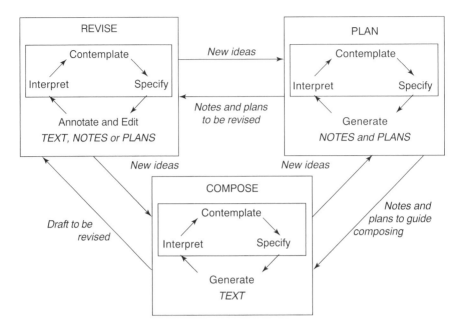

Figure 4.3 Model of writing as design

generates it on paper (or some other medium). Its visual appearance prompts the writer to interpret it and contemplate ways in which the plan could be extended, leading to a new round of planning. In revising, a writer reads and interprets all or part of the draft text, contemplates its form and content, decides on changes that need to be made and annotates or edits the draft.

The three core activities – planning, composing and revising – are bound together by external representations. Notes and plans guide composing. The draft text becomes material to be revised. The flow of activity, however, is not just in one direction. While reading the draft, new ideas occur which need to be incorporated into the text through further composing. Or the writer may realise that the draft text fails to match the plan, in which case either the text needs to be revised (in a new cycle of contemplation and editing), or the plans extended or changed. Thus, writing involves a flow of material (external representations) from planning to composing to revising and a flow of new ideas in the opposite direction.

The diagram is deliberately laid out in a form that shows planning, composing and revising as a cycle, rather than a series of stages leading up to a finished product. The links show that any of the three core activities can be followed by any other. It is fairly unusual for a writer to move from revising back to planning, but it does occur, particularly for complex writing on a new topic (such as a research paper where ideas that occur on reading a first draft can cause a writer to rethink the entire structure).

What does the diagram indicate about how we write? First, it emphasises the importance of external representations in mediating the entire writing process. External representations bind together the activities of writing. Second, the diagram shows no start point and no end to the process. Writing can begin at any of the three activities, and it never ends – that is what makes writing (and other design activities) so flexible and so frustrating. An episode of writing can start by the writer making a plan to guide composing, or it can begin with a session of free writing to explore ideas or it can begin with an existing text that the writer reworks for a new purpose or audience. Third, each arrow in the diagram indicates a choice about how to continue writing. The choices each writer makes form an approach and strategy of writing. The next four chapters look in more detail at the three core activities of writing and at writers' approaches and strategies.

Chapter 5
# Planning

When we talk of 'making a plan' we can mean two things. A plan is a diagram or representation on a flat surface. It is also a scheme to accomplish some purpose. We sketch out a route plan on paper. It helps someone to reach a destination. An architect creates a plan on the screen of a computer-aided design system. It guides the construction of the building. Plans for writing have that dual purpose of mapping out the structure of the intended text and acting as a guide to composing. But unlike a route map or an architect's plan they are not normally tight specifications.

A street plan shows the fixed layout of buildings and roads. However much we might like to shorten a journey or to add some new parkland, we cannot change a town by revising the street plan. Architects can revise their plans, but once the building work has begun it would be foolhardy to make major revisions since these could mean tearing down bricks and mortar, or at the very least an increase in cost due to delay.

A writing plan is more flexible. Like the architect's drawing it is a guide for action still to be performed. The only physical resources that the act of writing consumes are paper and ink and undoing the work involves only pressing a delete key or making a stroke of the pen. Plans for writing can be amended at very little cost.

A written plan or outline is always an expression of the 'writer then'. The act of writing brings into being ideas and intentions that the writer never had at the start of the task, or that could not be expressed in any detail. As the writing progresses the plan gets increasingly out of step with the 'writer now'. The plan does not become redundant, but it needs to be continually reinterpreted to fit the changing situation. A writer who regards a plan as a fixed specification for the text is missing its distinctive quality: a writing plan is a mechanism for idea exploration and creative design.

Writing plans serve multiple purposes. In the same way that writers are guided by mental constraints of content and rhetoric, so external plans can refer both to content (*what* to say) and rhetoric (*how* to say it – how to shape the text to meet the demands of style, structure, audience and task). Content plans capture and organise ideas and mental structures. Rhetorical plans specify the argument and form of the intended text. No single type of representation can show both the associativity of ideas and the linearity of text. So although some writers prefer to use one consistent means of planning (and some teachers of writing promote one particular approach, such as outlining) there are good reasons for using a variety of methods for different types of text and at different stages of the writing. The skill in planning a text is to choose a method that suits the purpose, one that is precise enough to guide composing but flexible enough to be explored and altered.

Figure 5.1 shows a spectrum of types of plan, from content to rhetoric. At one extreme are rough notes and sketches that capture ideas and mental images. At the other extreme is a draft of the text. The spectrum is not just a progression from ideas to text, it also indicates 'semantic potential', from broad to narrow.

Notes and sketches have what Charles Wood has called *broad semantic potential*.[1] They are open to many interpretations and even the person who wrote them may gain different meanings from them at different times. Most writers have had the experience of making notes that seem to capture a vitally important idea and then coming across them a few days later and finding they either make no sense or lead to a completely different train of thought.

A writer can use this slipperiness constructively, to record ideas that are important but not fully understood. Jotting down the words 'art nouveau' (for, say, an article on interior design) indicates a set of ideas that the writer might want to use in the text, but it does not require the writer to understand the concept of art nouveau or how it relates to the other topics.

| Notes and sketches | Idea lists | Mind maps | Notes networks | Rhetorical templates, tables | Content lists, document outlines | Draft text |
|---|---|---|---|---|---|---|

*Content*                                                     *Rhetoric*

Figure 5.1 Spectrum of plan types

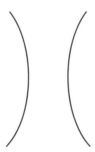

Figure 5.2  Sketch by a pair of authors to represent the 'shape' of a text

Similarly, a simple sketch can indicate intentions that are too fluid to express easily in words. Wood studied pairs of writers making plans for a jointly-written article. One writer sketched the simple funnel shape shown in Figure 5.2 to illustrate the overall 'shape' of the proposed article (a broad introduction, becoming more narrow in slope, leading to a general conclusion). Later, they both referred back to the shape, pointing to parts of it when talking about how to write the various sections. For them, a quick sketch captured the gist of their rhetorical plan in a way that would be difficult to express in words or as a more structured diagram.

The most versatile and underrated external representation is the humble list. A list is a flexible structure. It can contain words, phrases, notes or sketches. The items can be set down in the order that they occurred to the writer, or they can be clustered together into sets. They can easily be reordered, either by cutting and pasting, or by annotating the list with arrows. The ordering of items can indicate a sequence (as in a list of instructions, or table of contents) or a set (as in a list of topics or reminders of intention).

A list can indicate both the organisation of ideas and the intended structure of the finished text. But this ambiguity is a source of problems for student writers: they treat a list of ideas as if it were a table of contents. It is very unlikely that the order in which the writer generates ideas is the best way to present them in text. Thus, planning with lists involves making a conscious decision to rearrange the order from one based on ideas to one that shows the structure of the text. Figure 5.3 is a step-by-step method to plan with lists, for a complex piece of expository or argumentative writing (such as a newspaper feature, a lab report or an essay).

I am not proposing list making and outlining as the best method of planning, but rather as one of a range of techniques that writers use. The main problem with lists and outlines is that they prevent you from making multiple associations. Ideas in the head are non-linear. They form a rich web of inter-connected and over-lapping meaning. With a linear outline, you can only express one ordering of ideas. There is no means to indicate the other, potentially fruitful, connections and arrangements.

1. Start with a pile of blank cards, each about the size of a visiting card.
2. Think about the ideas you want to express (content) and also how you want to express them (rhetoric). Write them down one by one on separate cards, as single words or short phrases (no more than about ten words per card). Stop when you have about twenty to thirty cards, or have run out of ideas.
3. Separate the content cards from the rhetoric cards.
4. Group the content cards into clusters according to topic.
5. Make a stack for each topic and add to the top of each stack a new card with the name of the topic.
6. Look at the stacks of topics and see how they match up to the intentions as shown by the rhetoric cards. Are any topics short of ideas? Do they form the basis of a coherent argument?
7. If necessary, add further idea and topic cards.
8. Form the topics into a list in an order that they could be presented in the text.
9. Use this ordering as an outline, with the topics indicating section headings, and the ideas as a guide to the content of each section. At this point the plan should look something like a table of contents.
10. Reflect on how the outline communicates your ideas to the reader. Alter it to make the flow of explanation or the structure of the argument clearer.
11. Use this outline as a guide to writing the first draft.

Figure 5.3 Step-by-step approach to planning with lists

The simplest way to map out the inter-connections of meaning is to make an informal plan that combines lists with sketches and annotations. Figure 5.4 shows an informal plan for a research article I wrote on the design of computer environments for writers. It follows no particular technique, but mixes together many notations. At the top left is a list of some key concepts. The top right shows some rough notes intended as memory aids, such as 'external representations are cognitive metaphors' (I have no clear idea now what that phrase means, but at the time it captured a train of thought). The list at the bottom left is a more complete set of concepts and the one at the bottom right is an attempt to organise these into topic clusters ('consensus', 'conflict', 'social') that might form a structure for the article. In the centre of the page is a rough sketch of the design process, with references to Hayes and Flower's influential model of the writing process and some other reference sources. Although I added few explicit links (a somewhat cryptic arrow to the set of concepts and another one indicating a change of order) the arrangement of the different types of list on the page allowed me to make mental connections between the concepts, topics and text outline.

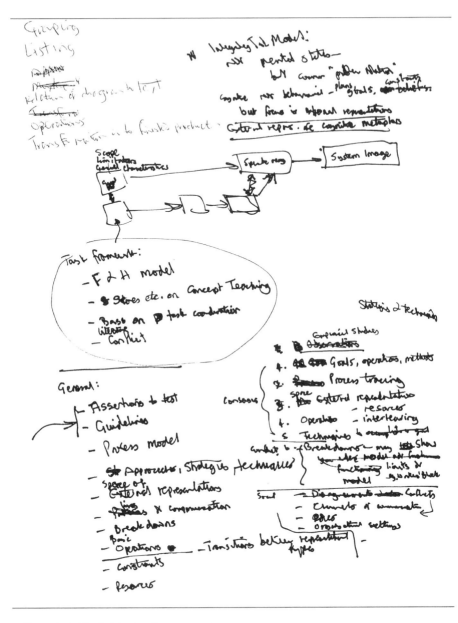

Figure 5.4  My sketch plan for a research paper

Mind mapping was developed by Tony Buzan[2] as a technique for overcoming the restrictions of linear lists, by mapping out explicit links between ideas. It comes nearest to capturing and illustrating the conceptual spaces discussed in Chapter Three. Mind mapping is a more orderly method of concept planning than the ones described so far. To profit from it requires some investment of time, and faith in its power.

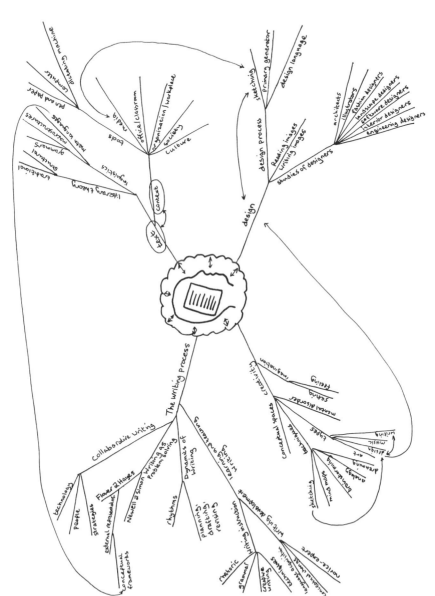

Figure 5.5 Mind map on the topic of writing as creative design

To create a mind map, you start by sketching a central image to illustrate the main topic, and then draw in branches for the main themes radiating outward. On each branch you write a key word or phrase, and the less central topics are joined to the main ones by smaller branches to form a connected network, as in Figure 5.5.

The mind map in Figure 5.5 shows my exploration of the topic of 'writing as creative design'. I started with a simple diagram that seemed to me to sum up the topic. Then I drew lines to indicate the main concepts. Three of them ('the writing process', 'design' and 'creativity') were easily labelled. The other was more difficult to capture, so I divided it into two linked branches to indicate the close relationship between 'text' and 'context'. I carried on adding sub-branches and cross-links until I had mapped out the topic. At various points the map suggested new ways forward: a branch was too sparse and needed more items; a twig of one topic could be linked with a branch of another.

Mind maps have been invested with almost miraculous powers. One convert, Lana Israel, a 13-year-old American schoolgirl, co-wrote a book with Tony Buzan entitled *Brain Power for Kids – How to Become an Instant Genius*. I must confess that I am not a regular mind mapper. I prefer to make a more disorganised mixture of lists and annotations. This is partly because I have never set aside the time to become familiar with the technique, but also because they are not particularly suited to rhetorical planning. Mind maps leave limited space for writing notes and there is no easy way to re-organise the network as a text structure. The easiest way is to write down each major branch as a main heading and the minor branches as sub-headings. This forms an outline for the text, but it ignores the cross-links which are one of the main benefits of a mind map. Like any other technique for writing, mind mapping has its uses (particularly for understanding a topic or exploring ideas) but it is no panacea.

One type of writing plan that retains the associativity of mind mapping while also allowing space for writing notes is a notes network.[3] In a notes network the ideas are not attached to links as with a mind map, but are written as individual notes. These are then linked together into an visual map. The advantage of a notes network over a mind map is that each note can be either a simple idea or a piece of draft text.

By starting with a network of idea notes, then clustering them into groups according to the main sections of the text, then sorting them into a linear draft, you can move in manageable steps from organising ideas to structuring a text, with the network as a visual guide. Figure 5.6 shows a step-by-step approach to creating a draft text from a notes network.

Figure 5.7 is a notes network on the topic of 'Should some drugs be legalised?' The network shows the basic structure of the argument. It has four main strands: youth culture, what is socially acceptable drug taking, dangers of drugs and crime. They all feed into the 'liberal' conclusion that drugs should be assessed according to their

1. Start with a pile of blank cards, each about the size of a visiting card.

2. Write down notes on the writing topic as they come to you, with each note on a separate card (no more than about 20 words per card). Stop when you have about 20 to 30 cards, or have run out of ideas.

3. Arrange the cards in rough clusters of related topics on a whiteboard or a large sheet of paper.

4. Link together related notes.

5. Try to label the links. A basic general set of link types is: *argues for, argues against, causes, comments, compares, contrasts, describes, develops, supports, example, explains, problem, solution, then*, but use other labels if they seem appropriate.

6. Add new notes to the network, using its structure as a guide. The shape of the network will indicate gaps in the notes and will prompt refinements.

7. When you have explored and extended the network then re-organise it for presentation as a text. You can do this either by collecting together notes on the same topic and organising them into an outline, as with lists, or by following the main paths through the network gathering up the notes as you go.

Figure 5.6  Step-by-step approach to planning with a notes network

harm, not by whether they are socially unacceptable. The absence of any 'supports' links indicates that the statements are not backed up by evidence. The word 'crime' features in three of the strands of argument, which suggests it might be an important linking theme in the article. The structure of the network reveals some issues that still need to be resolved, such as whether the widespread use of legal drugs is an argument for or against legalising other drugs. The network can then fairly easily be turned into a first draft by following the main paths for the two strands of argument in favour and the two against, and fleshing out the notes with additional text.

Creating a notes network can be a useful technique for planning a difficult text, such as an argumentative essay or a scientific article, where the ideas and the structure need to be created and organised in harmony. A slightly simpler approach to planning a complex text is to fit the ideas into a pre-set template for a rhetorical structure such as an argument or a thesis.

Figure 5.8 shows a template for an argumentative text. It is not the only way of structuring an argument, but it is a prototypical one, based on classical rhetoric. It starts with a set of issues and their background, then gives the central thesis,

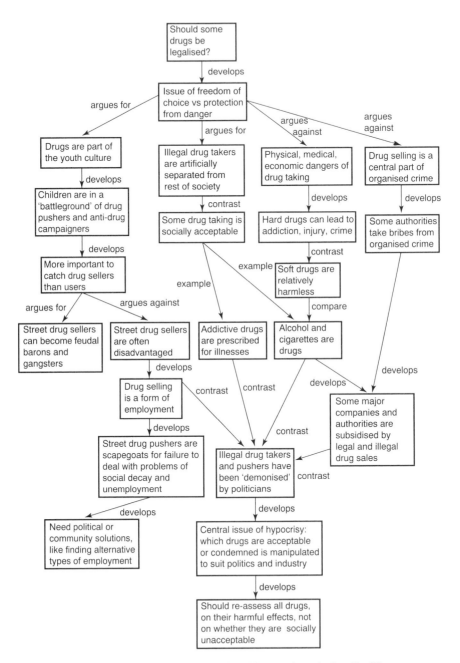

Figure 5.7 Notes network on the topic of 'Should some drugs be legalised?'

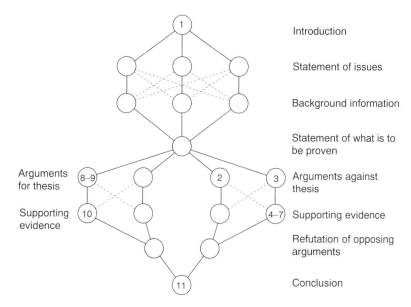

Introduction

Statement of issues

Background information

Statement of what is to be proven

Arguments for thesis — Arguments against thesis

Supporting evidence — Supporting evidence

Refutation of opposing arguments

Conclusion

Figure 5.8  Rhetorical template for an argumentative text

followed by arguments for and against the thesis with supporting evidence, leading to a refutation of the counter-arguments and a conclusion.

Each circle in the diagram indicates one element in the argument, which can then be filled with an appropriate piece of text. The uppermost circle, for example, indicates the introduction to the argument. The ones immediately below stand for the main issues or facts (they are just an indication of the elements; there may be more or fewer issues depending on the topic). The links show the most likely conceptual relationships between the elements.

To use this as an aid to planning, you first brainstorm a set of ideas for the topic and then associate each one with a circle in the template. This will provide a framework for the essay. That framework can then be turned into linear text by traversing the framework item by item. This can be done in a number of ways, for example by moving along each row of the template, giving an argument that balances the pros and cons step by step, or by first collecting together all the arguments for the thesis and then the arguments against. The arguments in favour of the thesis could be presented before the arguments against, or vice versa. Each linear ordering of the text will produce a different effect on the reader. One way may seem logical and irrefutable, another tentative and ill argued, despite the fact that they stem from the same underlying argument.

In addition to guiding the flow of text, a rhetorical template can also indicate missing parts of an argument. Take, for example, the list of notes shown in Figure 5.9 on the topic of 'Can computers think?' They were produced from an initial session of brainstorming. The items have been numbered to make it easier to refer

1.  Can computers think?

2.  Think in non-human ways

3.  Think like humans

4.  Turing – operational definition, Turing Test

5.  Test of whether machines can reason by conversational game

6.  Behaviourist approach

7.  Turing – machines could reason like humans

8.  Searle: nonsense to talk of machines thinking

9.  Machines don't have intentionality

10. Syntax but no semantics

11. Machine thought impossible in principle

Figure 5.9  List of notes on the topic of 'Can computers think?'

to them. They are in a rough order and can easily be turned into a first draft of an essay by fleshing out the text and adding connectives such as 'but'. Figure 5.10 shows how that might be done. By re-ordering the elements in the list we could, for example, make a stronger case for computers being able to think. But however the elements are ordered, they do not make a convincing argument.

To see why this is so we can place the list of ideas into the argument template of Figure 5.8. The numbers shown in the figure correspond to the items of the list. The partly-filled template shows clearly the limitations of the argument. The issues and background information are missing and there is no clear statement of what is to be

*Can computers think?*

Computers may be able to think in non-human ways, but some people suggest that they can think like humans. Alan Turing proposed the Turing Test as an operational definition of thinking. It is a way of discovering whether machines can reason, by means of a conversational game. This is reminiscent of behaviourist psychology. Turing suggested that machines would soon be able to compete with humans at intellectual reasoning. But others suggest that it is nonsense to talk of machines thinking. John Searle argues that machines do not have intentionality. They have syntax but no semantics. He concludes that machine thought is impossible in principle.

Figure 5.10  First draft of an essay from the list in Figure 5.9

proven (is it 'Computers cannot think', or 'Computers cannot think like humans'?). The argument that computers might be able to think in non-human ways (item 2 in the list) is left hanging, with no supporting evidence, and there is no attempt to rebut the counter arguments.

The template, then, serves as a guide to planning and a check on the completeness of a complex rhetorical structure. Notes networks and rhetorical templates bridge the gap between content and rhetoric, supporting both in a single representation. Another way of moving from ideas to text is to create a table of the main points along two important dimensions (for example in the essay on 'Can computers think?' the dimensions might be 'ways of thinking' and 'types of computer program').

Next on the spectrum of plan types is outlining. Outlining is a way of creating a precise rhetorical plan, at increasing levels of detail. Top-level headings indicate the structure of the text, while sub-headings fill in the detail. The outline can be constructed out of idea lists or notes networks, or it can be produced by a self-contained session of planning.

Outlines can help in two ways. They provide a framework for the text and they split the writing process into fairly independent tasks so that a writer is not faced with the burden of planning while composing. Outlines work best when there is a clear set of ideas ready to be fitted into an overall structure and are less use for more personal or experimental writing where the ideas emerge through composing.

Figure 5.11 shows my original outline for this book which I wrote before I began to draft Chapter One. Some items are cryptic and personal, such as 'bridging the dip', but the outline as a whole provided a firm structure, indicating the order of chapters and topics within each chapter. The outline served as a guide but not a blueprint. As I wrote the first draft of the book a new structure began to emerge, of writing in the head, writing with the page and writing in the world. I saw how that would offer a better way of organising the main perspectives on writing.

A draft text is itself a plan for further writing and, as we shall see, composing a free and unconstrained draft and then organising this into a more coherent text is one successful approach to writing. The writer begins by engaging with the text and expressing ideas through a flow of prose rather than a staccato list of ideas. The difficulty for many student writers of planning by drafting is that it can produce a sprawling mass of verbiage that drifts off the topic and takes a considerable effort to pull back into a well-organised text. It is harder to see the underlying structure and then reorganise a flow of continuous prose than it is to move around topic elements in a list.

This discussion of planning methods begs an important question: is planning any use? If we can write quite successfully without planning, then there is no point in

Chapter 1 INTRODUCTION
- motivation for the book
- general theory of writing as creative design

Chapter 2 THEORIES OF WRITING ??

Chapter 3 LEARNING TO WRITE
- development of writing abilities
- knowledge telling and knowledge transforming
- representational redescription
- u-shaped learning
- conceptual frameworks
- teaching: bridging the dip; freewriting??

Chapter 4 CREATIVITY
- creativity and idea generation
- road map analogy
- constraints
- high and low focus thinking
- externalisation of cognition

Chapter 5 WRITING AS DESIGN
- primary generators
- external representations
- plans, mindmaps etc.
- draft text

Chapter 6 HOW WE WRITE
- drafting and revising
- habits and motivations
- individual differences: approaches, strategies, habits

Chapter 7 THE TOOLS WE USE
- pen and paper
- word processors/new tools

Chapter 8 NEW WAYS OF WRITING
- collaborative writing
- online writing
- the future of writing

Chapter 9 CONCLUSIONS ???

Figure 5.11 My original outline for this book

wasting time on elaborate techniques. As with most investigations of writing, research into the value of planning is inconclusive, but interesting.

The most straightforward way to investigate the value of planning is to compare the written products of writers who plan with those who do not. A more sophisticated variant is to also take account of the quantity and quality of writers' plans. One study found that the quality of a finished text was strongly related to the quantity and quality of initial planning. Another study reported that the quality of texts written by 10th grade students was related to the quality of their plans.

But correlation does not necessarily imply cause. The more we plan, the more time we devote to the writing task. It may be that just spending more time on writing improves the quality of the finished text, because it gives more opportunity mentally to explore and develop ideas. If so, planning on paper is just a way of keeping one's mind on the task – it has no value in itself.

This possibility is backed up, to some extent, by a series of experiments with 10th graders that studied the interaction between text quality, planning and time-on-task. They found that the relationship between planning and text quality is due, at least in part, to the time spent on writing. Similarly, a study of adult writers found that, if time-on-task is held constant, there is no positive relationship between planning and the quality of the finished text. All this suggests that planning on paper does not necessarily lead to good writing.

Another way to test the value of planning is to carry out controlled experiments where writers are asked to plan and then to compare their texts with those of writers who wrote without planning. Again, the results are inconclusive. Asking students to produce a written outline before they wrote improved the quality of the text, but so did asking writers to prepare a mental outline.

These results are surprising. Students of writing are taught that making a plan will improve their writing, and it seems intuitively obvious that planning will help a writer to sort out ideas and organise the text better than just launching straight into a draft. The studies, however, suggest that the main benefit of planning is that it prolongs the writing time. Broadly, the longer a writer spends on the task, the better the product.

This could suggest that it doesn't matter what a writer does before starting a draft so long as it involves thinking about the task. Kellogg[4] tested this possibility by randomly assigning student writers to four conditions: a control group was given no instructions about planning or pre-writing; a 'list' group was asked to write a list of ideas in the order they should appear in the text; a 'cluster' group was asked to cluster their ideas into a graphic plan (similar to a notes network); and an 'outline' group was told to create a structured outline. The students were set the task of writing essays on the pros and cons of professionals joining an 'anti-greed club', and these were rated by two judges. The results are shown in Figure 5.12. There was no difference between the essays produced after making a graphic plan and those with

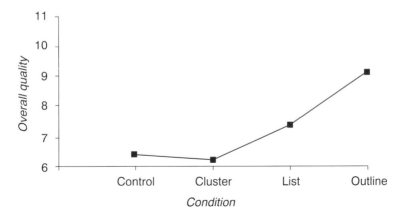

Figure 5.12  Overall quality of student essays as a function of type of pre-writing
Source: Kellogg, 1993

no planning at all. The list group performed significantly better than both the cluster and the control group, and the essays of the outline group were best of all.

Kellogg's experiment seems to offer conclusive evidence that outlining works. Again, however, the results should be treated with caution. Making an outline or list in the head may be just as successful as doing it on paper. The poor results from the cluster group may be due to the fact that these students were less familiar with creating notes networks than they were with listing or outlining: they didn't know how to make good use of a network plan. (Kellogg did test for this effect by training the writers in how to make network plans and found no difference between the trained and untrained ones. But learning a new planning technique may be a long-term investment.)[5] Lastly, the experiments were all carried out with students writing 200- to 300-word essays in a laboratory. The results may well not transfer over to planning a novel, a business report or a thesis.

To put the results of these experiments into a broader context, we can return to the purposes of planning given at the start of this chapter. Making a writing plan organises thought and it guides the production of text. A plan needs to satisfy both of these purposes. If it is illogical and fails to organise ideas then it will not form the basis for a coherent argument. If it does not offer a coherent rhetorical structure, then the resulting text is likely to be shapeless and rambling. This probably accounts for the results above. Cluster planning is a way to organise thought but it does not ensure that the ideas fit into a rhetorical structure that guides writing. Outlining is more likely to produce a well-structured text, but one that may be lacking in ideas. Making a list of ideas and then reorganising it into a hierarchical outline is the simplest and most effective general method of planning for all but the most complex of texts.

At the very least, time spent on planning is time well spent. It gives an opportunity to reflect on the content and structure of the text, and this appears to pay dividends in improved quality. What type of plan to make, and how long to spend on planning depends on the circumstances. If you already know what you want to write, then there is little point in organising ideas, though it may be worth creating a structure for the text. Conversely, if you are struggling for ideas, then creating a structured outline might well impede creativity. It would be better to start with a session of brainstorming, note networking or free drafting. As Hayes and Nash[6] point out, there are many different ways to plan, and writers appear to make sensible judgements about how much time to devote to planning and what method to use. Though their judgements may be imperfect, writers would be better advised to rely on their own sense of how to write than to simply to follow the imperative of 'plan more'.

# Chapter 6

# Composing

Composing is the central activity of writing, the familiar process of producing text on a page or screen. A common misconception is that composing is essentially concerned with generating words. This is the wrong level of description. It is like saying that the essence of driving is turning the steering wheel, or the essence of marathon running is moving one leg then the other. These are basic activities involved in driving and running, but they do not capture the essence of the task. The essence of composing is not to write words, but to design text.

Designing text is not just a matter of making the words visually appealing, of laying them out in columns or lists and leaving white space, though that is one important aspect. It is primarily the way we create and structure language to achieve an effect on the reader. Chapter Four gave a definition of design as 'a conscious and creative communication with and through materials to achieve a human effect'. The material of composing is the text. How, then, does the writer communicate with and through the text? And what is the human effect of writing?

Figure 6.1 shows the main flow of communication in writing. The writer creates ideas and organises them into mental schemas, represents these as language and presents them as words. Readers interpret the written language as schemas and integrate them with their existing knowledge and experience.

If the communication were completely transparent then each reader would gain an exact version of the writer's ideas. This can never happen, first because no two

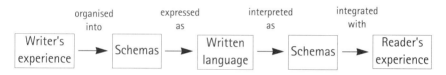

Figure 6.1 The flow of communication in writing

people share the same experiences, and second because language is a different type of representational system to mental schemas. Schemas integrate all our senses. They are pre-linguistic and must be converted into language before they can be expressed as words on a page. It is not just that language fails to capture the richness of the senses, but that it has a different web of meaning, in the form of dictionary definitions, synonyms and other linguistic associations.

Let's say I capture the scene now in front of my eyes as language:

A view of my garden wall framed by a curtain and a wisteria plant.

Each word and phrase in that sentence has connotations that supplement my visual impression. By expressing the image in words I am turning it into an artefact, a small piece of designed language. You will read it in the context of your own mental schemas for 'window', 'garden', 'framed by' and 'wisteria', enriched (or weighed down) by the linguistic and literary associations of these words ('Come into the garden, Maud', 'The Secret Garden' etc.) and the countless similar sentences you have read.

The connotations of written words also evoke new schemas for myself, the writer. I now see the scene in a new way as a result of having written about it. If writer and reader are the same person then the line of communication becomes a closed circle: the cycle of engagement and reflection. Thus, composing is a simultaneous process of communication to others and of self-discovery.

At any point in the composing process a writer is engaged in the current situation, consisting of mental schemas and constraints, the text that has just been written and the physical environment. The writer holds a representation of this situation in working memory and that provides a context for creative thinking through knowledge telling and knowledge transforming. Cues from this context activate long-term memory, retrieving further ideas (in the terminology of psychology these are called *propositions*) that meet the constraints of audience and purpose, style and structure. The product of this contemplation is stored in working memory.

The writer then selects and organises the propositions and turns them into language that fits the context. The language must maintain the flow of communication and connect to the existing text, through a sequence of words that refer to the given text and introduce new information. The writer then transcribes this language into text on the page or screen.

As the words emerge the writer interprets them with reference to the constraints at all levels, ensuring that the text is correct, coherent and cohesive, and that it communicates the writer's intentions. Already the text has become a thing in itself, a new stimulus that the writer re-interprets as propositions that interact with the writer's evolving ideas to prompt further contemplation. Although I could not avoid describing this as a sequence of activities, the processes are rapid and they interact to produce a fluid coordination of mental and physical activity.[1]

Composing, then, is a process not of emptying the mind, but of actively reconstructing it. The most recently written text is an external record of ideas in a handy form that the writer can re-read to refresh memory and drive composing forward. The act of scanning back over the text can also disrupt composing by interfering with the onward march of the text. A writer in the act of composing is in a continual mental tension between interpreting existing ideas and creating new ones. The arena for this struggle is working memory.

Working memory is the means by which we mentally store and process information. It also coordinates the interaction between the different processes. It has a limited capacity, so any activity that makes demands on working memory will interfere with composing. Demanding activities include writing slowly (increasing the time that ideas and language have to be held in memory), having to think about grammar and spelling, and continually scanning back over the text. Conversely, being a competent typist, writing on a familiar topic, having a good knowledge of spelling and written grammar, and being shielded from external distractions all reduce the load on working memory and so are likely to lead to more fluent composing.

Fluency also comes from working to a rhythm of reflection and engagement that matches the load on memory, which generally means writing in bursts of about the length of a clause or short sentence. Having mentally organised a clause or sentence the writer transcribes the mental content into external text. This relieves the load on working memory, to concentrate on generating the next idea. Writers make most errors of spelling at the end of sentences, when the load on working memory is greatest.

---

The most effective means of reducing the strain on working memory is to write within a familiar style and structure. In psychological terms, a writer's style and structure are determined by sets of mental schemas that pre-select language and so reduce the need to plan at the point of composing. A writer gains a distinctive style though a long process of mental development, during which all the aspects of that style become integrated and automatic. To copy the style involves either going through a similar developmental process, becoming so immersed in the works of an author as to absorb the style by a kind of mental osmosis, or alternatively analysing the many interacting factors that make up writing style and being able to imitate them.

Style is an elusive quality. A standard exercise in advanced creative writing classes is to write about an everyday event in the style of a celebrated author. Few writers can carry it off successfully. Jane Austen died before completing the novel *Sanditon* and another contemporary author finished *Sanditon* for publication, supposedly in the style of Austen. Recently, a researcher compared text from *Sanditon* with extracts from other novels written by Jane Austen, by means of a computer program that analysed aspects of style such as the type of punctuation and frequency of key words. He discovered that the ghost writer had successfully copied some, more obvious, aspects of Austen's style (such as the use of the word 'and' following commas, semi-colons and colons) but had failed to imitate many others (such as the ratio of the word *with* to *without*).[2]

Why is style so difficult to copy and to teach? Does it consist of a multitude of small mannerisms packaged into mental schemas? Or is it more than the sum of individual schemas and constraints? To examine writing style, I shall choose an example that is easier to illustrate, that of typestyle. Below is a sentence written only in the first 15 letters of the alphabet, in two different typefonts: Garamond and Futura bold italic. How can we describe the styles, in a way that someone who is unfamiliar with Garamond or Futura could also write out the remaining letters of the alphabet in the same style?

A black dog licked a bone.
**A black dog licked a bone.**

First, the typestyle is not the same as the meaning of the sentence. The sentence means the same whatever type is used to display it, and the terminology used to describe type ('font', 'weight' etc.) is entirely separate to that for describing meaning. Although some of the terminology can be easily understood ('bold', 'slant'), others are specialist terms, invented only for describing typestyle ('serif', 'ligature').

Second, to describe the typestyle in detail we need to refer both to global features (such as 'weight' and 'slant') and to local ones (such the curvature of the loops and whether the strokes finish with a short decorative foot or 'serif').

Third, to imitate a typefont in handwriting involves understanding the distinctive aspects of a typefont and then being able to execute them all simultaneously: making sure that the strokes have the correct thickness and a similar slant, that the loops have the correct curvature and also join the strokes at the appropriate point.

The same three points apply to writing style. The style of writing is separate to meaning. Although we can supplement meaning through style (for example signalling a quickening pace through shorter sentences), style imposes an additional set of constraints. We need a specialist terminology to describe writing style and this has been far less developed than the terms used by typographers. Apart from the well-defined terms of classical rhetoric, the words to describe written style such as 'tone' and 'formality' are broad covers for a set of more specific factors.

Writing style cannot be isolated in a single word or sentence but permeates the entire text. It lies in the choice of a word and the structure of a sentence, in the flow of the narrative and the rhythm of the dialogue.

Since a particular style needs to be described at many levels, books that describe how to write in a given style tend to be lengthy. The UK Benefits Agency designs documents that explain the rules and regulations of social security to people claiming welfare benefits. Because the regulations are complex and their customers may have eyesight problems or learning disabilities, the Agency takes great care to present their documents in a clear and readable style. The guide they produce to assist their authors covers style at every level of a document, including punctuation, vocabulary, patronising and sexist language, how to write questions and how to aim for the right tone. The guide cannot be summarised in a few lines. It does, however, offer two general rules for writing official documents: 'Be consistent' and 'If in doubt, spell it out.'

One broad area of style that can be taught, and copied, is formality. It is the most studied aspect of style, with the most extensive terminology. We all have some understanding of formal and informal language, from the experience of speaking in more or less formal settings.

A formal text, such as that found in an academic journal, tends to use words of a Latinate origin (such as 'cognition' rather than 'thinking'). The sentences are generally longer than an informal text, with more embedded or subordinate clauses. Swales and Feak offer some further basic rules for formal writing:[3]

- Avoid contractions (such as *won't*).
- Use the more appropriate formal negative forms (*little* rather than *not much*).
- Limit the use of 'run on' expressions, such as *etc.* or *and so forth*.
- Avoid addressing the reader as 'you' (except if you are writing a textbook).
- Limit the use of direct questions.
- Place adverbs within the verb ('The solution can *then* be discarded' rather than '*Then* the solution can be discarded').

Negating each of these rules can make the text less formal. To move further along the scale of informality, a writer can include personal reminiscences and address the reader more directly. To illustrate, here are two extracts on the same theme, reflection in writing. The first is from an academic article:

> The translation of ideas into text may be interrupted when the text needs revision, or when it prompts the generation of new ideas. Britton (1970) describes this latter action as idea generation 'at the point of inscription'. A good writer will make use of ideas that arise during production, either by noting them for later incorporation or by revising the plan to accommodate them.[4]

The second comes from a newspaper feature entitled 'How to sell your first novel for a quarter of a million and be even more happily married than before'.

Writing is an exposing business. You may find things out about yourself you had not expected or wanted to know. You abandon decorum, disobey your own protective rules of behaviour, allow yourself to become somebody else, experiment, fail, stare at your failure, begin again. It's an internal, invisible, disturbing process.[5]

Although the two passages express similar sentiments, the style of the second is more informal. Three of the sentences are short. There are no embedded clauses. It addresses the reader directly and uses everyday phrases ('find out things', 'allow yourself to become somebody else') rather than more scientific equivalents.

To write in a given style involves integrating the different levels of language – punctuation, word choice, word order, active or passive voice, organisation and length of sentences and paragraphs, and many more – so as to meet global constraints such as formality and readability. What makes style so difficult to copy is that all the constraints must be satisfied simultaneously, at the same time as creating meaning. It is possible to analyse a style by listing and counting all the factors that influence it (which is why computer programs can distinguish between text written by an author and an imitator) but writing in a given style involves more than just assembling the linguistic parts; they must be merged into a coherent flow of language that satisfies the general constraints. It is far easier to break the egg of style than to lay it. Style can be learned, but only through a combination of study and practice.

Whereas style pervades the entire text, structure can be divided and conquered. Structure, like style, serves two masters. It eases the load on a writer's working memory by dividing the task into pre-defined sections, like labelled sections in a personal organiser, for holding the content of the text. It also assists readers by supporting their expectations.

The most universal text structure is the 'what next?' narrative. We can't help forming narratives. They are the means by which we describe the jumble of sense impressions to ourselves and others. We impose order on our mental world by arranging events into a single orderly flow which we can then label and arrange. Narratives are easy to write because they can be generated by the method we use to make conscious our own experience: the 'what next?' strategy of recalling or imagining a single event and then responding to the (implicit) mental question 'what happened next?' with a further event. Similarly, narratives seem natural to read because they pre-interpret experience for the reader, arranging events one after the other with a single type of link between each one.

Combine the flow of narrative with two other structuring devices – descriptions of strong, identifiable characters and everyday dialogue – and you have a powerful force that can draw a reader through the most difficult scientific and philosophical terrain. Here are the opening words of two books for children.

'Turnip wants us to do a project,' Gedanken announced.

'Turnip?' repeated Uncle Albert.

'Mr Turner – the science teacher. We have to choose a topic – a scientific one. Then,' she added with an air of importance, 'we have to research it . . . '

'Research it!?' exclaimed Uncle Albert, looking as though he were going to burst out laughing.

'Yes,' said Gedanken indignantly. 'We have to research it – and write up the results in a folder.'

Sulkily she kicked a stone – hard. She was wearing trainers, so it hurt. But she didn't let on. She was very fond of her uncle, but he could be so annoying at times. She hoped one day to be a famous scientist like him. That's why she had hoped he would have been pleased at her news. She now wished she had stayed at home an watched television.

Sensing her disappointment, Uncle Albert apologized.

Sophie Amundsen was on her way home from school. She had walked the first part of the way with Joanna. They had been discussing robots. Joanna thought the human brain was like an advanced computer. Sophie was not certain she agreed. Surely a person was more than a piece of hardware?

When they got to the supermarket they went their separate ways. Sophie lived on the outskirts of a sprawling suburb and had almost twice as far to school as Joanna. There were no other houses beyond her garden, which made it seem as if her house lay at the end of the world. This was where the woods began.

She turned the corner into Clover Close.

Both books begin with the familiar routine of the school day. Both introduce a strong central character in the first sentence. Both continue with a conversation. Both books structure the text around a 'what next?' narrative that continues to bind together the first chapter. Both of the books were written to explain highly complex topics to children (the first extract is from *The Time and Space of Uncle Albert* which introduces children aged 10–12 to Einstein's theories of relativity; the second extract is from *Sophie's World* which interprets 3000 years of Western philosophy for young adults). And both books have been best sellers.[6]

The narrative flow of a text gives a powerful indication of how the underlying ideas should be interpreted. By structuring an argument as a narrative you can make your own viewpoint appear to be the natural one. Readers are led along a trail of argument, with contrary views falling by the wayside, until they end up at the writer's destination. The writer's preferred sequence of ideas is signalled by the linear ordering of the sentences. Any other interpretation has to be constructed by the reader pulling apart the text and re-creating the web of underlying ideas.

To escape from the lure of the simple narrative, writers organise their text into macro-structures. Macro-structures are the consensual equivalents of mental schemas. They save the writer from having to devise an overall structure for each type of text, and they cue the reader to expect an acceptable order and logic. By invoking a macro-structure a writer can impose a ready-made framework on the text, one that, even though it may not be signalled explicitly, will be readily interpreted by the reader. Conversely, by deliberately distorting a macro-structure – omitting elements, or altering their normal order – a writer can challenge the reader's expectations.

Macro-structure covers a range of more everyday terms for the organisation of text at different levels, such as 'text element', 'section', 'scene' and 'plot'. Writers through the ages have speculated on whether it is possible to enumerate these, so that composing a text becomes, initially at least, simply a matter of choosing from a list of available structures. At the end of the last century Georges Polti came up with a list of 36 dramatic situations[7] which, he claimed, covered all the possible story elements a writer would need. By assembling these in different orders a writer can create many different plots. Here are a few of the situations (title of the situation followed by main characters or components):

*Deliverance:* Unfortunates, Threatener, Rescuer
*Revenge:* Avenger, Criminal
*Self Sacrifice for an Ideal:* Hero, Ideal, Person or Thing Sacrificed
*Rivalry between Superior and Inferior:* Superior, Inferior, Object
*Enigma:* Interrogator, Seeker, Problem
*Adultery:* Deceived Spouse, Two Adulterers
*Mistaken Jealousy:* Jealous One, Object of Jealousy, Supposed Accomplice, Author of Mistake
*Faulty Judgement:* Mistaken One, Victim of Mistake, Author of Mistake, Guilty Person

An interesting diversion is to try and find a book or movie that fits each of the situations (the first should not be difficult!).

Polti described his dramatic situations in words, but it is possible to show a text structure more explicitly: as a list of embedded text elements, as a story grammar of the type shown in Chapter Three, or as a diagram showing possible transitions between elements. The easiest way is as a list. The list can either be a result of planning by the writer resulting in an outline of section headings, or it can be based on a conventional structure.

Figure 6.2 is an ingenious way of displaying the list of elements for a research paper. The diagram shows not only the order of the main sections but also, by the width of the shape, their generality.[8] Thus, an Introduction normally starts with a broad overview of the topic, narrowing down to the specific investigation or experiment. The Methods and Results sections are confined to the investigation. The Discussion section then broadens into a series of more general issues raised by the investigation, some of which refer back to statements made in the Introduction.

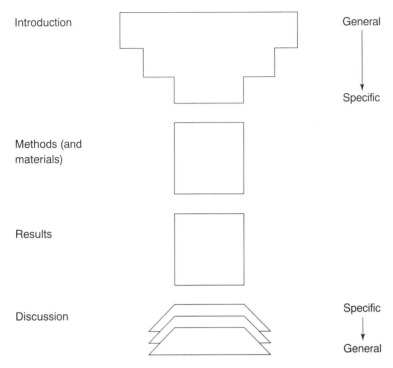

Introduction

General

Specific

Methods (and
materials)

Results

Discussion

Specific

General

Figure 6.2  Overall shape of a research paper
Source: Swales and Feak, 1994

A template such as this should not be seen as a rigid prescription for composing. A writer can add new elements, such as 'acknowledgements', can revise the structure or can abandon it altogether (I have written a published journal paper that was organised around a series of questions and answers). However, a macro-structure is not simply a convention, it also represents the way that readers organise their understanding of a particular type of text. Academic readers expect that a scientific research paper will have Introduction, Methods, Results and Discussion sections, arranged in that order. To write one in any other way will confound the readers' expectations. This implies, first, that a writer must be aware of the macro-structure that a reader will expect and, second, that altering it puts the onus on the writer to alert the reader to the new structure (for example by setting it out it in the Introduction) and possibly to give reasons for writing to an unconventional structure.

In fiction writing, the macro-structures are less apparent (they are not generally marked by section headings in bold type) but they nevertheless exist. Readers expect a detective story to have a sympathetic, but frail, main character, a corpse within the first few pages, and a neat but unexpected resolution.

Some writers have developed the systematic exploration of macro-structures into a lucrative craft. Umberto Eco wrote a penetrating essay called 'The narrative structure in Fleming'.[7] He showed that Ian Fleming's novels of James Bond are built around a series of contrasts between characters and values, such as Bond–M, Bond–Villain, Villain–Woman, love–death, luxury–discomfort, loyalty–disloyalty. He set out 14 of these 'oppositions' which, Eco suggested, include all of Fleming's narrative ideas. For example, in the contract between Bond and his boss 'M' there is a 'dominated–dominant relationship which characterizes from the beginning the limits and possibilities of the character of Bond and sets events moving'. The plots of all the Bond novels can be seen as games with the 'oppositions' as opposing pieces, governed by fixed rules and moves. The invariable scheme of moves is as follows:

A. M moves and gives a task to Bond.
B. The Villain moves and appears to Bond (perhaps in alternative forms).
C. Bond moves and gives a first check to the Villain or the Villain gives a first check to Bond.
D. The Woman moves and shows herself to Bond.
E. Bond consumes the Woman: possesses her or begins her seduction.
F. The Villain captures Bond (with or without the Woman).
G. The Villain tortures Bond (with or without the Woman).
H. Bond conquers the Villain (kills him, or kills his representative, or helps in their killing).
I. Bond convalescing enjoys the Woman, whom he then loses.

Although the scheme is fixed, in the sense that all the elements are always present in every novel, the order may change. In *Dr. No* the order is A B C D E F G H I, but for *Goldfinger* it is B C D E A C D F G D H E H I.

As Eco concluded, it is clear how the James Bond novels attained such a wide success. They translate the purity and order of epic stories into current terms, and transform a network of elementary associations into new but familiar patterns.

> In the novels of Fleming the scheme follows the same chain of events and has the same characters, and it is always known from the beginning who is the culprit, and also his characteristics and plans. The reader's pleasure consists of finding himself immersed in a game of which he knows the pieces and the rules – and perhaps the outcomes – drawing pleasure simply from following the minimal variations by which the victor realizes his objective.[9]

Fleming clearly knew how to explore the possibilities of macro-structures, and exercised this skill for all its considerable worth.

If we combine together content, style and structure, the result is genre. Genre provides a writer with a pre-prepared and labelled package of constraints. It is what turns composing from being a problem-solving activity into a largely pattern-matching one. A writer summons up an appropriate genre to cover the topic and then carries out a process of fitting the content into its text structure, expressing this in an appropriate style.

A highly incomplete list of everyday genres includes:

Narrative fiction
  Science fiction and fantasy
    Technological science fiction
    Space opera
    Science fantasy
  Period fiction
  Romantic fiction
    Historical romance
    Contemporary romance
  Utopian fiction
  Introspective fiction
  Detective fiction
  Thriller
    Spy thriller
    Psychological thriller
    Horror
  Epic fiction
  Westerns
  Sagas
  Children's fiction
    Fairy tales
    Adventure stories
Drama
  Tragedy
    Tragi-comedy
  Melodrama
  Naturalistic drama
  Soap opera
  Comedy drama
    Situation comedy
    Romantic comedy
    Slapstick
Poetry
Non-fiction
  Journalism
  Academic writing
    Research paper
    Thesis
    Student essay
  Popular science
  Criticism
  Biography

The list could be organised in other ways, for example by dividing it first into children's fiction and adult fiction. Some literary theorists have developed more analytic systems of genre, for example based on classical typologies such as 'comedy' and 'tragedy' or on textual structure. There can be no definitive list, since it is part shared currency and part a private catalogue of each writer. For writers, genre is best seen as a resource for composing, an index to different styles and structures of text and also a classification system that can itself be manipulated, merging and combining genres to invent further genres: romantic science fiction, a research paper in the style of popular science, tragedy journalism.

Some genres, such as romantic fiction, have a well-specified structure, thoroughly analysed both by literary critics and by authors of 'Earn a living as a writer' books. Popular genres are intended to be an easy, undemanding read, relying on a complicity between reader and writer. The reader, from having read many other books of the same genre, comes to expect books that follow the 'rules of the game'. The writers deliver a product that meets their expectations. Writing as design is at its most transparent in popular genres: from the illustration on the cover to the structure of the plot the formula novel is a carefully-designed commodity.

To summarise, a writer composes to communicate to achieve a human effect, by designing text within constraints. The human effect of composing comes from the way the text meets or confronts the reader's expectations. Texts that 'play by the rules' of a familiar genre are easier to read than ones that break the generally accepted constraints. At one level easy texts can be more satisfying to read because of their familiarity. As we read them the style and structure recede from consciousness and we are carried along by the flow of narrative, sometimes into understanding a complex topic or accepting a contentious argument. At another level, they fail to meet a human need to be challenged. As readers, we can feel commodified, participants in a game of marketing that reduces the world to chunks of easily assimilated information and the people in it to implausible heroes. We look instead for more demanding texts that reveal their structure and make fewer concessions to the reader.

Even when writing to a formulaic genre, a writer must make many decisions, of content, phrasing, variation of style and, in fiction, character, setting and development of plot. Some writers have been able to internalise the constraints of a genre to the extent that they can compose lengthy works (within that genre only) with a minimum of preparation and revision. For most writers, however, the choice is either to set out the constraints in the form of an explicit plan to guide composition, or to write freely and then pull the text back into line through a series of revisions.

Chapter 7

# Revising

So many people have been put off writing by being instructed to revise but not being told how or why. From the perspective of a child in the classroom revision seems an unnecessary chore. The child has worked hard to produce a respectable piece of writing. In the course of composing he has discovered new ideas and has captured them in his best handwriting. He presents the work to his teacher, perhaps pleased with the result, perhaps thankful that the pain of composing is over. Then back it comes, defaced in red ink. The teacher has clearly been able to make sense of the writing in order to comment on it, yet the child is expected to resurrect forgotten ideas and perform feats of grammar and spelling in order to make it conform to the teacher's idea of a good text. The whole process of revision in the classroom seems designed to sap the child's motivation, to emphasise that composition can never measure up to an adult's never-revealed ideal. It is hardly surprising that some people carry a hostility towards the process of revision into their adult writing.

I want to put forward an alternative, positive conception of revision as a productive activity. To begin, consider revision as part of design. Writers are privileged in being able to revise their products so easily. An architect who designs an ugly, impractical or unsafe apartment block cannot easily alter the shape, rearrange the rooms, or strengthen the structure once it has been built. Nor can an artist move around paint on a canvas at will.

The ease of revising in writing is due to the separation of a text from its physical form. Until recently a text had to be captured on paper to be stored, read and revised. The computer changed all that. By displaying text on a screen in patterns of light that can be manipulated by simple keypresses, the computer has made the act of revising easy.

It is not just the physical process that is easy. We are all amateur critics. Most adult writers are able to find faults in another person's text and to spot poor style or unintelligible jargon. Children as young as 11 can detect errors of grammar and spelling in a text. If revising is so straightforward, then why are most writers so bad at it?

One of the clearest findings in research on writing is the difference between the revising abilities of expert and inexpert writers. Expert writers revise more and the quality of their revisions is better. They alter the overall structure of a text whereas inexpert writers tend to make changes at word or sentence level. Good writers make revisions to the meaning of a text while poor writers tend just to correct the spelling and grammar. A study by Faigley and Witte showed that 34 per cent of revisions by expert adult writers resulted in changes of meaning, compared with 25 per cent by experienced college writers and just 12 per cent by inexperienced college writers.[1]

Worse than that, studies have found that in some cases revision can make the text worse. Thomas, Torrance and Robinson asked 48 social science research students to complete two argument-based essays.[2] For one of the essays each student was asked to produced a detailed outline plan and then a polished draft. For the other, each student had to write a rough draft and then revise that into a polished draft.

The experimenters rated essays produced by rough drafting then revision and by planning then composing. They also assessed the quality of the students' rough drafts. The main results are shown in Figure 7.1. As expected, the study found that the planned essays were significantly better than the essays that the students had revised from rough drafts. However, the scores for the rough drafts were, in general, better than for the revised versions. The students had failed to make any significant improvements to the structure or expression (appropriate and effective use of English) of the essays through revising. Moreover, the breadth and depth of content of the revised versions were *worse* than their drafts. Overall, the quality of the rough drafts was almost as good as the outlined, polished essays.

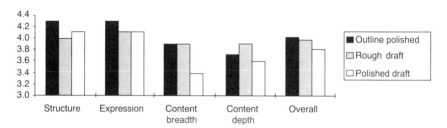

Figure 7.1 Mean quality rating for essays produced by outlining, rough draft, and rough to polished draft, on a scale of 1–7 (with better essays receiving higher scores)
Source: based on data from Thomas, Torrance and Robinson, 1993

From these studies it appears that the very ease of carrying out one aspect of revision – altering the surface structure of the text – causes inexpert writers to ignore other important aspects, such as depth and breadth of content.

Revising a text involves a number of interacting processes, the most basic of which is pattern matching. When we read over a text we match the shape of the words against stored mental schemas and the best match summons up the meaning. As we continue, the text becomes predictive: the new words fit into a pattern of grammar and style. If we meet a misspelled word or a badly constructed sentence it jars with our expectations and becomes a candidate for revision. From first learning to read, children begin to build up these patterns of correct and appropriate language, a process encouraged by school lessons in spelling and grammar.

Detecting and correcting badly-written sentences is an essential part of revision, but not the most demanding part nor the most productive. Expert writers revise for two main reasons: to make the text more appropriate and acceptable to their readers and to gain new understanding for themselves. Only the first purpose is taught to schoolchildren: they must revise to please readers (or more often a single reader, the teacher). The second is generally learned by experience: in the process of revising for readers, we learn to see the text from the perspective of both writer and reader. This self-revelation can often be the most pleasurable part of adult writing, but because it involves reflection and meta-cognition, it is not easy to explain to young writers. To complicate matters further, revising can either be carried out as a discrete activity or embedded into composing.

The first way of revising, as a separate activity, is shown in Figure 4.3. It is a deliberate, ritualised process. For young writers, a teacher performs the rite, by annotating the text with errors and proposed changes. This is an exercise of unalloyed authority: the teacher is the arbiter of good grammar and style, with the power to pull down a carefully constructed argument and to demand another painful revision. The child, understandably, often takes the easy option and carries out the more obvious sentence-level corrections while ignoring the more difficult revisions of content and structure.

This ritual is carried over into self-directed adult writing. At the end of each draft, the writer reads over the text and decides whether to spend time and effort in producing yet another version. The physical investment is far less now that computers allow words to be edited and sections moved without the need to re-write the entire text. But the mental barrier remains. So long as revising is seen as performing a service to some unsympathetic reader, then it carries the stigma of 'writing for teacher'.

In adult writing, the 'teacher' is internalised. Adult writers act as their own critics in a cycle of interpreting, contemplating, specifying and editing the draft text. Interpreting is a constructive process that goes beyond simple pattern matching. It involves reviewing the text as a reader who does not share one's own perspective, abstracting away from the detail of individual words and sentences to gain a sense of the overall meaning and structure.

The interpretation is then compared against the mental constraints and schemas that represent the writer's intentions, to detect mismatches. These may range from a misspelled word to an overall style that is inappropriate to the audience. As a result of this contemplation the writer specifies changes, to repair obvious faults and to construct a new version of the text that better expresses the intentions. This leads either indirectly or directly to annotating and editing the text.

A writer can go through the cycle of revision in small chunks, paragraph by paragraph or sentence by sentence, composing the text and then revising it. This can have the consequence of focusing on lower-level revisions, while ignoring more major ones. It also means continually switching between the mental state of reader and composer, juggling two different conceptions of the text.

Alternatively, the writer can perform a longer cycle of drafting and revision. The advantage of this is that the writer can enter into the rôle of reader, reviewing and interpreting the entire text before switching back to writing. It also allows the editing to be performed in more than one pass, for example by marking up the text with symbols and notes to indicate revisions, then making the major changes to content and structure and then tidying the style and grammar.

The second type of revision is *revising while composing*. As part of the Specify act of composing a writer expresses an idea as a form of words and mentally adjusts the language until it meets the constraints of style and structure. The part-written words and sentences mediate the activity, creating patterns on the page that spark ideas and suggest alternatives. On a handwritten draft this process leaves traces, in the form of false starts to sentences, phrases written and crossed out and words substituted. An analysis of the draft texts of great writers can give a fascinating insight into their thinking processes.[3]

Here, for example, is an extract from the completed 1799 draft of *The Prelude*, a long autobiographical poem that William Wordsworth wrote over a period of 40 years. (The analysis of Wordsworth's revisions is based on a study by Linda Jeffery.)

> . . . Oh, when I have hung
> Above the raven's nest, by knots of grass
> Or half-inch fissures in the slipp'ry rock
> But ill sustained, and almost, as it seemed,
> Suspended by the blast which blew amain,
> Shouldering the naked crag, oh, at that time,
> While on the perilous ridge I hung alone,
> With what strange utterance did the loud dry wind
> Blow through my ears! the sky seemed not a sky
> Of earth, and with what motion moved the clouds!

W
[?]ith what strange utterance did
                              wind
                              the loud dry
Blow through my ears, what colours
                         what motion did
                    The co        the cloud
                    the lou
                    the colours of the sky
                                            not
Wh                          The sky was    then
                                            no sky
Of earth & whith what motion move the cloud,
As on the perilous brink cliff

Figure 7.2  Depiction of part of Wordsworth's work sheet for *The Prelude*

Part of Wordsworth's work sheet for the first draft of the poem is shown in Figure 7.2. The revisions have been transcribed here, but retain roughly the same layout as the original handwriting.[4] The revisions are the public evidence of the poet's struggle to turn visual experiences into language. He appears to be testing out descriptions for the sky. He first qualified the 'utterance' of the wind with the phrase 'the loud dry' and then crossed it out. He played with describing the colours and then the motion of the clouds, crossed both out, tried again with 'The co' and 'the lou' and then wrote 'the colours of the sky'. It suggests that his memory for the scene was based on a mental image or sensation of the sky that he tried but failed to capture in words. He resolved the problem as a poet rather than an artist, through allusion: 'The sky was no sky / Of earth'.

Wordsworth's revisions are not simply a record of his thinking process, they are the means by which he transformed experience into language, enabling him to see lines of the poem as they would be read and to compare alternative phrasings. Revision on paper makes visual the patterns of language. It also helps to overcome the two great limitations of the mind: the restricted capacity of working memory and the inability to work consciously on two tasks simultaneously. For example, Wordsworth often wrote down a series of similar words, such as 'brink cliff' in the extract above, as though he used them to consider alternative wordings in parallel ('as on the perilous brink', 'as on the perilous cliff').

Revision is easy because symbols can be created, deleted and (with a word processor) moved at will. It is also difficult because many writers have only learned to revise for readers, as a separate activity.

In Table 7.1 we can see the two main dimensions of revising: 'why' (for oneself and for others), and 'how' (revising as a separate activity and revising while composing). This produces four main types of revising, all of which contribute towards creative writing. They also all have associated demands and problems. Each problem, rather neatly, fits into one dimension.

Thus, revising for oneself demands that a writer be able to interpret the text in relation to plans and intentions. Such self-reflection only comes with cognitive maturity.

Revising for another reader requires the writer to have a sense of audience, to be able to appreciate the reader's understanding while composing, and be able to re-read the text from the perspective of a typical reader while redrafting.

The difficulty with revising as a separate activity is gaining an overview of the text, moving beyond its surface patterns to see the implicit styles and macro-structures.

Revising while composing brings the need for a knowledge of language, to be able to see alternative ways of expressing an idea without holding up the flow of words. Revising as a separate activity also needs a knowledge of language, but then there is more opportunity to stop and think without fear of losing the thread.

*Table 7.1* Demands and problems involved in revising

|  | *For self* | *For external reader* |
| --- | --- | --- |
| *Revising as a separate activity* | Self-reflection<br>Gaining overview | Sense of audience<br>Gaining overview |
| *Revising while composing* | Self-reflection<br>Language knowledge | Sense of audience<br>Language knowledge |

The three most effective ways to overcome the demands and problems of revising are to:

- *offload thought onto paper* – instead of trying to think about multiple intentions and forms of expression, to write them down as notes and alternative phrasings; instead of struggling to gain an overview of the text, to mark up a draft with headings and sub-headings to indicate its macro-structure;
- *delay revision* – instead of attempting to imagine the audience while composing, to read over the draft text some time later in a fresh context; instead of revising the entire text in one pass, to make the easy revisions first while thinking about the more major changes;
- *use reference aids* – instead of coping with a half-remembered knowledge of language, to look up in a dictionary and thesaurus.

A draft text provides both the raw material for revision and a visual space for adding annotation. The head and foot of the page, the back of each page, the margins and

| Instruction to printer | Mark in text | Mark in margin |
|---|---|---|
| Insert new matter | ⋏ | New matter followed by stroke / |
| Delete | Stroke through character to be deleted<br>Line ⊢⊣through word to be deleted | ♂ |
| Correction to be ignored | _ _ _ under words to be left | stet |
| Change to italic | ___ under word to be changed | ital. |
| Change to roman | Circle round italic word to be changed | rom. |
| Change to capital letter | ≡ under letter to be changed | cap. |
| Change to lower case | Circle word to be changed | l.c. |
| Transpose letters or words | ⎵⎴ round matter to be transposed | tr. |
| Insert comma, apostrophe, full stop | ⋏ | ͻ/⸴/⊙/ |
| Insert hyphen | ⋏ | -/ |
| Insert space | ⋏ | #/ |
| Close up, no space | ⌢ round space to be closed | ⌣ |
| Run on; not new paragraph | ⌐ between matter to be run on | run on |
| Make a new paragraph | ⌐ before first word of new paragraph | n.p. |
| Move to the right | ⊏ before matter to be moved | ⊏ |
| Move to the left | ⊐ after matter to be moved | ⊐ |
| Damaged letter or mark on film | Circle round damaged letter or mark | × |

Figure 7.3 Publisher's proofmarks from Routledge's *Instructions to Authors*

the spaces between lines and characters all have different relationships to the words. Each of these spaces can be filled with marks to guide the revision. The most obvious way to indicate revisions is by annotating the text with publishers' proofmarks. When an author submits a manuscript to a publisher it is read by an editor and marked up to indicate deletions, substitutions, additions and movements of the text. Although the set of proofmarks is fairly standardised, each publisher has minor variations. The proofmark set for Routledge is shown Figure 7.3.

Proofmarks need not just be part of the publishing process. They are a valuable, and under-used, resource for the individual writer. As well as indicating revisions to be made, they also form a checklist: Can words be deleted? Are the words correctly capitalised? Is the punctuation correct? By working through the text, testing each sentence or paragraph against the set of proofmarks a writer can at least be sure to have thought about the errors of grammar and punctuation.

Variations on the proofmarks can be applied to higher levels of text organisation than a single sentence. Deletion of a paragraph or section can easily be indicated by crossing through a chunk of text. Major additions can be indicated by marking the insertion point with an arrow and number, then writing the additional text on a separate numbered sheet. Substitution is a combination of deletion and addition. The movement of a large section of text can be shown by drawing a line down its margin with a number, and an insertion arrow in its new location with the same number.

Proofmarks were designed to assist the public communication between writer and publisher, not to record a writer's more private plans and intentions. For their own use writers employ a variety of personal marks and diagrams. As part of a study of writers' external representations at the University of Sussex, Claire O'Malley observed two people as they drafted and revised. These were not particularly expert writers – one was an academic administrator and the other a postgraduate student – but they both marked up their draft texts extensively before revising.

The first person was observed while writing a document about the work tasks involved in computer administration. She began with an existing job description and a list she had already made of items to be included in the document. These served both as an outline for the document and as a checklist of items to include. She wrote by first expanding each item on the list (which became headings for sections) into draft text and then making a second draft by going through each section and extending the 'easy bits' first. As she expanded the headings, she often made notes on the text: for the reader (e.g. about what the reader of the document should do) and for herself (e.g. reminders to go back and change wording). The main marks she used were simple asterisks, to indicate items for revision. The headings played an important (and possibly confusing) part in her revisions: as reminders of unfinished sections, as a plan to guide writing and as a framework for the eventual document.

The second person was working on a thesis proposal. He had already made several drafts and, at the time of the observation, was working from two documents: a first printed draft of the proposal, and a handwritten note that he intended to include in the text. He had marked up the draft with his own conventions: arrows and numbers to indicate sections to be moved around, lines and notes in the margins, circles around items for which changes had been made, boxes around items that he had changed his mind about altering.

His main method of working was, like the first writer, to pick off the 'easy bits' of the revision first. In this, the two writers did not work as experts. Expert writers generally first make more global revisions and then later consider the more minor corrections. The advantage of this strategy is that the higher-level revision may involve deleting a major section, and so making changes within that section would just be wasted effort.

Some of the more generally useful conventions that these and other writers use for annotation include:

- marking up the text with headings and sub-headings in the margin to indicate its macro-structure (the headings need not be those that will be used in the final version, they just need to mean something to the writer);
- making a note of intentions beside the text (Often the text only captures part of the intended meaning and the writer's original intentions become lost between revisions. It can help to mark up paragraphs with notes to say 'what I'm trying to express here is . . . ');
- marking up the text with different coloured highlighter pens to indicate its status (blue for 'reads well', yellow for 'read this again', red for 'needs revising', etc.);
- making a brief summary of each paragraph or section in the margin, to be considered along with the headings as an overview of the text;
- making notes on how a reader might respond to the text ('boring', 'long-winded', 'too technical', 'inspired', etc.).

There is no need to be scrupulous about following the conventions exactly. What is important is that the annotations should cover the higher-level aspects of revising as well as punctuation, spelling and grammar, and that their meaning should be obvious later when the text is being re-read and revised.

---

Revision is not the end of the line for the writing process. It forms an essential link back to planning and composing. In reading over a text for revision we gain new ideas that demand to be written down. Embedded within each part of the revision process is the seed for further complete cycles of writing.

This notion, that one part of a process can become a new version of the entire process, is called *recursion*. It is fundamental, not just to writing but to productivity in language, nature and science. For example, the power of language comes from being able to embed one complete structure, such as a clause, within another. It follows from this that the structure of a text can be described in a very compact way by means of a recursive formula.

Look again at Pemberton's rules for generating story structures from Chapter Three, shown again in Figure 7.4. A story contains an 'active event'. An active event has, as its second part, an 'action sequence'. An action sequence contains an 'action'. And within one type of action is another story. This story contains an 'active event', and so on round the recursive cycle. The set of rules break out of an infinite loop by offering an alternative type of 'action', one that does not contain an embedded story.

| | |
|---|---|
| *story* → | INITIAL-SITUATION active-event FINAL-SITUATION |
| *active-event* → | complication action-sequence |
| *complication* → | MOTIVATING-MOTIF* MOTIVATION |
| *action-sequence* → | plan qualification action RESOLUTION |
| *action* → | ACTION* story action \| ACTION* |
| *plan* → | INFORMING-ACT* PLAN-PROPER |
| *qualification* → | QUALIFYING-ACT* QUALIFICATION-PROPER |

Figure 7.4  Rules for generating story structures

If we regard the rules as a kind of mechanical specification for writing, then while composing or revising the text for an 'action' within a story (i.e. a basic event that happens to a character) the writer has the choice of either continuing with the action sequence, or making an action be the originator of a story within the story (a sub-plot, or a flashback, for example).

At a more basic level, any note to add some more text to a draft becomes a prompt for composing, which may itself lead to further revision and composing. The hallmark of a good writer is the ability to capture ideas during composing and revising and feed these back into a new cycle of composition.

Recursion in writing is both daunting and empowering: daunting because any minor revision could be the gateway to a complete new round of composition; empowering because each piece of written text is a resource for composing. Seen this way, revision is the start of the writing process. As we read over texts written by ourselves or others, we gain ideas for writing. No writing is truly original, because it relies on the ideas, language and literary styles of others. All writing is productive and creative, because we recursively build a complete work out of a series of fragments.

# Chapter 8
# Being a writer

The account I have built up so far of writing as creative design, with recursive cycles of planning, composing and revising, still leaves open many different ways of writing. The poet Stephen Spender was the first person to claim that there are broadly two types of writer: those who write as a way of finding out what they want to say (which he called Beethovians) and those who write to record or communicate what they have already prepared (which he called Mozartians). Recently, researchers have given these types of writer the more helpful names of Discoverers and Planners.

Dividing writers into Discoverers and Planners is too simplistic. Many writers are, indeed, wedded to one approach. They often find it difficult to see how anyone could write differently and justify the way they write through statements like 'I can't think until I've started writing' or 'It's essential to do *some* planning to get your ideas straight.' Some writers, however, are able to adapt their composing process to the task and the audience. So it is better to think of Discovery and Planning as approaches to writing rather than as unchangeable traits.

Writers with a Discovery approach are driven by engagement with the text. For them, self-understanding arises from writing. They may prefer to begin by scribbling out a draft that reveals their thoughts to them. Then, they often rework their text many times, reading and revising until it 'shapes up' to the constraints of the task and audience. The rhythm of their writing is often one of long periods of engaged composing, followed by extensive revision.

Writers with a Planner approach are driven by reflection. For these people, writing flows from understanding. They spend a large proportion of their time on exploring ideas and on preparing mental or written plans. The plans guide composing and when there is a mismatch they either edit the text or revise the plan. Their rhythm of composing is, typically, one of rapid alternation between engagement and reflection, continually making minor adjustments to keep plan and text in harmony.

The Discovery and Planning approaches are the visible result of two different types of communication through the text. Discovery writing is, initially at least, a communication with oneself – a means to understand a complex topic by turning ideas into language and then reading and reflecting on the product. Through the act or re-reading and revising, the writer gradually becomes an objective reader, separated from the original ideas, and can shape the text to the needs of an audience. A Planning approach is, from the start, a communication with the external reader. The plans are made with a reader in mind, and these constrain the composing.

Neither approach is a better way to compose. They are suited to different types of writer and different writing tasks. Academic works or business reports are often governed by external constraints, such as the need to construct a balanced argument or to fit the text into a conventional structure such as a company report. For these, a Planning approach allows the writer to set down the constraints and to ensure that the text stays within their bounds.

Fiction writing normally encourages longer periods of engagement, with the writer creating an imagined scene and characters then acting it out through Discovery writing. Discovery writing is not only the preserve of novelists. Some great philosophers and scientists worked that way, including Jean-Paul Sartre, Bertrand Russell and Jean Piaget.

At the polar extremes of Discovery and Planning approaches are the pathological dispositions of writers who are caught in prolonged engagement or reflection. The rhythm of their composing has come to a halt. At one pole are writers who engage with the text for long periods of time, leaving no opportunity for monitoring or critical appraisal. The following quotation is from the author Thomas Wolfe:

> I wrote too much again. I not only wrote what was essential, but time and time again my enthusiasm for a good scene, one of those enchanting vistas which can open up so magically to a man in the full flow of creation, would overpower me, and I would write thousands of words on a scene which contributed nothing of vital importance to a book whose greatest need already was ruthless condensation.[1]

At the other pole are the overly reflective writers who plan but cannot turn on the flow of words. Trying to think too hard about planning can result either in a complete breakdown due to over-constraint, or in interminable tinkering with plans and text:

> Dorothy Parker reported that it often took her six months to write a story: 'I think it out and then write it sentence by sentence – no first draft. I can't write five words but I change seven.'[2]

Getting the right balance between discovery and planning is central to composing. A writer needs to work within constraints that will guide the composition without, on the one hand, stifling the imagination or, on the other hand, leading to a ramble of unconstrained creativity. The balance comes from creating appropriate constraints and then choosing a strategy for writing that matches the task.

Two studies, using very different approaches, have come to remarkably similar conclusions about writing strategies. The first, by Luuk van Waes,[3] was a detailed analysis of 80 writing episodes, under experimental conditions. The second study, by Ali Wyllie[4], was based on a questionnaire survey to uncover the writers' own conceptions of the strategies they use.

In the study by van Waes, 20 subjects wrote two reports each, using computers and pen and paper (making 80 writing episodes in total). Van Waes used a combination of video observation and computer logging to record the times, pauses and activities of writing. This allowed him to reconstruct each writing episode in detail.

He selected 12 variables (such as 'share of revisions in the first draft phase', 'duration of initial planning', and 'degree of recursivity (number of times a formulating pause is followed by a revision pause)') that could be abstracted from the data. Then he performed a cluster analysis (a method of forming the data into clusters with similar properties) which came up with five 'writing profiles', indicating general strategies used by the writers. These were:

*Profile 1: Initial planners* (n=7)
These writers spend relatively longer planning at the start. They make few revisions, mostly during the second phase of writing after they have produced a first draft.

*Profile 2: Average writers* (n=24)
This strategy combines aspects of all the other profiles, with close to average values for each of the variables.

*Profile 3: Fragmentary first-phase writers* (n=19)
These writers revise extensively during the first phase, less later. They make frequent short pauses.

*Profile 4: Second-phase writers* (n=9)
They take time to plan the writing, but once they start composing a draft they rarely pause. When they pause it is for a relatively long time. They mostly revise during the second phase. There is little recursion – once they have completed the draft they do not return to planning or composing.

*Profile 5: Non-stop writers* (n=20)
These writers tend to 'get it down in one'. They plan less, revise less and make fewer pauses.

I should emphasise that although van Waes devised the names for the strategies, the profiles were not his invention. They were the direct result of the cluster analysis that grouped the writers according to the variables their writing processes had in common. It would lend powerful support to his method if we could show that the five profiles revealed by statistics match the writers' own accounts of their strategies.

Wyllie carried out a survey of student and academic writers, questioning them about the strategies they used. She also discovered five types of strategy, and these bear a remarkable similarity to the five profiles of van Waes. She described them by the evocative names (based on a typology by Chandler) of Watercolourist, Architect, Bricklayer, Sketcher and Oil Painter. The main characteristics of the strategies, drawn from the responses to the questionnaire, are shown in Table 8.1

Watercolourists tend to write in one pass, from beginning to end, with few pauses or revisions. They may make mental plans, but there is little evidence of planning on paper. When writing with a computer, they tend to review the text on the screen, rather than printing out drafts, and even typing on a small screen they rarely lose the overall sense of the text. This might seem like an enviable way of writing, but few people are able to achieve it, with only 15 of the respondents describing having used this strategy.

The Architect strategy is the Plan, Compose, Revise method traditionally taught in schools. Architects make detailed plans and set down headings to guide the composing. They compose a draft with only occasional pauses and then review and revise it. They may not compose in sequence, but instead start with the easiest sections. With a computer they tend to print out a draft of the text and make the corrections on paper then repeat them on screen.

Bricklayers build the text sentence by sentence, revising as they go. They tend to polish up one sentence before moving on to the next. They revise frequently, but mainly at the sentence level, correcting grammar and altering the style. Having completed a draft they may sometimes, but not always, make further revisions. They can find it difficult to gain an overall sense of the text, particularly when writing on computer.

The Sketcher did not appear in Chandler's original list of strategies, falling somewhere in between Architect and Oil Painter. But the Sketcher strategy is not just a mish-mash. It was the strategy that the students and academics used most frequently, perhaps because their work demands flexibility: academic documents can range from discursive essays to highly structured reports. Sketchers produce rough plans that organise the text under broad headings, though they may stray from or abandon these once they have started composing. They tend to be

Table 8.1 Wyllie's characteristics of the five writing strategies

| Watercolourist (n=15) | Architect (n=33) | Bricklayer (n=30) | Sketcher (n=58) | Oil Painter (n=36) |
|---|---|---|---|---|
| Planner (mental) | Planner (external) | Planner / Discoverer | Discoverer / Planner | Discoverer |
| Similar to 'Non-stop Writer'. | Similar to 'Initial Planner'. | Similar to 'Fragmentary first-phase writer'. | Similar to 'Average Writer'. | Similar to 'Second-phase Writer'. |
| Single draft of whole paper with minimal revision. Usually sequential. | Plan mostly before writing, then write, then review. | Polish one sentence, paragraph or section before moving to the next. | Rough plan, revise later. | Jot down ideas as they occur, organise later. Rarely sequential. |
| Plan in head with broad headings. | Detailed plan. Compose with broad headings. | Type of planning depends on combination of strategies. | Compose with broad headings. | Compose with broad headings. Sometimes have a rough plan. |
| Always sequential. | Often sequential. | Sometimes sequential. | Sometimes sequential, sometimes jump about. | Sometimes sequential, sometimes jump about. |

Table 8.1 continued

| Watercolourist (n=15) | Architect (n=33) | Bricklayer (n=30) | Sketcher (n=58) | Oil Painter (n=36) |
|---|---|---|---|---|
| Rarely start easiest part first. | Sometimes start easiest part first. | Rarely start easiest part first. | Occasionally start easiest part first. | Often start easiest part first. |
| Little revision – some changes. | Revise a fair amount, mainly sentence level. | Fair amount of revision, mainly spelling, grammar and re-sequencing. | Much revision, mainly meaning and sequence changes, and sentence level. | Much revision, particularly meaning and sequence. |
| Tend not to correct. | Rarely correct as they go, mainly on printout. | Correct at both stages, but mainly later | Correct as they go, also later. | Correct as they go, but mainly later. |
| Tend to review more on screen than other strategies. | Tend to review on printout. | Will review on screen, but prefer printout. | Review on screen and on printout. | Least tendency to review on screen, mainly printout. |
| Don't find screen restrictive. Rarely lose overall sense of the text. | Occasionally find screen restrictive. | Often find screen restrictive. Often lose overall sense of the text. | Occasionally find screen restrictive. | Occasionally find screen restrictive. |

pragmatic in composing, sometimes writing from start to finish and sometimes jumping to a section that can be written more easily. They revise frequently, making changes to the meaning and the ordering of the text as well as altering the grammar and style. Often they will correct the text as they compose and then read over the draft and make the more global revisions. When using a computer they may review the text as they write it and also print out a copy to annotate and revise.

Oil Painters are classic Discovery writers. They often start by drafting and they may note down new ideas as they occur, later working them into the text through many sessions of revision. Writers with an Oil Painting strategy are most likely to use a word processor for their writing, but they tend to print out their drafts and review them on paper rather than on the screen.

---

Surprisingly, none of these strategies are immature or ineffective. They have all had their champions among professional authors. The thriller writer Frederick Forsyth is an archetypal Watercolourist. Here, he describes the approach he took to writing The *Day of the Jackal* and which he continued for his subsequent novels:

> I wrote 4,000 words a day . . . seven days a week. When I finished the manuscript it was 450 pages – about 120,000 words. It was written on a typewriter, journalist style with two forefingers. I don't like writing in longhand; it's hardly legible.[5]

After 35 days of composing in this fashion he had produced a complete manuscript that required little editing. He claims that meticulous research, saved as handwritten notes, allows him to write rapidly without suffering from writer's block:

> If you've prepared well enough, it's like a choreographed dance, the next step must follow. If you're wondering what to do, searching for inspiration, you will get writer's block when it doesn't come. Minds are much more mechanical. I don't sit there thinking, Oh, what can I write about? I know what I'm writing about.[6]

Another of the more unusual strategies, Bricklayer, matches the way that novelist Beryl Bainbridge writes:

> I make notes about the story before I begin writing. What I like to do is work out how many words and then chapters I am going to have, making notes of what I want in each chapter. That takes up a lot of time. After that, it's a process of getting down to it.
>
> On the word processor, I keep all the different versions, as I only do one draft of the novel. I can't work on the second page until I've got the first page as right as I can get it. It means doing about six drafts for each page, but once I'm satisfied with that page, that's it, more or less, and I go through it like that to the end, although I cut all the time.[7]

Many professional writers characterise the way they work in terms of an unchanging strategy. This is understandable. They have generally achieved success by adopting a distinctive style of prose and the composing strategy is their method of production. Some writers have an almost superstitious reverence for the strategy that has brought them success. Watercolourists, in particular, can see their strategy as a precious and delicate communion with the unconscious, as in this quote from the novelist Ray Bradbury:

> I do a first draft as passionately and quickly as I can. I believe a story is only valid when it is immediate and passionate; when it dances out of your subconscious. If you interfere with it in any way, you destroy it.[8]

Those who have a more mundane and varied relationship with their writing, such as journalists, business writers, students and academics, normally adopt a more flexible strategy, such as the Sketcher, or they vary their strategy to suit the task. Thus, a writing strategy should not be seen as a description of a type of writer, but the result of an interaction between a writer, the writer's previous experience and learning, the writing task and audience, and the writing environment. All of these are infinitely varied. We cannot hope to understand writing by isolating just one of these factors, nor can we ensure that someone will become a successful, or even a competent, writer by teaching them just a single writing strategy.

In the remainder of this chapter I shall cover some of the factors that contribute to individuality in writing. Because of the complexity of the interaction between writer, task and environment, it cannot be a predictive analysis. It is not possible to say: 'If you adopt these habits then you will become a successful writer.' It can, however, illustrate the diversity of habits and rituals that contribute to the rich ecology of writing.

An extensive survey of the habits and rituals of writers was carried out by Ron Kellogg.[9] He questioned 121 science and engineering academics and compared their responses with their writing productivity, measured by the number of reports and publications they had prepared over the previous three years. This is a measure of quantity rather than quality of writing, but it may at least give an indication of habits that produce words.

Walking and coffee were the two most frequent accompaniments to writing. Although many of Kellogg's respondents drank coffee while writing, there was great variation, with some writers drinking it frequently and others never touching it. Vigorous exercise was the only habit associated with productivity, though this does not necessarily imply that exercise causes creativity. It may be that the most productive writers were also the youngest and healthiest! Kellogg also found intense concentration to be the most frequent mental state while writing, but that no state of consciousness was more productive.

Not surprisingly, Kellogg found that the academic writers tend to work between 8 a.m. and 8 p.m. with the most popular times being between 8 a.m. and noon, and noon and 4 p.m. More surprising was that no particular time of the day was associated with productivity.

Anecdotal evidence from novelists and professional writers suggests that they find early morning to be a suitable time for writing. Of the eight novelists who described their daily schedule to Alison Gibbs[10] all of them start early in the day, generally between 6 a.m. and 7 a.m. A general pattern is to work on composing in the morning and on revising and planning in the afternoon, so that they complete a cycle of composing and revision within the day, and leave plans and notes to inspire them the following morning.

However strange and habitualised one's writing may have become, it cannot approach the bizarre rituals enacted daily by some celebrated writers. Balzac dressed as a monk and drank strong black coffee. Somerset Maugham wrote from 8 a.m. until precisely 12.45 p.m., after which he indulged in a one-martini lunch, a nap, golf or tennis, a cocktail hour and then a formal black-tie dinner, always with champagne. He rarely varied his routine throughout 65 years of writing.

Many successful writers describe ritual or habitualised ways of working. They start precisely at a given time of day, or perform an unvarying activity before or after writing. The bestselling author Jeffrey Archer, for example, writes in precise two-hour stints – from 6 a.m. to 8 a.m., 10 a.m. to noon, 2 p.m. to 4 p.m. and 6 p.m. to 8 p.m. – with the passing time marked by a one-hour silver egg-timer. Hemingway used to start each day by sharpening twenty pencils. Frederick Forsyth ends a day's writing by taking a walk.[11]

It would be tempting to subject these rituals to Freudian psychoanalysis, but there is probably a far simpler explanation based on the rhythms of writing. Both writing and reading are rhythmic activities. Our appreciation of prose and poetry is charged by the writer's systematic variation of grammar and metre. The modern text is structured around patterns of word, sentence, paragraph and page. A sentence is the mental unit of organisation. We can hold and manipulate approximately one sentence in working memory. A paragraph is the basic external chunk. A writer can easily stop and scan back over a paragraph, perceiving within the field of view as a single unit. A page is the largest integral unit of text. By scanning a page we can gain an overview of the text's style and structure. The reflective writer is aware of, and governed by, these epicycles.

We write to short rhythms of engagement and reflection – moving between engaged composing and reflective reviewing of sentence, paragraph and page – and to the larger recursive cycle of planning, composing, revising and rewriting. These patterns of writing activity all interweave with the daily cycle of work and rest. The circadian rhythms of human activity have been well researched. The studies show that human mental and physical abilities follow a daily pattern, with mental alertness rising to a peak in the morning and physical and perceptual abilities peaking in the afternoon and evening.

This agrees with the general writing patterns of novelists. These writers are engaged in a project that spans many days. They generally have control over their daily routine and they often choose to spend the morning in the more mentally demanding task of composing, then the afternoon and evening in the more routine but perceptually and physically taxing activity of reading and revising. Many professional writers finish the working day by writing plans or notes to prime the next day's cycle. A similar technique for a Bricklaying strategy is to revise all the day's work apart from the last few lines. The activity of re-reading and revising this material summons up ideas to launch the next day's session of composing.

Professional writing is a solitary activity. The writers must rely on their own mental resources and find the time for uninterrupted work. The more successful they become, the more they need to create a structure to the working day, one that forms a barrier against interruption by publishers, agents, journalists and readers, and allows them to slide rapidly into a productive frame of mind. The precise starting and finishing times for writing, and the small rituals at its beginning and end, are the means by which professional writers disengage from the distractions of the outside world.

Few people have the luxury to shut off all distractions and to organise their day around writing. Most of us write to a mêlée of interruptions. Some writers, such as school students, may have their daily schedule organised for them so that they are instructed to write at a set time. For these people, writing must be interleaved with many other activities. The Sketcher writing strategy provides this flexibility, with the writing process divided into phases of rough planning, composing and revision, and the revision divided between minor edits during composing and later more substantial rewriting. The cycles of engagement and reflection can be long or short according to the time available. A Sketcher strategy makes full use of paper and screen as an external memory, to capture the changing context of the task. If the writing process is suddenly interrupted, the writer can rapidly pick it up again by referring to the written plans, outlines, notes and edits.

The Sketcher may be no more than a coping strategy, a compromise that allows writers to work with reasonable productivity against the pressures of the outside world. Given the opportunity, experienced writers may prefer to block off a longer period of time and alter their writing strategy from the Sketcher to one that relies less on external representations and offers more scope for creative mental engagement. A study by Hartley and Branthwaite[12] of productive psychologists (academics with a successful record of publications) reported that these academics tended to package their writing into a few lengthy sessions when they could set aside other work and concentrate on the task.

The poor alternative is to be forced into another strategy when a deadline looms and the task is still unfinished. A survey of academic writers by Boice and Johnson[13] found that they often wrote against a deadline in an intensive binge.

Procrastination and binge writing may not just be an inevitable result of the pressures of daily work. Many people fear and loathe writing, sometimes to the extent of feeling physically sick. A survey by Freeman[14] of college students reported that 45 per cent found writing painful, 61 per cent found it difficult, and 41 per cent lacked confidence in their ability to write. Another survey[15] found that the most difficult aspect of writing was judged to be motivating oneself to get started.

The relationship between attitude towards writing and motivation to write is not a simple one. It is not always the case that people who dislike writing avoid it. Some professional writers actively dislike writing. Elizabeth Jane Howard is a full-time writer, the author of seven published novels, 14 television scripts, a biography, a cookery book and two film scripts. She describes her attitude to writing thus:

> Towards the end of a novel I sometimes get a high, usually after a day when I have done a good scene, but it's not very often. Most of the time I don't think the novel I am working on is any good. It's very, very depressing.[16]

This appears to be a paradox. Why are some writers successful despite a crushing lack of confidence in their own abilities? Why do some people write for a living, when starting a new project fills them with dread at the thought of failure? What is the link, if any, between motivation to write, fear of failure and writing ability? The answers to these questions come in part from new psychological studies of writing apprehension (the fear of writing) and in part from observations of mental disorder among writers.

Psychologists at the University of Alaska Anchorage have teased out the various factors that combine to form writing apprehension.[17] Their work is a good demonstration of how detailed experiments can sometimes give answers to broad and important questions of human psychology.

The Alaska team set out to resolve the apparent paradox of why people who are apprehensive about writing, who find it distressing and distasteful, perform just as successfully on some writing tasks as people who find the work pleasant and rewarding. They devised a series of experiments to test factors that might influence writing apprehension and mapped out each factor's contribution to writing ability and success.

First they tested whether fear of writing does affect the writer's ability. They divided 75 psychology students into three groups based on a survey of their attitudes towards writing. They then set aside the group in the middle, leaving 30 'low-apprehension' writers and 28 'high-apprehension' ones. Both groups were asked to write essays on topics requiring analysis and argumentation.[18] The students were given as long as they wished to complete the task (most took less than 30 minutes) and the results were judged for general quality, and also on a number of more specific measures designed to test the writer's fluency. On every measure the apprehensive writers performed only slightly worse than the non-apprehensive. No difference was significant – the researchers found no evidence that the products of apprehensive writers were substantially worse than those from students who enjoyed the task.

The researchers suspected, from previous studies, that apprehension might be related to the writers' tendency to make negative mental comments to themselves while writing, such as 'This isn't working out' and 'Nobody would want to read this.' Apprehensive writers, they surmised, may be continually judging themselves and their text too harshly. This is not always unhelpful. In some cases the negative comments may be self-fulfilling – the negative thoughts crowd out useful ideas – but in others self-criticism may help the writer to view the text as a critical reader.

To investigate these possibilities, the Alaska team set a similar writing task to another group of 101 students. This time, the researchers also asked the writers to complete a questionnaire to assess their self-talk. The students had to indicate whether they had had 'an idea, thought or feeling while you were working on your writing assignment' by selecting from a range of positive statements such as 'I am doing a good job' and a list of negative ones such as 'I'd rather that other people didn't read this.' The researchers also tested the students for their general level of anxiety and neuroticism ('trait anxiety'), and their general aptitude for writing, as measured by the span of their working memory span and their general language ability ('language usage').

A technique called structural equation modelling enabled the researchers to put figures to the relationships between each of these factors, to show how one trait or ability influences another. The results are shown in Figure 8.1. The arrows show the relationships between the various constructs and measures and the numbers

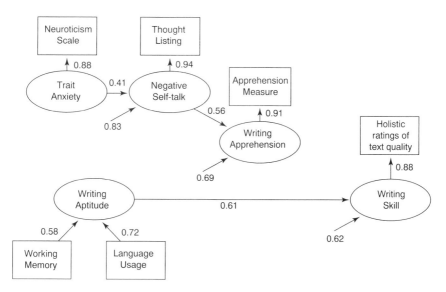

Figure 8.1 Structural model showing the relationships between factors that influence writing apprehension and writing performance
Source: adapted from Madigan, Linton and Johnson, 1996

indicate the relative contribution of each of the constructs. (For example, trait anxiety contributes 0.41 units towards negative self-talk. In the case of single direct measures, such as the neuroticism scale, the number gives the reliability of the measure.)

The most important information is in the absent links. There is no significant relationship between writing apprehension and writing skill, nor between writing aptitude and writing apprehension. In other words, apprehensive writers are no less skilled than confident ones, and people with a good memory and language ability are just as likely to be apprehensive about writing as those who lack the aptitude.

The team did find a path of causation from trait anxiety to negative self-talk to writing apprehension, suggesting that people who are generally anxious tend to make negative comments to themselves while writing, and that this leads to them viewing writing as an unpleasant, unrewarding activity. There was also, as expected, a link from general aptitude to writing skill.

An ingenious further study tested this theory of negative self-talk by distracting both the apprehensive and the confident writers as they wrote. Each student wrote two essays, one in a quiet room and one while being played a dry and irrelevant lecture through headphones. The distraction made little difference to the apprehensive writers, but it caused the non-apprehensive ones to make significantly more negative and less positive comments to themselves while writing. Thus, the experimenters concluded, apprehensive writers appear to be little more distressed by a difficult, distracted writing task – they dislike writing, whatever the occasion.

Although dislike of writing has little effect on the outcome for argumentative and explanatory writing tasks, there was a difference for more personal narrative writing, and for writing under pressure of time. In both these cases, apprehensive writers performed worse than non-apprehensive ones. The researchers suggest that when apprehensive writers are required to write about themselves this may add to their self-doubt to the extent that it interferes with composing. And when apprehensive writers are pushing against a deadline, the negative talk may cost them valuable time.

These findings have clear implications for teachers of writing. There is no point in simply giving further instruction to students who lack confidence in their writing abilities. On the other hand, a scheme that addresses the cause of apprehension may bring results. A treatment that helped anxious writers to eliminate negative self-talk and substitute positive coping thoughts was found to be successful in improving their performance.[19] For the individual writer, the message is: try to think positive!

---

Having come to some understanding of apprehension, we can now turn to motivation, and why some people write despite a lack of confidence in themselves. People are motivated to perform a task for two general reasons: because they want

*Table 8.2* Motivation and writing

| Motivation | Apprehension | Activity | Problems |
| --- | --- | --- | --- |
| Extrinsic | High | Reward-oriented | Procrastination |
| Intrinsic – process | Low | Self-satisfying | Lack of focus on product |
| Intrinsic – product | High/low | Achievement-oriented | Relies on reader Over-confidence/ fear of failure |

to and because they have been told to. This distinction between *intrinsic* and *extrinsic* motivation applies equally to writing. Table 8.2 shows the different kinds of motivation in writing.

Extrinsic motivation is fairly straightforward. The person has been put in a situation, such as a classroom or a job, where they are expected to write so as to pass an exam or to satisfy their manager. The person may or may not enjoy the process of writing and the main motivation is to complete the task, to avoid criticism or to gain reward. Often, extrinsic motivation is accompanied by apprehension (at not completing the task to the satisfaction of someone in authority) and procrastination (putting off as long as possible the pain of writing to order).

A person may be intrinsically motivated to write either because they enjoy the process of writing or because they gain pleasure (or release from pain) through the finished product. As one might expect, pleasure from the process appears to be the main motivation for professional writers, but a few are driven by a need for their product to be appreciated. This is not the same as extrinsic motivation. The impetus to write comes from within. By completing a text you are offering yourself, or whatever self you wish to portray, up for judgement. The reader acts as a stimulant and critical success is an affirmation that your ideas are worthy of being heard. The quotation from Elizabeth Jane Howard given earlier in this chapter continues by mentioning how her publisher helps to motivate her by praising her results. She describes the need not so much to write, but to have written:

> It's very, very depressing – and that's where a good editor comes in. Jane Wood at Macmillan cheers me up and I trust her judgement. Most of the time it's really hard. I often feel very disparaged and it doesn't get any easier. Some people write x thousand words a day and don't find it at all difficult as they have a compulsion to write. I don't have that. I love being interrupted and often I'd rather be doing something else, but I feel writing is all I can do. It interests me. I've tried not writing and I felt worse.[20]

Achievement-oriented writers such as Elizabeth Jane Howard are often balanced between a desire for success and a fear of failure. Desire and fear are both strong motivators, but the balance between them can be delicate. If the expectation of success dominates then the writer can become over-confident and extravagant with words. If the fear of failure takes hold then the writer can be stricken into inactivity. Lurching backwards and forwards between over-confidence and petrification can be the most destructive of the rhythms of writing.

Here, we come to a strange twist in the account of writing habits. Some of the most celebrated of writers have suffered from manic-depression. The list of great writers who alternated between mania and depression includes Eliot, Dickens, Goethe, Swift and the poets Coleridge, Byron and Pushkin. Among the twentieth-century writers who were driven to suicide were Ernest Hemingway, Sylvia Plath, John Berryman, Anne Sexton and Virginia Woolf. These and many lesser authors lived and wrote while straddling a see-saw of impatient hyper-activity and stultifying despair.

In the manic state, manic-depressives are filled with uncontrollable energy.[21] They take on new projects and write with a restless fluency accompanied by a lack of direction or restraint. As the mania intensifies they may work for days with little or no sleep, spurning friends in the rush to create, or sometimes becoming wildly gregarious and argumentative. Their writing becomes a drive to record the unrelenting, formless flow of thought, often with no pause to reflect or revise. In the words of the German author E.T.A. Hoffman, 'disorderly ideas seem to rise out of my mind like blood from engorged open veins'. This is the pathological form of engaged Discovery writing, where the writer abandons all form of pre-planning and is drawn along by the rush of ideas.

When the balance tips towards depression, manic-depressives become withdrawn and defensive. They see events in a negative light and tend to be pessimistic, conscientious or long-suffering. In the mild state of depression, work seems difficult and people irritating. As it intensifies, sadness takes over and the sufferer loses interest in work, friends and self, lapsing into dishevelment and apathy.

Neither the severe manic nor the depressive state is conducive to creative writing – success comes from managing the see-saw of moods and matching them to the rhythms of engagement and reflection. Some manic-depressives experience a daily fluctuation of mood, with the manic phase early in the day and depression later, or vice versa. Such mild changes of mood can be valuable. The hypo-mania can be conducive to both creativity and productivity; the mild depression can foster empathy, sensitivity and the discipline needed for reflection and revision. Composing when high and revising when low brings the advantages of unfettered creativity regulated by painstaking examination. Longer cycles of mood change can fit into stages of a project. George Eliot and Charles Dickens generally began to write their novels in states of depression that lifted as the work progressed. Dickens usually finished each book in a burst of mania.

A study by Nancy Andreason[22] raised the relationship between mental disorder and creative writing above the level of anecdote. She investigated 30 creative writers, interviewing them over a period of 15 years to discover their patterns of creativity and their history of mental illness. She found that the writers were no more likely than a matched group of similar age, sex and status to suffer from schizophrenia or drug abuse. The writers had higher rates of alcoholism (nine writers, compared with two in the control group). The most significant difference was in manic-depression. Twenty-four of the writers showed some form of manic-depression compared with nine of the control subjects. Of these, 13 of the writers suffered severe manic-depression and two-thirds of the ill writers received psychiatric treatment during the 15 years. Beyond statistics was the fact that two of the writers she studied committed suicide.

In Chapter Three I referred to the mental state that most writers have experienced for short periods, and some manic-depressives for longer times, when the ideas and words flow freely and there is a feeling of being completely absorbed in the task. Process motivation is related to such a 'flow state'[23] in that writers commonly report feeling enjoyment, even euphoria, during a period of creative flow. The relation is not inevitable and probably not causal – enjoyment of writing does not necessarily cause creative flow, nor does the flow of creativity always lead to enjoyment – but rather enjoyment and flow interact in a mutually harmonious way. When the words are flowing the writer is enjoying the process, and the pleasure of writing encourages the flow to continue.

Is it possible to maintain that charmed state of mild euphoria in which writing is both pleasurable and productive? There does not appear to be any simple formula for enjoyable creative writing (had there been, it would long ago have been packaged and sold around the world). Factors that might appear in any such formula include education and training in writing, knowledge of the subject, self-esteem and general outlook on life, engagement with the task and the writing environment.

Successful process-motivated writers will most likely have learned the craft of writing through a long apprenticeship, experimenting with different styles and strategies to find ones that feel natural and effortless. They may well work within a well-defined genre. They will be immersed in the subject matter and have researched the topic thoroughly so that the basic information and additional detail that give authority to the writing (and give the writer confidence to invent and embellish) are all ready to hand. They know and respect their readers. They can control their moods and working schedules and be able to put aside distractions.

The science fiction writer Isaac Asimov is celebrated for never having had a moment of writer's block. He claimed to be able to compose a draft at 100 words per minute on a typewriter.[24] Asimov carefully cultivated a Watercolourist writing strategy (he reported having changed from making outlines, when he first started as a writer, to thinking up a 'snappy ending' and then 'making it up as I go along' for his later works). He researched his subject matter until he knew it intimately. He was a deliberate optimist and self-publicist who enjoyed attending science fiction conventions and meeting his readers. He embraced new technology for writing. Asimov was perhaps the archetypal self-made writer.

Being a writer is, above all, having control over how you write and trust in your ability to make progress. If you try to walk with your eyes closed you find that the first few steps are easy, but after about ten paces you begin to slow down, to tread carefully, sensing the terrain and feeling for obstacles. You lose faith in your ability to continue. Open your eyes again and the terrain guides you onward.

Writing is similar. In some ways it is easier, because a writer can design the contours of a text. There is no need to map it out completely in advance, though it helps to have an idea of the end point and some landmarks on the way. As you write you need to know in which general direction to progress and be able to see far enough ahead to take the next few steps. Then writing becomes a self-perpetuating process. You become guided by the unfolding ideas and text and you are able to create, within those bounds, your own momentum and route. You may not see the destination, but you know how to keep going.

Chapter 9

# Writing images

A game of chess does not depend on its visual appearance. It is the same game whether it is played on an ornate marble chess set, a cheap pocket set, with human players, against a computer or by sending the moves through the mail. The nature of the game is determined by the laws of chess, not by the design and construction of the chess set.

This, too, is the conventional view of writing: that the nature of a text lies in its linguistic content and structure, not its layout or its materiality (the physical form, such as ink on a paper page). To most people, illustrations are not part of writing. They are added to the text, to brighten up children's books or to supplement the information contained in textbooks and encyclopedias. Layout and typography are considered (if they are considered at all) as the way a text is presented or marketed: of interest to a printer or publisher but of little concern to a writer.

This is surprising, since we gain a first, immediate impression of a text from its visual appearance. However hard a teacher, parent or examiner may try to ignore the presentation of a text and concentrate on its message, a scruffy piece of paper containing spidery writing full of crossings-out will put the reader in a less receptive frame of mind than one that is presented on spotless paper in a copperplate script. That the illustration, layout and materiality of text have been so comprehensively divorced from the process of writing is a legacy of nineteenth-century technology and thinking.

In medieval times, a writer (more usually a copyist) would have considered illus-tration and presentation as indissoluble parts of the text. A medieval manuscript was an infusion of words and pictures, with individual letters sometimes almost disappearing under elaborate ornamentation. The writer would know how to mix inks to ensure the blackest lettering and the most vivid illuminations. He would consider carefully the best choice of paper or parchment, to balance cost against durability, to absorb the ink without smudging or diffusing it and to offer the text in a form that was suited to its purpose and audience.

In *The Name of the Rose* Umberto Eco describes the complex materiality of a medieval writing desk:

> Each desk had everything required for illuminating and copying: inkhorns, fine quills which some monks were sharpening with a thick knife, pumice stone for smoothing the parchment, rulers for drawing the lines that the writing would follow. Next to each scribe, or at the top of the sloping desk, there was a lectern, on which the codex to be copied was placed, the page covered by a sheet with a cut-out window which framed the line being copied at that moment. And some had inks of gold and various colours.[1]

Ornate illustration survived the introduction of the printing press, though in a much degraded form. Then, in the nineteenth century, two coincident events led to the separation of text from its visual appearance and physical form. The first was the mechanisation of publishing, with the invention of the typewriter and mechanical typesetting. Publishing became a production line, with the writer typing out a manuscript and the publisher controlling the layout and design of the page. The second event was the promotion of the densely printed page as a symbol of literacy. It suited those who controlled the mass media (illustrations cost money!) to join forces with nineteenth-century academics and literati in promoting the purity of the written word. A scholarly writer should be able to present an argument or scientific principle through the logic of language. A learned reader should have the analytic skills and imagination to comprehend a scientific text or enjoy a novel without being distracted by pictures. Where illustrations are essential, as in a geometry textbook, they should be sparse and used only as sources to be discussed in the text.

This notion of illustration and layout as separate to the written text persisted well into the latter half of the twentieth century. It is disappearing only as a result of another technology: computer-based publishing. The computer makes no distinction between text and illustrations; they are all represented at the lowest level by binary digits. Desktop publishing packages allow a writer to wrap text around images or to superimpose images over the text. Most professional writers now have a passing understanding of and interest in typefaces and pagination. Some produce camera-ready copy for publishers.

In most cases, though, writers are self-taught in the art of text design. Schools and colleges encourage children to produce their own newsletters, but usually without teaching them any more than the rudiments of page layout. And in one important area, the materiality of text, we are less knowledgeable than our nineteenth-century counterparts. Most nineteenth-century writers would have a knowledge of the weight and quality of paper, and of different styles of bookbinding. Few contemporary writers can tell a 'saddle-stitch' from a 'perfect' binding. The time is ripe for a re-integration of illustration and text design with writing, not just as an aspect of 'visual literacy' but as an essential part of the process of writing as design.

The language, visual appearance and physical form of a text together constitute the writer's communication with the reader. They embody, or *encode*, assumptions about the nature of that communication. A writer designs a text for a reader that, at least passively, shares and responds to the code. A paperback novel is an 'easy read' because the language, appearance and packaging are carefully designed to be natural and familiar to a typical reader. It seems natural only because we belong to the culture of which that novel is a part. A book that is designed for a different culture (even cultures with much in common, such as those of the United Kingdom and the United States) may seem unnaturally garish, exotic or dull.

By becoming more aware of the code, and how it will be received by readers in different cultures and contexts, a writer can deliberately manipulate all its aspects – not just the language – to achieve effects on the reader. The manipulation is most obvious in advertising which arrests and persuades the reader by adding elements from one genre to another, by mixing codes and by employing visual and verbal puns.

The advertisement in Figure 9.1, for example, uses the visual device of the warning label to catch the reader's attention. The text on the label inverts the standard warning messages on medicines and foodstuffs ('Keep in a cool place', 'Keep out of reach of children'), to engage the reader with a visual and linguistic pun and thus to advertise the product. We encountered the technique of taking a familiar schema and inverting it in Chapter Three, where the expert writer altered part of a restaurant schema to create a story of Luigi rejecting his own wine. There, the negation of a schema was used as a device to create a macro-structure for a story, which the reader would need to discover from the surface text. Here, the negation of the warning labels is presented quite explicitly. The reader is expected to share the pun with the advertisers, and so be drawn into a complicity of shared culture (it is because we are familiar with warning labels that we get the joke) and, by implication, of shared interest in the advertised product.

Visual appearance can persuade. It can also clarify, enliven and beautify. Plain English forms and instructions are examples of texts designed to be clear. The layout of the form complements the text but does not intrude on it. At the other pole are texts whose visual design is intended to be beautiful or intriguing, but not necessarily the most readable. The presentation forms a large part of the appeal of the text. Examples of texts where clarity gives way to visual appeal are concrete poetry (such as Lewis Carroll's 'Tale of a Mouse' in Figure 9.2) and calligraphy.

Figure 9.1  Advertisement that manipulates verbal and visual codes

Clarity and elegance need not be in opposition. A text that is laid out to be clear and understandable is generally also a pleasure to read. Like style, clarity and elegance are holistic attributes that cannot be analysed or learned by decomposing them into constituent parts. They can be acquired, though, by understanding their constraints and properties.

```
    Fury said to
       a mouse, That
          he met in the
               house, 'Let
                   us both go
                  to law: I
                  will pros-
                 ecute you. —
               Come,  I'll
            take no de-
         nial; We
      must have
      a   trial:
       For really
         this morn-
            ing I've
            nothing
             to do.'
               Said the
                  mouse to
                     the cur,
                     'Such a
                     trial, dear
                  sir, With
               no jury
            or judge,
         would
       be wast-
      ing our
     breath.'
     'I'll be
     judge,
       I'll be
        jury,'
           Said
             cun-
              ning
               old
                 Fury:
                  'I'll try
                      the
                       whole
                     cause
                    and
                   con-
                 demn
              you
           to
        death.'
```

Figure 9.2   Lewis Carroll's 'Tale of a Mouse', from *Alice's Adventures in Wonderland*

The starting point for understanding the visual design of text is the page. Pages are a relatively new invention. Ancient books were written onto scrolls some 20 to 25 feet in length.[2] These were the basic units of text and authors wrote to fit a scroll (rather as a movie fits into an integral number of reels). Because the only boundaries were the edges of the scroll, and the reader could not easily jump to a particular place in the text, early texts tended to be long, linear narratives. Each line of the text was a row of about 20 letters with no spacing or punctuation.

The codex or paged book was developed around the second or third century AD. At first it imitated the dense lines of lettering in scrolls, but as cheaper paper replaced parchment the medieval copyists began to organise the text visually, creating spaces, punctuation and illumination. Around the central text they wove a web of marginalia such as glosses and critical notes. The page became a space for both textual and visual organisation.

A page creates a pictorial frame for the text. In their book *Reading Images*,[3] Kress and van Leeuwen discuss the meanings created by the composition of objects within a frame. They analyse visual design from the point of view of the reader, revealing to readers and viewers the implicit codes of composition. But the same analysis can become a tool for writing. As writers we can deliberately organise the text and illustration in order to create particular informational or emotional effects on the reader.

I should stress that these effects are cultural. They have arisen organically over the centuries from the ways in which artists and designers have organised the frame of a picture or book, connecting or emphasising its parts to create conventions of meaning. Some aspects of visual composition are fundamental and independent of culture, such as size to indicate importance. Others are quite culture-specific: Western culture tends to organise the frame from left to right and top to bottom, whereas in Asian design the centre tends to be the dominant region.

Kress and van Leeuwen describe three aspects of visual composition that encode meaning within a visual frame:

- *salience:* from the ways in which the elements attract a viewer's attention (e.g. relative size, foreground/background, tonal contrast and colour, sharpness);
- *information value:* from the placement of elements within the frame (e.g. left/right, top/bottom, centre/margin);
- *framing:* from devices such as lines and edges of objects within the frame that connect or disconnect elements.

We are all aware of size as an indication of salience, probably because it is such a fundamental part of our visual-motor system (if an object looms large then it is either close or sizeable – either way, we pay it attention). In writing we can control salience by altering the size of the type or of an illustration. Other more or less obvious ways to increase the salience of an object include:

- increasing the 'weight' of the type by making it bold;
- separating the object from the body of the text, by surrounding it with white space or placing it within a box;
- distinguishing its visual style or placement from the surroundings, for example by putting text in italics, or raising it above or below the line;
- greying out the surrounding text or employing colour contrast (some colours, such as yellow, appear to 'stand out' while others, such as deep blue, appear to recede);
- within illustrations, placing an object in the foreground of the picture, or making it sharp against blurred surroundings.

If salience affects the basic human visual system, information value is more a product of cultural attunement. The left side of a frame conventionally holds the 'given' information, that should already be familiar to the reader or viewer. The right side contains new or unfamiliar material. Kress and van Leeuwen illustrate this visual code with pages from magazines. For example, they show a double page spread from a women's magazine on the changing rôle of women. The left page contains a small picture of people working at a gold-mining furnace. The right page has a larger (i.e. more salient) picture of two women, in 'space-age gear' to protect them from the heat of the furnace. The left shows the traditional industry; the right depicts the 'new women' workers.

The top and bottom of a frame connote the ideal and the real. Placing an object at the top of a page idealises or generalises it. The title, for example, as a generalisation of the topic, is normally placed at the top of a page. Footnotes that ground or amplify the topic are put at the bottom of the page. By placing a picture above text, you lead with the image and the text serves to elaborate it, as in a caption or legend. By reversing the positions, the text takes the lead and the image provides an example or consequence of the written message.

The centre of the frame is the dominant or focal area of vision, the margin the peripheral. As I indicated earlier, Western culture tends to emphasise elements in other ways – by devices of salience or by placing them at the top of the frame. Modern magazine and newspaper design, with more flexibility in wrapping text around images, sometimes uses a central image or 'pull quote' (a key sentence taken from the main text) to focus attention and illustrate the theme of the surrounding text.

Framing produces a visual grid within the page, linking and separating objects by the use of borders and connecting lines. The horizontal rule is the simplest framing device, to separate disconnected areas of text. Generally, dividing lines should be used sparingly since they can create a harsh linear grid that detracts from the flow of the text. Sometimes, though, framing can be emphasised to give a sense of geometric composition. As you might imagine, the back cover of Kress and van Leeuwen's *Reading Images* is an essay in textual design, and the temptation of trying to 'read' the book's cover is too great to resist. It is shown in Figure 9.3.

Its geometric design, with each block of text separated by a linear rule, suggests both the grid used to lay out a newspaper and the geometric abstractionism of Mondrian, neatly encapsulating the book's twin themes of formal design and visual imagery.

The dark flash (crimson on the colour page) carries multiple meanings. It serves to emphasise the title of the book. It is reminiscent of a banner headline in a tabloid newspaper. It connects the miniature image of the front page on the right with a legend indicating its contents on the left. It separates the 'ideal' of the book synopsis from the 'real' of the author details.

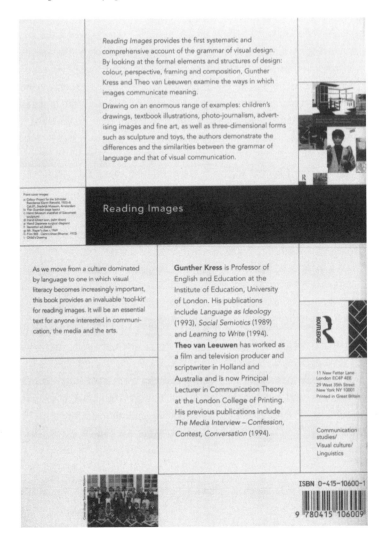

**Figure 9.3** The back cover of *Reading Images*, by Kress and van Leeuwen, 1996

The text is in a simple sans-serif typeface, in keeping with the connotation of modernity and abstractionism. Bold and italics serve to emphasise the key information of the authors' names and their previous publications.

The three pictorial images on the cover are all visual puns. The faces in profile on the Routledge symbol also form part of the letter 'R'. The miniature copy of the book's front cover (shown at the top right) becomes an image to be read and also illustrates the recursivity of visual form: how part of a composition can itself be a composite object. The photograph at the bottom left of the frame is the most deliberate verbal-visual pun. It shows a class from a British secondary modern school and, as the tiny caption beside it reveals, the cover was designed by a company named Secondary Modern.

The structure of the cover mirrors that of the front cover, inviting a comparison between each element on the back and its corresponding one on the front. The biography of the authors, for example, is in the same position as a detail from a Benetton advertisement which shows an ambiguous and ironic figure in a designer 'Mao suit', with an elegant female hand draped over the shoulder, holding a red book and proffering a limply clenched fist. I leave it to the authors and cover designer to sort out the semiotics of that one.

The general point I want to make by this 'reading' of the book cover is that the design of a page sends two types of message. The design helps to support and clarify the information contained in the text and also conveys its own message through the codes of visual imagery. The layout of the back cover helps to organise and segment the publisher's information, author details and book synopsis, and it also indicates visually the book's themes of modernity, composition and visual encoding.

The same double effect is found within each element on a page. It assists in the communication of information and also expresses the language of imagery. Each choice we, as writers, make in laying out text and images on the page generates multiple meanings for its readers. This is impossible to avoid. Take something as simple as underlining a piece of text, <u>such as this</u>. The line draws attention to those words and singles them out as being significant. It pre-interprets the text on behalf of the reader. Writers of instructional and educational texts use many different kinds of emphasis – larger size, bold face, ruled lines, boxes around text, white space, bullet points – to reveal the macro-structure of a text and guide the reader towards items to be remembered.

The visual imagery of the underline suggests the ground: it places the phrase on a firm foundation. The image is also intrusive, it breaks up the white space between the lines. Underlining is not generally used for emphasis in a printed text, partly for this reason. Using **bold** or *italic* provides emphasis without intruding on the space needed for a reader to scan text a line at a time.

A writer who selects one visual effect where another is possible creates a *motivated* conjunction of meaning and form.[4] The writer selects particular objects, or features of an object, to be significant at that point, in that context. In the case of the underlined text in the context of this book, the reader is entitled to ask 'Why has the writer chosen that form of emphasis? Why use a visual device left over from typewriting? Is this an implicit rejection of new technology?'[5] All writing creates a web not only of textual meaning, but also of visual connotation.

A more complex conjunction of meaning and form in visual design comes from the way a writer chooses to present data to the reader of a textbook, business report or academic paper. One choice is between a table or a diagram. Take, for example, the histogram of quality ratings for essays from Chapter Seven (reproduced in Figure 9.4). The data for the diagram come from a paper by Thomas, Torrance and Robinson.[6] In the original paper the results were shown as a table (reproduced as Table 9.1).

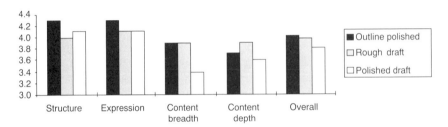

Figure 9.4 Histogram of quality ratings for essays
Source: Thomas, Torrance and Robinson, 1993

The table presents the raw data and leaves the reader to interpret it. This is appropriate for the paper's audience of experimental psychologists who are trained in extracting meaning from data. A less trained reader would need to rely on the writer explaining the implications of the table through the accompanying text. A table also has a connotation of exhaustive regularity, of laying all the permutations of data before the reader. It offers the scientific audience a display of technical competence and honesty.

Representing the data as a graph helps to clarify its message. It offers the reader a visual image whose undulations show, at a glance, the differences between the three experimental conditions. It indicates visually that the 'outline polished' condition is rated better overall, but that its relation to the other conditions varies according to the different types of scoring. The immediate clarity of the visual presentation is suited to this book's wider range of readers, some of whom will not be used to picking out implications from a table of experimental data. The diagram also breaks up the monotony of text on the page through a visual image, as well as offering connotations appropriate to the book of 'design' and 'rhythm'.

But the clarity of the graphic presentation is deceptive. By interpreting the experimental data on behalf of the reader I have highlighted some implications of the experiment and hidden others. For example, the histogram leaves out all the standard deviation scores that are an important indicator of the spread of the data. And by starting the vertical numbering at 3.0 rather than 0, the diagram

Table 9.1 Reproduction of the table printed in Thomas, Torrance and Robinson, 1993

| Condition | Draft | Rating | | | | |
|---|---|---|---|---|---|---|
| | | Structure | Expression | Content breadth | Content depth | Total |
| Outline | Polished | 4.3 (1.2) | 4.3 (0.69) | 3.9 (1.5) | 3.7 (0.80) | 16.2 (2.85) |
| Rough draft | Polished | 4.1 (1.1) | 4.1 (0.70) | 3.4 (1.4) | 3.6 (0.95) | 15.3 (3.02) |
| | Rough | 4.0 (1.1) | 4.1 (0.82) | 3.9 (1.6) | 3.9 (1.1) | 15.9 (2.70) |

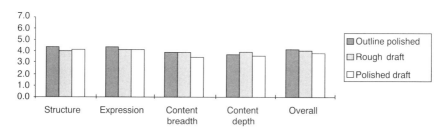

Figure 9.5  A version of Figure 9.4 showing the full seven-point scale

exaggerates the differences between the results of the three conditions. If I had used the full seven-point scale on a graph of the same size, the diagram would have looked like Figure 9.5.

Although Figure 9.5 presents the data in a more 'honest' format, the apparent transparency conceals the fact that its data are themselves the end result of a complex process of experimental design and interpretation. Each rating, for example, is an average of figures taken from three different assessors. The authors of the paper have chosen to combine the ratings rather than present the scores of each individual judge. This is no criticism of the authors. They have presented the table and discussed it in the text in a way that is entirely fair and appropriate to the audience. It simply indicates how constructing a table or illustration is as much a part of creating meaning as writing the words. A writer needs to know the conventions of text layout and visual design in order to use them wisely in guiding and influencing the reader.[7]

The most obvious way that a writer can influence the layout of text is through the use of white space. White space is created within a character and between characters, sentences, lines, paragraphs and columns. All these can be varied for effect. Some typefaces produce a more 'open' look than others for the same type size. Generally, sans-serif typefaces such as Rotis (used for this book) are more open and unadorned. They are easier to read at small sizes and so are often used within tables or diagrams. Sans-serif faces suggest 'modernity' and 'simplicity'. By contrast, serif typefaces, with the short decorative strokes on each character, suggest classical elegance. Serif faces such as Times Roman or Garamond are often used for the body of texts and sans-serif faces for the headings, but there is no clear evidence as to which typefaces are more legible or appropriate for which purposes.[8]

At first sight it is surprising that the extensive research into legibility of text has not been able to answer the simple question of which typefaces are easier to read, but part of the problem is that the faces were designed by printers, not psychologists. One notable exception is Sassoon Primary. Rosemary Sassoon is both a psychologist and a type designer. She noticed that young children had great difficulty in reading certain typefaces and set out to design a face that was matched to children's reading processes and preferences.

He was right out of the water and away from the waves and he lay still.  He rolled on to his back, and lay very still.  He lay there for a long time.  He blew and puffed, and lay there on the sand.  And as he lay there, the wind blew more softly and the clouds began to blow away.  There was a little blue sky.  The sun began to shine a little.

Figure 9.6 Text printed in Sassoon Primary typeface

She showed children different typefaces and asked them for their preferences. The children had clear favourites, their general preferences being for text that is unjustified (ragged right border) with sans-serif, slightly slanted characters. Sassoon designed a typeface that possessed these characteristics along with some additional features to improve legibility, such as longer ascenders (upstrokes on characters such as 'k'). The letters also had terminal strokes (curly bits on the end of letters such as 'l' and 'h') to help group them together into words and to make them look more like handwriting. The result is Sassoon Primary[9], an elegant and readable typeface that has been adopted by publishers of children's books and software. Figure 9.6 shows an example of the typeface.

Unless they are type designers or are writing by hand, writers cannot vary the shape of individual letters. With a modern word processor, though, a writer does have complete control over the layout of the text and illustrations. The difficulty is in knowing which combinations of visual devices cause which effects on the reader.

In general, if the aim of the writer is to draw the reader into a narrative flow, as in a short story or novel, then the spacing should be uniform, with little to distract the eye. The writer holds the reader's attention by punctuation, dividing the text into sentences and paragraphs that create rhythms of prose. In a novel, the writer's implicit contract with the reader is that, in general, the writer will make it as easy as possible for the reader to keep moving from one word and sentence to the next. The reader, in turn, guarantees to read the text in a linear way from start to end, and to mentally reconstruct the macro-structure of the plot.

For an instructional or a reference text, the contract between the reader and writer is different. Here, the writer employs visual design to reveal the overall structure of the text and to guide the reader towards important and appropriate information. The task of the reader, then, is to follow the writer's cues and make best use of all the writer's devices of text design.

White space is, perhaps, the most important, and most misused, aspect of writing as visual design. According to James Hartley, a psychologist who studies the visual design of text, good use of white space can help a reader to:

- see redundancies in the text and thus read faster;
- see more easily which bits of text are personally relevant for them;
- see the structure of the document as a whole;
- grasp its organisation.[10]

A page can be spaced both horizontally and vertically – horizontally by increasing the space between letters and words and by leaving additional space at the start and end of lines; and vertically by altering the space between lines, by splitting the text into paragraphs, and by adding space at the head and foot of a page.

Each type of spacing can serve to assist reading and indicate the text structure. One basic method is to leave space between lines in proportion to the importance of the structural break between text elements. Thus, we can leave one line space between paragraphs; a gap of two lines above and one below sub-headings; and put four lines above and two lines below main headings. This may seem to be a waste of space, but research suggests that readers prefer text to be set in a more open manner.

With horizontal spacing, a writer can group text into meaningful components (for example by tabulating items) and can vary the length of each line. In most printed works, such as newspapers or books, the lines are right justified: extra space is added between words, or words at the end of lines are hyphenated, so that the text stops at the same position on each line to create a straight right border.

This is one case where elegance and readability are in conflict. A justified text can look neat and orderly, but can be less readable, particularly for less able readers such as children or older adults. Unjustified or 'ragged right' text gives the writer more control over layout. The text can be organised so that there is no 'stray' word at the end of a line (for example, a word that begins a sentence or one that follows a punctuation mark). It also removes the occurrence of distracting 'rivers' of white space running down the page (caused by accidental alignments of the extra space between letters in a justified text).

By combining the use of white space to indicate breaks in meaning with appropriate headings to describe the topic, a writer can signal the macro-structure to a reader. There is good experimental evidence to show that laying out an explicit structure results in more readable and acceptable academic texts. Hartley and Sydes[11] rewrote abstracts from social science journals in a structured form, organised around the sub-headings of Background, Aims, Method, Results, Conclusions and Comment. They found that the structured abstracts can be easier to read, easier to search and easier to recall than the original ones. Figure 9.7 shows an example of a structured abstract, from a paper by Hartley and Sydes.[12]

ABSTRACT.

BACKGROUND. Structured abstracts – which include subheadings such as this one – have replaced traditional abstracts in most current medical journals. However, the number and detail of the subheadings used varies, and there is a range of different typographic settings.

AIMS. The aims of the studies reported in this paper were to investigate readers' preferences for different typographic settings of (i) the subheadings and (ii) the overall position and layout of such abstracts on a two-column A4 page.

PARTICIPANTS. Over 400 readers took part – students, postgraduates, research workers and academics in the social sciences.

METHOD. A series of studies was carried out in three main stages in order to narrow down readers' preferences for different typographic settings of the subheadings in structured abstracts. The most preferred version emerged from the final study. Two additional studies were then carried out to determine preferences for the overall position and layout of this most preferred version on an A4 page.

RESULTS. The most preferred version for the setting of the subheadings was that used in this present abstract, i.e. to have them printed in bold capital letters. Readers also preferred the abstracts to have a line-space above the main headings (as here), and (unlike here) for the abstracts to be centred over the top of the subsequent two-column article (on an A4 page).

Figure 9.7 Example of a structured abstract
Source: Hartley and Sydes, 1996

To the basic elements of space and headings, a writer can then add a variety of other devices to structure the text and guide its interpretation. These include:

- *boxes*, to set off material to be remembered or recalled from the main text;
- *self-assessment questions*, to prompt the reader to reflect on the text and draw inferences from it;
- *activities*, such as questionnaires for the reader to fill in;
- *advance organisers*, that have a similar aim to abstracts of introducing the text and alerting the reader to its content and structure;
- *summaries*, at the end of a section or chapter, to help the reader to remember the main points;
- *margin notes*, to summarise a paragraph or draw out its implications;
- *content lists and outlines*, that present the overall macro-structure of the text;
- *indexes*, to help the reader to find particular pieces of information;

- *glossaries*, to explain the terminology;
- *footnotes*, that give references to related texts, or that provide useful amplifications or interesting digressions;
- *topic maps*, that give a visual indication of the text's content;
- *frequently asked questions (FAQs)*, that anticipate and answer questions a typical reader might ask;
- *tips* on how to use the material.

All these devices can help readers to interpret and remember a complex text, or to find the information they need. They are particularly useful in books for self-directed learning (such as user guides or distance-learning texts).

The problem with structured texts is that the text itself can disappear under a profusion of structuring devices. Pages of badly designed reference manuals and instructional texts can look like an urban highway, strewn with signposts, diversions, cryptic symbols and warnings. The skill (which many text designers have not acquired!) is to use structuring devices and study aids to complement the main text, not obscure it. Shown below are some types of text, in rough order of the need to add explicit structure. For those around the middle of the list, a writer needs to balance the need to direct the reader's attention against the need to avoid breaking the flow of narrative.

| Novel | Biography | Popular non-fiction | General academic | Reference | Textbook | User guide, instruction manual |
|---|---|---|---|---|---|---|

Just as text has layers of internal structure and conveys multiple meanings, so do images. I have alluded to the language of imagery in my discussion of the cover of *Reading Images* and that book covers the topic in detail. A writer may not need to understand the semiotics of soap adverts or the modality of Mondrian, but it is useful to have some idea of the ways in which images can communicate with readers.

First, you cannot assume that readers will study the image at all. Any item that is set outside the flow of text (including pictures, tables and blocked quotations) is a diversion. The reader must make a conscious decision to give it attention. If the image stands alone in the text, the reader may not examine it at all, or may not do so at a point that relates to the written information. To control when a reader views an image, the writer needs to divert attention from the text, either by inserting the image into the text or by adding a reference to it, at the point where studying the image is most appropriate. A difficulty for writers is that unless they lay out the page themselves they have little control over where the image appears. In a book, the position is usually chosen by the publisher to be at the top or bottom of a page, with the result that the reader has two stopping points: one a result of the constraints of publishing and the other controlled by the writer through a reference in the text.

Figure 9.8

A writer normally has more choice over the content of the image and how it is described in the text. An image placed within text forms a pictorial question mark. Why has it been placed there? What purpose does it serve? What aspect of the image am I meant to attend to? How does it relate to the text? The writer provides a guide to interpretation by the caption and the referring text. Take, for example, the two images in Figure 9.8. Without a caption for guidance, the meanings they convey are limited only by the images themselves, their position within the page and the content of the book so far. Are they intended to show how the reader's attention can be distracted from text? Or to introduce a section on naturalistic pictures? Or to show how to divide up a rectangle? In fact, the images are taken from an article on 'Affecting Instructional Textbooks Through Pictures'[13] and the original caption reads: 'Dynamic images are more interesting than static ones'.

In this case, the original writer picked out one aspect of the images – their dynamism – to illustrate a point he was making. The images of the horses might have been reproduced from another publication. In that case it would have selected different aspects of the images as being important (perhaps the shape of the horse). In this book I have, once again, reproduced the images in a new context and re-interpreted them for another purpose. As with the earlier example of underlining a piece of text, a writer creates a motivated combination of form and meaning by selecting particular aspects of a visual element to serve a purpose. In the case of the underlined text I did so by marking out the important element; in the case of the picture I created the interpretation through the text.

It is not only a one-way direction of meaning. The text does not just influence the image. The image also affects how the reader interprets the text. It breaks the text at one particular point and inserts the visual into the verbal. As well as the aspect to which the writer draws attention, the image has other symbolisms, other connotations. Every picture tells a story, one that varies with the reader and context. Its meaning will influence the way the reader makes inferences from the surrounding text.

For example, the cover of a recent paperback edition of one of Enid Blyton's *Famous Five* stories shows the children in 1990s clothes. To children, the picture will influence the way that they understand the story and identify with the characters. It might also, in a deeper sense, influence their perception of history. If they realise, from reading Enid Blyton's text, that the stories are set in the past, in the childhood of their parents, then they may also infer that t-shirts, jeans and trainers have always been the universal children's fashion. The single image, when interpreted by a child in the context of Enid Blyton's text, asserts the dominance of the present over the past. To an adult viewer, the cover might well be interpreted differently, as a cynical attempt at re-packaging worn out stories.

Rather than continuing to look separately at how we write text and images, it makes sense now to consider how they combine. In recent years, the printed page has once again become a composite object, with illustration merging into text. Unlike medieval manuscripts, the illustration does not serve to glorify the text; in many cases the text is fragmented by the image.

Look, for example at the two pages (Figure 9.9 and Figure 9.10) from popular science books for children, one from the 1930s[14] and the other from the 1980s.[15] Both pages are somewhat peculiar hybrids. The 1930s one combines a chatty avuncular style of writing ('Let us, therefore, first find out what a lens does') with illustrations in the style of a learned scientific paper. The text meanders around the images, but it still maintains a continuity of visual and narrative flow.

The page from the 1980s book draws on the imagery of the comic book, with cartoon characters and speech bubbles. The images spread out and (in the picture of the fruit) merge with the words. The pictures have taken over. There is no primary flow of text. The page uses a variety of structuring devices – headings, boxes, speech bubbles, labels, numbers – that a child would need to understand in order to navigate the page. The page itself is split vertically into two columns and then again into two images. The left column is boxed off, and it is not clear whether that is a supplement to the right hand column, or a text in itself. The relationship between the images at the bottom right and the text below them is ambiguous. Which should the child attend to first, picture or text? The text acts both a caption to the image ('fruits, like the ones in this picture') and as a set of instructions for performing the experiment illustrated by the picture. Modern texts may be visually more appealing, but the visual complexity can make them harder to interpret.

A tour of pages on the World Wide Web shows the perils of indiscriminate visual complexity. Web-page designers are offered power without modesty. They can command an arsenal of devices for positioning, sizing, colouring and illustrating

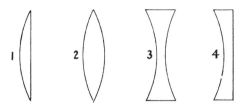

PLANO-CONVEX   BI-CONVEX   BI-CONCAVE   PLANO-CONCAVE
Fig. 1.   1 and 2 are convex or converging lenses; 3 and 4 are concave or diverging lenses.

# HOW A TELESCOPE WORKS?

EVERY tele-scope (except a reflector) contains two lenses, one large lens, the objective, and one small one, the eye-piece. Let us, therefore, first find out what a lens does.

There are two sorts of lenses: the first sort is the convex lens, thickest at the centre: the second sort is the concave lens, thinnest at the centre.

The convex lens makes rays converge, as in Fig. 2. On the other hand, the concave lens makes diverging rays diverge still more, as in Fig. 3,

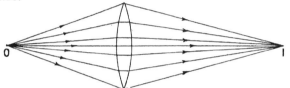

Fig. 2.   A convex lens causing rays from a point O to converge to a point I.   I is said to be the image of O.

where the rays diverging from O proceed from the lens *as if* they had started from I.   The image I is, therefore, said to be *unreal*.   In Fig. 2 the rays from O are focussed at I.   But there is a special point (or rather pair of points) for any particular lens which is known as its principal focus, and the distance of this point from the lens is called its focal length. Rays from the focus become parallel after leaving the lens; whilst, conversely, parallel rays falling on the lens converge to the focus.

These two foci are at equal distances on either

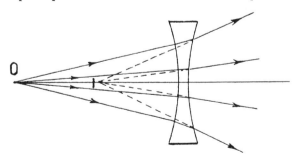

Fig. 3.   A concave lens causing rays from a point O to diverge still further, so as to appear to come from I.   I is the image (unreal) of O.

Figure 9.9 Children's science book from the 1930s

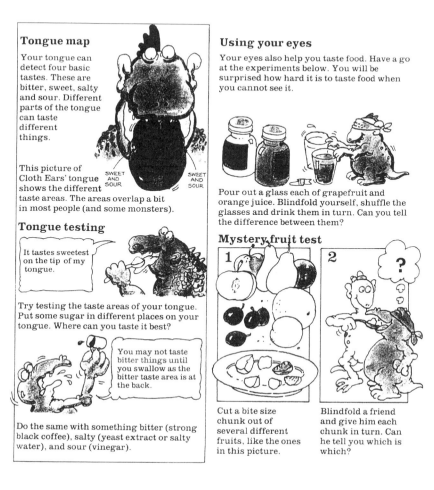

**Tongue map**

Your tongue can detect four basic tastes. These are bitter, sweet, salty and sour. Different parts of the tongue can taste different things.

This picture of Cloth Ears' tongue shows the different taste areas. The areas overlap a bit in most people (and some monsters).

SWEET AND SOUR

SWEET AND SOUR

**Tongue testing**

> It tastes sweetest on the tip of my tongue.

Try testing the taste areas of your tongue. Put some sugar in different places on your tongue. Where can you taste it best?

> You may not taste bitter things until you swallow as the bitter taste area is at the back.

Do the same with something bitter (strong black coffee), salty (yeast extract or salty water), and sour (vinegar).

**Using your eyes**

Your eyes also help you taste food. Have a go at the experiments below. You will be surprised how hard it is to taste food when you cannot see it.

Pour out a glass each of grapefruit and orange juice. Blindfold yourself, shuffle the glasses and drink them in turn. Can you tell the difference between them?

**Mystery fruit test**

1

2  ?

Cut a bite size chunk out of several different fruits, like the ones in this picture.

Blindfold a friend and give him each chunk in turn. Can he tell you which is which?

Figure 9.10 Children's science book from the 1980s
Source: Walters, 1985

text and are tempted into applying these indiscriminately, splattering the Web page with clashing colours, irrelevant illustrations and distracting text separators. Even worse, they discover how to make things move, so that the long-suffering reader must watch and wait while the web site transmits an arcade of flashing words and spinning icons. Fortunately, the culture of the Internet mocks such displays of nerdishness. The Web also contains some excellent examples of good visual design.

I shall end the chapter with a prime example of writing as creative visual design, in the guidebooks of Alfred Wainwright. The guides are a publishing phenomenon. Wainwright was a private man who detested publicity, yet his name and signature have become icons. He originally published his guidebooks privately and never sought a major publisher, yet his works have reportedly sold over one million copies worldwide.

Producing a guidebook for walkers is a particularly demanding task for a writer. The visual must be balanced against the textual, information against opinion. The guide must tell a walker precisely how to get from one place to another across a sometimes desolate landscape, and at the same time it must inspire the reader with a love of the countryside and an appreciation of the sights along the route.

Alfred Wainwright worked as an accountant in a local government office, meticulously writing out longhand ledgers. He was a pen-and-ink man, in the days when accountancy was an art of precise visual reckoning. For relaxation he roamed the hills of the British Lake District. As he put it:

> On a day when I didn't have to wear a collar and tie I was a boy again. If I was heading for the hills, and not the office, I could set forth singing, not audibly, heaven forbid; just in my heart. I was off to where the sheep were real, not human.[16]

After spending many years walking and sketching, he decided to put his training to good use in producing an account of the Lake District for his own pleasure. In 1952, at the age of 45, he sat down with the highly-detailed 6-inch maps of the area that equally meticulous Victorian cartographers had produced and planned out a project that he knew would take the remainder of his time until retirement, to interpret the maps as seven guidebooks of the Lakeland fells. He would climb every fell and record not just the ways up and down, but his own impressions of the journey and the sights along the route.

Rather than handing his art to a machine, he decided to print the text by hand, but he wanted to achieve the precision and legibility of metal type. So he invented his own handwritten fonts, in roman and italics and bold forms. With typical obsession he planned each line of text to be right justified (or aligned with an illustration) and without hyphens. The handprinted typeface was as legible as a printer's font, but subtly varied (a university team attempted to produce a 'Wainwright' computer font, but it looked overly bland compared with the original). He never erased a word. If there was a mistake on the last line he would throw away the page and start again. Since he had complete control over the layout (not a word of his original guidebooks was typeset) Wainwright could experiment with merging text and illustration.

What makes Wainwright's guides such a pleasure to read is that he was far from an artless copyist. An academic article on the design of walkers' guides[17] starts as an objective comparison of different approaches and ends as a hymn of praise to Wainwright's style and innovation. For example, Wainwright developed a method of displaying the route up a mountain as a stylised map at the bottom which turns into a profile or elevation as it rises up the page (as with the example in Figure 9.11[18]). It is as if the viewer were hovering some 200 feet above the mountain, looking down at its foot and then raising his eyes to the summit. The text combines the precision of an accountant with the verbal fancies of a man steeped in the

## ASCENT FROM THRELKELD
### via HALL'S FELL
### 2400 feet of ascent : 2 miles

Gategill Fell Top

BLENCATHRA (Hallsfell Top)

Doddick Fell Top

The last half-mile of the ridge, from 2000, is entirely delightful. This section, known as Narrow Edge with good reason, is a succession of low crags, with steps and gateways and towers of rock. A distinct track on grass is available for walkers — at first this keeps mostly on the Doddick side and later prefers the other, occasionally being forced along the crest. Care is needed in places but there are no difficulties. Scramblers will enjoy following the crest throughout.

Under ice and snow the ridge is for experts only

An enchanting track climbs the broad base of the fell. Unseen from below, this track reveals itself in the heather a few yards at a time, beckoning irresistibly upwards to the exciting ridge above.

For active walkers and scramblers, this route is positively the finest way to any mountain-top in the district. It is direct, exhilarating, has glorious views, and (especially satisfying) scores a bulls-eye by leading unerringly to the summit-cairn.

arete
pinnacle
tower
care needed in traversing rockface by horizontal crack
From the ridge there are tremendous views down to Doddick and Gate Gills

Middle Tongue

Gategill Fell

Gate Gill

heather

Doddick Gill

Doddick Fell and Scales Fell come into view

Hall's Fell

heather

Doddick Fell

level

Gategill Mine (disused)

bracken

hut

weir
fold
fall

Gategill

kennels (the home of the Blencathra Foxhounds)
Woodend Mine (disused)
spoil heaps
SCALES 1¼
PENRITH 13

THRELKELD HALL (from which Hall's Fell is named)

MAIN ROAD

looking north

Threlkeld (east end of village)

Figure 9.11 Page from a Wainwright guide
Source: Wainwright, 1992

countryside of Wordsworth. Each page is a harmonious blend of text and image, with the words acting as an accompaniment to the visual journey.

Few writers will have the patience or obsession with detail needed to create a handwritten manuscript, but modern methods of page layout can achieve some of the same effects, so that words can be wrapped around images and images can fade into the text. Increasingly, a writer is becoming a visual designer and it no longer makes sense to look at illustration or text design as the preserve of a publisher.

# Part Three

# Writing in the world

# Chapter 10

# Messages in bottles and cultures

A message in a bottle is an evocative and enduring image. It is the vision of a shipwrecked sailor on a deserted island writing a plea for help, placing it in an empty rum bottle and throwing it into the sea. It is the etching on the plaque bolted to the Pioneer spacecraft of a naked Average Man, hand raised in greeting, standing beside his Average Woman.[1] It is also the standard view of how writers communicate with their readers.

In this information processing view of communication, a writer produces a message that captures some information in words and pictures. The message is sent, in the form of a book or other medium, to one or more readers who then interpret the message and so gain the writer's information. Providing that the writer knows how to put information into text, the message is delivered safely through time and space (and the entire postal, publishing and telecommunications industry is dedicated to ensuring that it is), and the reader can turn the text back into information, then the information has been transmitted successfully from writer to reader.

Unfortunately, safe transmission does not guarantee that the writer will be able to communicate anything interesting, useful or even understandable to the reader. When a reader receives a message in a bottle, spacecraft or book, he or she may not be able to make sense of it. The reader may communicate in a different language to the writer or, in the case of Pioneer, may come from an entirely different civilisation. Carl Sagan, the designer of the Pioneer plaque (Figure 10.1), came up with the ingenious idea of basing his message on hydrogen, the most common element

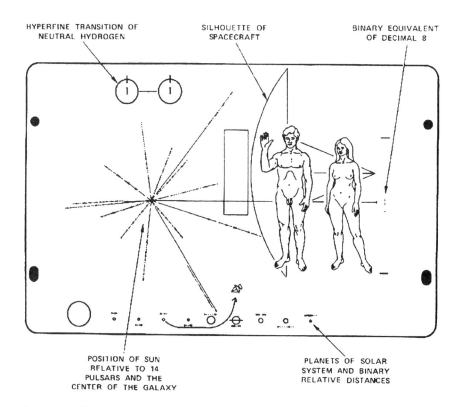

HYPERFINE TRANSITION OF
NEUTRAL HYDROGEN

SILHOUETTE OF
SPACECRAFT

BINARY EQUIVALENT
OF DECIMAL 8

POSITION OF SUN
RELATIVE TO 14
PULSARS AND THE
CENTER OF THE GALAXY

PLANETS OF SOLAR
SYSTEM AND BINARY
RELATIVE DISTANCES

Figure 10.1 The plaque on the Pioneer 10 and 11 spacecraft, the first man-made objects to leave the Solar system (with annotations)

in the universe. In the corner of the plaque is a small diagram that illustrates the structure of hydrogen. According to NASA, anyone from a scientifically trained civilisation having enough knowledge of hydrogen would be able to translate the message. To this we might add that they would also need to be possessed of eyes, to realise that lines etched in gold constitute a message, and to be sufficiently inquisitive to bother to decipher it.

Thus, a message is a message not because it is written in words on paper or etched in gold, but because it forms a conceptual link between different minds. This relationship was shown as a diagram in Figure 6.1. The Pioneer plaque can, NASA hopes, carry a simple message to other possible civilisations because the universe is bathed in hydrogen and we share with an Arcturan Zarg an understanding of the structure of this most common element. If the planet Arcturus has no hydrogen, or Zarg scientists cannot understand its structure, then there is no communication.

In general, the closer in time and culture a writer is to a reader, the more they will have in common and the easier will be the communication. The further apart, the more reading becomes a struggle to understand. To give a simple example, Figure 10.2 shows part of *The Bothie of Toper-na-fuosich*, a long narrative poem written by the nineteenth-century English poet Arthur Hugh Clough.[2]

And from his seat and cigar spoke the Piper
    the cloud-compeller.
Hope with the uncle abideth for shooting. Ah
    me, were I with him!
Ah, good boy that I am, to have stuck to my
    word and my reading!
Good, good boy to be here, far away, who might
    be at Balloch!
Only one day to have staid who might have been
    welcome for seven,
Seven whole days in castle and forest — gay in
    the mazy,
Moving, imbibing the rosy, and pointing the gun at
    the horny!

Figure 10.2  Extract from *The Bothie of Toper-na-fuosich* by A.H. Clough

We can understand what most of the words appear to mean and the most unusual of them (apart from Balloch, the name of a village) is 'mazy' and that is defined in a modern Chambers Dictionary as 'winding or convoluted as a maze; confused, dizzy (*dialect*)'. At the most superficial level the poem (with the aid of a dictionary) has successfully transferred information from the nineteenth century to the present day. But a contemporary reader would find it hard to make sense of the extract (and the poem as a whole), not only because the word 'gay' has taken on a new meaning in recent years and 'horny' has lost any connotation other than as sexual slang, but also because the poem describes the alien environment of a nineteenth-century reading party of Oxford students in Scotland. The reader cannot enter into the writer's world; there is little shared understanding. In most cases, though, a reader shares many aspects of culture with the writer. The reader understands a text and its author by negotiating the similarities and differences between their two cultures.

What this implies is that a message is not a fixed impersonal entity, but is formed by the comparative cultures of writer and reader. The first people to make this observation were a group of Soviet linguists, literary theorists and philosophers in the 1920s, led by M.M. Bakhtin. They argued that the meaning of a written text or a spoken utterance does not lie in the text itself, but in the context of its use. When we speak or write we engage in a situated dialogue.

But it takes two to make a dialogue. How can a writer be said to hold a dialogue with an unknown reader, when there is no obvious channel of communication back from reader to writer? There are three kinds of dialogue that a writer can hold with a reader. At increasing levels of abstraction they are: directly with the reader, with an imagined reader and with the culture shared by the writer and reader.

The first and most obvious means of communication is the reader's direct response to the text. A newspaper prints a critical review of a book that the writer then reads. A teacher gives a student spoken or written comments on an essay. These are highly circumscribed kinds of dialogue, generally restricted to passing judgement on the text. They are also fraught with problems.

The common-sense notion of literary criticism is that the duty of a writer is to 'tell it like it is', to communicate the truth to a responsive reader. The reader, in turn, assesses the text in terms of how well it directs the mind towards objects, people and events worthy of contemplation and how faithfully it represents their essential truth. Telling the truth is the basis of our literary tradition. The nineteenth-century philosopher and critic John Ruskin asserted that 'I shall look only for truth; bare, clear, downright statement of facts; showing in each particular, as far as I am able, what the truth of nature is, and then seeking for the plain expression of it.'[3]

To Ruskin, as to other nineteenth-century critics, the great writer or artist is possessed of an exquisite sensibility and, through text, can reveal truths about the world not open to the untutored reader. Lesser writers may never be possessed of such insight but must at least learn how communicate clearly and faithfully. Echoes of Ruskin's words can be found in the response of every teacher to children's writing.

Ruskin accepted, indeed relished, the idea that some ennobled writers and artists can perceive nature differently to the untrained mind, but he did not follow this through to its logical conclusion, that there can be no *ideal* view of the world, free of perception, only *different* ones. There is no single truth for a reader to unpack from the text; rather each reader evokes a different interpretation at each reading. The message is not in the bottle, but in the interaction between writer and reader.

To anyone trained as a scientist, this is deeply troubling. Surely there are some absolute truths, enduring facts that can be communicated across time and culture. $E$ equals $mc^2$ whatever the context. This is the essence of Pioneer's message, that some truths hold sway throughout the universe.

Bakhtin tackled the problem of truth and text by distinguishing between the natural and the human sciences. The natural sciences, such as physics and chemistry, study objects; the human sciences study subjects, or the discourse created by subjects. In the natural sciences there is a subject – the scientist – and a mute object, and the aim is for the subject to gain knowledge of the object. Human sciences consist of those disciplines whose primary data are the texts created by subjects. ('Subjects' are not the same as 'people'. We can study people as objects, their anatomy or biochemistry for example. Subjects are people actively engaged in the world as thinkers and doers.)

Texts, according to Bakhtin, can include thoughts, speech, gestures and actions, all of which are interpreted by subjective intellects trying to understand other intellects, in a continual dance of mutual interpretation. The only way we can gain an understanding of subjects and their unfolding texts is by engaging them in dialogue.

What about texts that address the natural sciences, such as textbooks in physics or chemistry? Are these objects or subjects? Bakhtin and his colleagues would answer that such texts are subjects, they are constructed by minds in society and they can never be read neutrally.

> Every sign . . . is a construct between socially organized persons in the process of their interaction. Therefore, the forms of sign are conditioned above all by the social organization of the participants and also by the immediate conditions of their interaction.[4]

Take $E=mc^2$ for example. A physicist can only make sense of the equation because of an agreement amongst scientists that $E$ stands for energy, $c$ for the speed of light and $m$ for mass, and because these letters are arranged in a mathematical formula whose form and meaning has been socially negotiated. It does not mean that $E$ only occasionally equals $mc^2$, or that it only does so in certain cultures. What the formula describes is part of the voiceless and objective world, but the formula itself is a text charged with cultural meaning. To a generation raised during the Cold War $E=mc^2$ evokes the genius of Einstein, the promise of unlimited energy and the threat of nuclear annihilation.

Writing as well as reading is shaped by context. Each writer is capable of creating unique, personal texts, yet each text is wholly determined by the writer's culture and context. It speaks with 'other voices', the subtle influences of society on what we write and the way we express ourselves. As we write, we draw on and are conditioned by both our immediate resources – physical, mental, social – and our wider cultural values and influences.

This is as true of scientific texts as it is of personal expressive writing. Again we must distinguish between the natural world and human texts. We may write about enduring, impersonal entities, such as the structure of hydrogen, but the texts we produce are social constructs.

Here is a paragraph from the first page of the introduction to a computer user manual:

> The computer is equipped with a Pentium® processor with Voltage Reduction Technology (VRT). It operates at 133 megahertz and incorporates a math co-processor and a 16KB cache memory. To save battery power, the effective processing speed can be set to Low by the MaxTime and TSETUP program.[5]

The text ostensibly describes the features of a personal computer (the one I am using to write this book). The principles by which the computer works – the properties of silicon chips, the structure of binary logic – are socially neutral, yet the computer itself is a social construct, designed by an organisation to gain profits by selling goods in society, and so too is the user guide. The reason why readers are being told that they can save battery power with the MaxTime and TSETUP program is not primarily that they need to know, or are likely to be interested in this fact on page one of the manual. It is that the writer wants to, or has been told to, praise the features of the company's new product. It is, in part, a piece of persuasive rhetoric masquerading as technical description.

Some companies employ independent firms of technical authors who are not prey to the need to praise the company product. They may also use methods such as focus groups and user critics to encourage discussion between writer and reader as the documentation is being prepared, to ensure that the text meets the reader's needs. If we accept Bakhtin's analysis that the goal of scientific, technical and other 'objective' writing is not to tell the truth – because words are always filled with meaning drawn from human culture and behaviour – but to communicate understanding, then dialogue between writer and reader is vital. If they are to communicate effectively then both must work together to bridge their differences in understanding and to make shared meaning. That is why attempts by scientists to popularise their work are so important: they build bridges of shared meaning between the culture of a scientist and the (often sceptical) public.

The second kind of dialogue is an internal one that comes from the writer actively anticipating the reader's response. In the process of composing, a writer is continually making adjustments on behalf of the reader, bridging cultural differences by adding explanations, leaving out parts that can be assumed from a shared understanding. A writer is also in a dialogue with things, such as a thesaurus or a style guide, that stand for aspects of the reader. By consulting an English dictionary or a guide to colloquial English, non-native speakers can find ways to reconcile their own inner voices with the expectations of their English-language readers.

Our inner dialogues are directed forward to the reader and backward to the words, concepts and actions that have shaped our current understanding. It is as if, as writers, we are forever caught up in a universal conversation about the meaning of words and the nature of understanding. If this is so, then how do we ever manage to write? Why aren't we forever delaying putting pen to paper, while we wrestle with meaning and struggle to communicate with an absent reader?

For some authors, the inner dialogue is, indeed, a constant source of torment. They worry about the way their words will be received and try to out-manoeuvre the reader by expanding and explaining every idea. Just telling a young writer to 'be clear' and 'think of the reader' has the danger that they too will lapse into this pathological dialogism, continually trying to second-guess and adjust to the needs of every conceivable reader.

We survive as writers by being lazy. As part of writing development we have learned to push the dialogue below consciousness, so that it becomes part of the process of finding words to express meaning. We also avoid conscious dialogue by thinking and writing in set ways, in Bakhtin's terms by subscribing to a particular ideology. An ideology in this sense is not a set of political beliefs, but a package of cultural and social assumptions that influence a person's understanding and action. Ideology is what seems to you to be entirely natural and obvious, but to others appears strange, annoying or threatening.

Ideology also influences the way we act, and believe other people ought to act, as writers. To one writer it is natural that we should make a plan before starting to write; to another it is obvious that people should write from felt experience and so must compose first and organise later. These are both ideological positions. Both can be justified by reference to research findings, but for many writers their source is a deep and inexplicable feeling about how we *ought* to write.

If an ideology is the totality of ways in which we make sense of ourselves in society, then it follows that it is difficult to take on someone else's ideology and to write with another person's authentic voice, because to do so involves adopting that person's unarticulated view of the world. The only way we can appreciate someone else's experience is by observing their signs: their actions and their spoken and written texts. But these signs can never be read neutrally; they are forever coloured by our own experience, our own ideology. This goes back to Bakhtin's distinction between knowledge and understanding. We cannot *know* how someone else feels, we can only try to *understand* their experience.

The struggle to understand the world and to interpret it in writing is a large-scale rendition of the cycle of engagement and reflection that was discussed earlier in relation to a single writing episode. Writers continually analyse their own experiences in relation to the actions of others, internalise these as resources for writing, and then re-analyse the written work to see how it matches up to their understanding of reality.

---

This is the third type of dialogue: between the writer and society. Each person lives in a complex and changing social environment of many voices and influences. We are moulded by these influences and we, in turn, fashion the social environment through words and actions. We cannot sit outside society, we must always engage with it, through behaviour and ideology. As Bakhtin put it, 'Life by its very nature is dialogic. . . . To live means to participate in dialogue: to ask questions, to heed, to respond, to agree and so forth.'[6]

What this means for writing is that conceptual spaces are social constructs, coloured by ideology and patterned by the myriad influences of the writer's context and social interactions. The mapping, exploring and transforming of conceptual spaces, discussed in Chapter Three as a source of mental creativity, is also part of a wider dialogue with society, as we struggle to present the world in our own terms and to re-employ language that has been used down the ages for our own purposes and contexts.

Our ideologies are revealed in the words we use and what we make them stand for. Not only do the words change in meaning as society moves on, but people and organisations can also deliberately manipulate words to promote or deny particular ideologies. The Reagan and Thatcher governments endowed the emblems of their ideology of individualism – the words 'enterprise', 'freedom' and 'market' – with almost magical qualities ('leave it to the market', 'free enterprise works'). They singled out other words – 'society', 'union', 'socialist', – to signify the opposing ideology. Repeatedly, in television interviews and advertisements, they placed these words in the company of negative phrases and images ('union demands'; 'socialist dogma') so that the vocabulary of the opposition, and by association anyone who used it or had ever used it, became soiled.

Similar contests are played out on a smaller scale in every conversation and piece of writing. Words are never neutral and by using them for our own needs we deny them to others. As writers, we need continually to think about how others might read and be affected by our words through their own contexts and ideologies. Usually these little differences go unnoticed. If they do emerge then the consequence can be sudden and inexplicable conflict.

Linda Flower describes a project with inner-city teenage writers at the Community Literacy Centre in Pittsburgh.[7] College students acted as mentors for the teenagers and the project was supervised by adult literacy leaders. The aim was for the three very different groups to work together to develop writing on issues that affect the lives of the teenagers. One particular task was to produce a joint document for their parents, educators and local politicians on *Street Life: Dealing with Violence and Risk in Our Community.*

As one of the literacy leaders, Linda Flower introduced the teenagers to strategies for writing. In a session on 'revising' she gave a brief introduction to techniques for revising (such as reading out loud, tracking a topic, spell checking) and then reminded the writers that they would need to make decisions about when to use Standard Written English and when to use Black English. She stressed that both codes of language were valued, but that the writers would need to make rhetorical decisions about how they use language, given their audience of both peers and policy makers.

Flower expected her brief introduction to trigger a discussion on which form of language to use. Instead, in the middle of her remarks, one of the student mentors, Drena, an African American, abruptly challenged not the use but the very existence of Black English. As the introduction turned into a discussion it became clear that the teenagers and most of their college mentors had never before met the notion that there might be a label for the way that 'teens really talk'. As one teenage writer put it: 'If this is true, why didn't they [the school] ever tell us we were speaking Black English?'

Furthermore, they had been presented with the label by a white academic. Linda Flower describes the growing scepticism of the group: 'the mentors, responding to

Drena's tone, began to see it as a suspect, potentially racist construct, if not a figment of racist imagination.' Over the following days and weeks the participants worked through the consequences of that encounter: feelings of guilt and anger, miscomprehension and later a more sympathetic understanding.

At its centre was a two-word phrase, 'Black English', that became a totem for many contrasting and intersecting ideologies: African American and White American; teenage and adult; teacher and learner; student and mentor. To Flower the phrase was a useful way to describe a particular form of speaking and writing. To Drena it was an attempt to push her into a white person's category of bad speaker. To many of the teenage writers it may have been a tedious irrelevance: an excuse for academic and mentor to talk over their heads. There is no 'true' meaning for the phrase 'Black English', nor even one that we can assign to races or types of person. Each person who took part in Flower's discussion (and each person reading this chapter) forms a meaning that is both individual and socially constructed. And uttering the phrase, as Flower did in that meeting, draws on and transforms those meanings and so initiates a new dialogue.

This applies to writing as it does to speaking. The writer's dialogue with the world is shaped by other people's past utterances and actions and it results in a text that forms part of the continuing dialogue.

The written text, though, is a strange participant in this universal discourse. As soon as a writer finishes working on a text and places it before readers – by showing it to colleagues or teachers, or by formally publishing it – it dies. It becomes fixed, no longer part of a writing process. (The writer may later produce and distribute another version, but that is a different text.) Although the text cannot change, society does, and so do readers. They interpret the unchanging text in new ways, and from it draw conclusions, about its meaning and its author.

We know about writers of the past mainly through the textual remains that they have left behind. This poses all kinds of problems for both reader and writer. How can we write in a way that will not be increasingly misinterpreted, as society moves on? How can we gain a true understanding of what a writer meant, if the only evidence we have is a text that is continually being re-interpreted?

The answer to both these questions is: we can't. Anything we write will be interpreted in terms of other people's cultures and ideologies. We can never know 'what Shakespeare (or any other writer) really meant', only how generations of commentators have interpreted his words.

The consequence for writers of this *post-structuralist* analysis has been a loss of faith in the reliability of language, and in text as a means of conveying essential truths. Instead of the author being in charge of a text, filling it with meanings to be uncovered by the reader, suddenly readers are empowered to find whatever meanings they wish. Because the reader can question everything, nothing in a text can be taken for granted. 'Characters' in a novel are no longer depictions of real human beings. They need to be re-cast as 'participants', to be analysed in terms of the effects they have on the plot, rather than their psychological traits. Textbooks do not present eternal truths or unquestionable facts, but are social constructs, representing a view of education and of the world that can be interpreted only by reference to the cultural and ideological assumptions of the author.

Post-structuralism is a giant step into the unknown. Concepts that seemed intuitive suddenly become complex and uncertain. Consider genre. In Chapter Six we described genre as a combination of content, style and structure that allows us to place texts into categories, such as 'romance', or 'science fiction'. It is how we classify the message in the bottle. But if there is no stable message, if content, style and structure are determined by the relative cultures of writer and reader, then genre dissolves into uncertainty.

One approach to genre is to argue that the everyday categories may be unstable, but they are nevertheless helpful. Libraries manage to place books on shelves according to genre and the library classification generally helps readers to find the books they need. If it works, why decry it? The problem is that books seldom fall into a single category. By selecting one aspect of the book as its shelfmark, a librarian is denying its other characteristics. Take, for example, the book shown in Figure 9.10 of Chapter Nine. By classifying it as a 'children's science book' we ignore its use of cartoon imagery. The combination and subversion of traditional genres is often what makes a book interesting.

Figure 10.3 shows three verses of a typical moral verse for parents and children from the nineteenth century.[8] Its aim of encouraging parental love and tolerance may still be seen as laudable, but most people nowadays would balk at its sickly expression of the sentiments. Even in Victorian times the poem was ridiculed as over-sentimental, and Lewis Carroll included a wicked parody of the poem in *Alice's Adventures in Wonderland* (Figure 10.4).

---

Speak gently! It is better far
    To rule by love than fear;
Speak gently; let no harsh words mar
    The good we might do here!
Speak gently! Love doth whisper low
    The vows that true hearts bind;
And gently Friendship's accents flow;
    Affection's voice is kind.
Speak gently to the little child!
    Its love be sure to gain;
Teach it in accents soft and mild;
    It may not long remain.

---

Figure 10.3 The first three verses from 'Speak Gently'

'Speak roughly to your little boy,
    And beat him when he sneezes:
He only does it to annoy,
    Because he knows it teases.'

CHORUS.
'Wow! wow! wow!'

'I speak severely to my boy,
    I beat him when he sneezes;
For he can thoroughly enjoy
    The pepper when he pleases!'

CHORUS.
'Wow! wow! wow!'

Figure 10.4 The 'Duchess' Lullaby' from *Alice's Adventures in Wonderland*

To classify Lewis Carroll's verse as, say, 'children's poetry: nineteenth century' is to miss its point. Carroll wrote it as a satire on the moralistic verse of the times. Like all good satires, it communicates on many different levels. Children enjoy its violent imagery, and adults in the know can appreciate its clever inversion of the moral verse. Many nineteenth-century readers were shocked that such subversion might issue from a clergyman. Nowadays, we can interpret it not only in those ways, but also in relation to the effect that Lewis Carroll had on children's literature in general, imbuing it with a sense of adult satire and irony. Carroll hijacked the traditional genre of children's literature to carry a gamut of adult messages (about celebrating and provoking children's curiosity, about logic and scientific enquiry and about the cloying Victorian morality).

So we arrive at a more sophisticated notion of genre. We can define genre as a set of expectations shared by writers and readers and codified by society into categories. To a writer, the traditional categories are important. They are how books are displayed in libraries and bookshops, and how readers will describe the text, to themselves and others. Writers can use these categories to their advantage. By writing to a familiar genre we meet readers' expectations; by altering or subverting the genre we draw readers' attention to it (as Lewis Carroll did) and to its rôle in organising literature to suit the purposes of writers, readers, teachers, booksellers, librarians and critics.

Genre, therefore, is culturally determined and forever changing. What makes people in one culture laugh or cry may leave others unmoved. A book such as Swift's *Gulliver's Travels* may be read in one context as a children's story and in another as a political satire. Literature that a hundred years ago seemed poignant and moving may, in our more ironic times, be interpreted as trite or melodramatic. The traditional categories of 'romance' or 'science fiction' are the ways in which an organised society at one point in time attempts to contain this slippery substance, to arrange it on the bookshelf or the school curriculum.

Post-structuralism unsettles not merely the traditional categories of text, but the fundamental tenet of writing as the communication of meaning. Meaning, like genre, say the post-structuralists, is formed by the reader's cultural expectations. A writer can make a text 'easy' by ensuring that it meshes with the expectations of its assumed readers, or 'difficult' by confronting their assumptions through disorienting techniques of style and structure. Writers can play games with texts, by using familiar styles (such as the detective novel in Umberto Eco's *The Name of the Rose*) to raise deep issues, or by including an unreliable narrator whose views and values diverge from that of the story.[9]

Some people have taken this to be an agenda for despair. If writers cannot tell a universal truth, then one piece of writing is as valid as any other. Writing is just the pursuit of ideology. Furthermore, if texts can mean what we want them to mean, and if texts are the main evidence we have of the past, then the past can mean whatever we want it to mean. This is a Looking-glass world, in which the past is unknowable and writers are villains who seek to defend their interests by creating the world in their own ideological image.

We cannot simply agree or disagree with this position; it calls for analysis. Writers do promote their own views of society and in some cases they can seem extremely narrow and one-sided. The textbook account of history has been formed by (mostly male) academic writers. Until recently it has mostly been a parade of kings and queens, battles and power struggles, in which workers, women and minority groups are absent or are reduced to 'bystanders', 'heretics' and 'dissenters'.

Fiction writers, too, can create a lop-sided view of the past. Some particularly influential ones have moulded entire societies to fit their own ideology. Walter Scott was celebrated in his own time not just as a writer but also as the voice of Scotland. It was Scott who created the 'tartan and bonnet' image of Scotland, striking a chord with a downtrodden nation by inscribing a past in which heroic and romantic Highland clans battled against the English oppressors. In 1822 his association with Scottish nationhood was such that he was put in charge of organising the state visit of King George IV to Edinburgh. Scott arranged a royal reception for the clan chieftains and ordered each chief to appear in his clan tartan.

At that time tartans were the trademark of individual weavers, and thus were associated with towns rather than individual clans. Each chieftain hurriedly commissioned a weaver to put together a clan tartan and the clan chiefs duly paraded in front of the King wearing their team colours (the portly King was also bedecked in what he was told was a Royal Stuart tartan). Nowadays, visitors to Scotland who purchase their 'ancestral tartan' from the Highland Gift Shop are themselves participating in Scott's elaborate literary fiction.[10]

All this adds weight to the idea that writers do not describe society; rather they invent it, and invest it with their own moral, aesthetic and political preferences. This idea needs to be countered.

First, the past did happen. As the historian Richard Evans points out:

> the insistence that all history is discourse diverts attention from the real lives and sufferings of people in the past. Auschwitz is not a text. The gas chambers were not a discourse. It trivialises mass murder to see it as a text.[11]

We do not need to rely on a single writer to find out about history, we can uncover many sources of evidence including contemporary writings, such as diaries and tangible products (the radioactive remains of Hiroshima for example), that have survived into the present day.

Second, writers do not generally set out to corrupt the minds of readers or to invent history. Even if they had that intention, it is unlikely that their writings would be published: there are too many checks and constraints in the business of commercial publishing. There are, however, real dangers in the kind of writing that blurs the boundaries of reality, such as stories of miracles or alien abductions recounted as fact, or theories of history founded on pseudo-science. Such writing can be persuasive, particularly in a culture where strength of belief is valued above the need for proof or justification. It is, however, at odds with writing as design.

An architect who designs a building on the basis of popular belief or pseudo-science would not be employed long. The Challenger Space Shuttle disaster was, in part, the result of engineering designers putting consensus before professional judgement. Architects, and every other type of designer, adhere to sets of design principles, the 'rules of the trade'. These principles are not arbitrary, or the product of a personal ideology, they are based on the collected knowledge and practice of the profession about what kinds of designs are known to be sound and well-founded and how the integrity of a design can be checked and justified.

Writers, too, are bound by design principles. They specify that, for scientific and factual writing, although we cannot tell the truth we can, and should, do our best to promote understanding. We should, for example:

- not present unwarranted belief as fact;
- provide justification for assertions, by reference either to the publicly observable world or to an acknowledged authority;
- reference the sources of ideas;
- not selectively ignore facts, but offer all the information that is relevant to an argument;
- acknowledge the limitations of an argument;
- present the text in a form that is designed to assist, not mislead, the reader.

Fiction writing does not escape the bounds of professional design. For example, a writer should not mislead a reader into treating fiction as fact. (The broadcast of

Orson Welles' adaptation of *The War of the Worlds*, which caused mass panic amongst listeners who thought that the United States was being invaded by Martians, is an indication of what can happen when fiction is dressed up as fact.)

Most writing does not directly affect the material world and so its design principles are not formulated by governments, standards organisations or professional associations. They are the result of centuries of scholarship, passed on by the apprenticeship of essay and report writing in college and university. Because they have evolved through consensus and the success of writers in communicating ideas and explaining the world, design principles for writing are more powerful than any government regulation.

As with a writer's mental constraints, the purpose of design principles is not to stifle creativity but to make a writer aware of what readers expect from their product. Writers are at liberty to ignore the principles (though as many experimental writers have discovered, they may not be able to find a willing publisher or a receptive audience) and the more a writer understands these 'social constraints', the more breaking them becomes an act of creativity rather than ignorance.

We need to distinguish between two types of social constraint: those that make the product more comfortable, and those that maintain the integrity of the design. A furniture designer may produce an uncomfortable chair for good reasons – to be provocative, to exhibit a product that is visually appealing rather than useful or to challenge assumptions of what constitutes a chair by creating an unusual example. A writer might create a text that is difficult or uncomfortable to read for similar

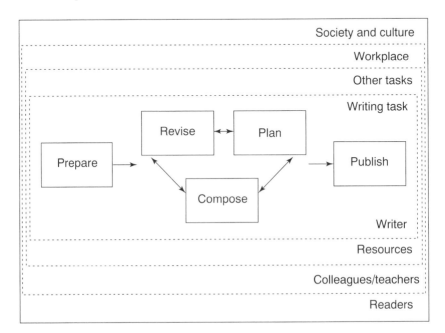

Figure 10.5 An extended model of the writing process

reasons – to provoke people, to display the art of writing or to break the bounds of convention.

But a furniture designer who sells a chair that is unsafe, that collapses when someone sits on it, is simply a danger to the public. In this case the designer is breaking an integrity constraint: the chair just doesn't hold together. That too is the case when a writer presents falsehood as truth, neglects to check sources or writes in a way that simply fails to communicate with the reader. There may be no objective way of detecting such writing, it may depend on the discernment of an educated reader, but that does not exonerate it. Post-structuralism is no excuse for bad writing.

We can now put together a complete picture of the writing process. Figure 10.5 shows the writer within a context of resources (including other texts), colleagues and teachers, and readers. All of these are in a more or less explicit dialogue with the writer, offering ideas and criticism, and providing a context for writing. The writing task is interleaved with many other activities, within the writer's workplace, which is itself situated in a society and culture. The task itself consists of an inter-linked cycle of planning, composing and revising, preceded by preparation and followed by a process of publishing (in the broadest sense – it might just involve handing the text to a teacher or mailing it to a friend).

So far I have covered all these aspects, apart from the influence of colleagues and the activities of preparing and publishing. These are the topics of Chapter Eleven.

Chapter 11

# Writing together

All writing is collaborative. It has to be. Writers are in constant dialogue with the surrounding world and that world includes other people. Guidance from a teacher, support from a partner, criticism from a reader, a letter from a friend, a conversation in a bar can all alter the course of writing by offering ideas and constraints. The influences may be subtle but they are nonetheless direct.

In 1816 Mary Shelley spent a summer in Switzerland with the poets Lord Byron and Percy Shelley. To amuse themselves during a spell of unseasonal rain they decided to each write a ghost story. Mary was the only one to finish a story, which she named *Frankenstein, or the Modern Prometheus*. In her introduction to what has now become the archetype for gothic science fiction Mary Shelley wrote:

> At first I thought but of a few pages – of a short tale, but Shelley urged me to develope the idea at greater length. I certainly did not owe the suggestion of one incident, nor scarcely one train of feeling to my husband, and yet but for his incitement it would never have taken the form in which it was presented to the world.[1]

Percy Shelley was certainly not a co-author of the novel, yet his influence was decisive. *Frankenstein* arose out of the talk and activity in which Mary Shelley found herself during that long wet summer. This in no way denies her profound achievement. The book was the product of her own creative mind, a mind working in a particular context of friends and circumstances.

Other writers have drawn on a brief overheard phrase, or a long correspondence by letter. The collected letters of the scientist Charles Darwin fill seven volumes. For much of his life Darwin was in poor health and he used his position at the centre of a network of intellectuals to clarify ideas and carry out investigations by correspondence.

Authors of fiction have formed into literary groups for mutual support and as a safe haven from which to sail out and challenge the literary establishment. The other great romantic cliché of writing – besides that of the penniless author starving in a garret – is the group of intellectuals gathered in a Parisian café, sipping black coffee and exchanging *bon mots*. Gertrude Stein was one inspiration for that vision. In 1902 she moved to Paris and founded a literary salon and art gallery that became a home to avant-garde painters and writers including Picasso, Matisse, Hemingway and Pound. In a later era, Jean-Paul Sartre, Simone de Beauvoir and friends expounded revolution and existentialism over beers in the cafés of the Boulevard Saint-Germain.

Few of these collaborations, however, appear on title pages of books. There are too many disincentives to more formal co-authorship. Of the few attempts to write fiction as a group, most have been unsuccessful. In 1908, 12 authors, including Henry James, published a novel, *The Whole Family*. According to their editor,[2] the project 'was a mess' with the writers competing rather than collaborating and 'each author trying to impose his vision on the entire work'. Despite being an almost unique exercise in mass collaborative fiction, the novel gains no mention in the *Oxford Companion to English Literature*. Publishers' catalogues, book-signing sessions and chat show appearances, the entire publicity machine is built around the single author, who appears in print or in person to represent the book.

Where co-authorship has been more successful, or at least tolerated, is in scientific writing. Research in physics, biology and medicine is often carried out in large teams and it is not unusual to see seven or eight names above a paper in a scientific journal. Whether all eight contributed to its writing is another matter – often one person writes the text while the others appear by virtue of having contributed ideas and scientific research.

Two-person partnerships can be more successful, for example in science fiction, where one person is the main author and the other contributes the scientific ideas, or autobiographies, where a celebrity dictates his or her life story and a ghostwriter turns the reminiscences into a readable book. Once again this does not fit with the publicity process, so ghostwriters, the session musicians of the literary world, are rarely given credit in print.

One of the strangest literary partnerships was between the fantasy author Terry Pratchett and himself. When he was 17 Pratchett wrote *The Carpet People*, an epic tale of the tiny folk who live between the hairs of a carpet. The book was published, had modest sales, and went out of print. Many years later, when he had risen to fame as the author of the Discworld books, Pratchett began to get requests from fans for his early novel and so he decided to revise *The Carpet People*. As he says in the Author's Note: 'It's not exactly the book I wrote then. It's not exactly the book I'd write now. It's a joint effort but, heh heh, I don't have to give him half the royalties. He'd only waste them.'[3] Needless to say, only one name of Terry Pratchett appears on the cover page of the book.

Thus, we can distinguish two general types of collaboration in writing: *writing support*, and *co-authorship*. Writing support may involve proffering ideas, advice, emotional help and criticism. Sometimes, as with Mary Shelley, it may influence the content or the entire direction of the writing. Co-authorship is where one or more collaborators make an explicit, identifiable contribution, by planning, drafting or revising the text.

For co-authorship many of the difficulties of single-author writing – setting and satisfying constraints, organising ideas, managing time – are multiplied and amplified. The writers need to make their intentions explicit and to agree on the scope of the text, they need to communicate ideas and changes of plan that affect the other contributors, they need to agree responsibilities and divide up the work, they need to organise the text from multiple sources and to reconcile the different voices and approaches to writing. Lastly, whenever people work together there are conventions to be followed, statuses to be respected, conflicts to be resolved and partnerships to be forged. All these can be troubling and time-consuming, so why bother? Writing support is generally simple and painless, at least for the receiver. What are the added advantages of co-authorship?

The benefits of co-authorship are those of teamwork. Just as a factory or a football team can accomplish more by a group of people working together, so a well-coordinated group of co-authors can bring the benefits of teamwork to writing. At the most general level we can describe co-authoring in terms of three general types of teamworking: *parallel*, *sequential* and *reciprocal* (see Figure 11.1).

*Parallel working* is the classic 'division of labour' where a job is divided up among the workers into sub-tasks. In writing, the sub-tasks are either to write different parts of the text (Introduction, Section One, etc.) or to do jobs that can be carried out in parallel, such as checking spelling at the same time as tidying up the references. Each job is given to a different person, according to the person's skills or interests, and the co-authors work simultaneously.

*Sequential working* is like a production line. The job is given to the first person in the line who takes it to the first stage of production. The first person hands the part-completed product on to the second person who works on it to the second stage and so on down the line. Sequential working fits a 'plan–draft–revise' approach to writing, with the first person creating a plan, the second composing the first draft of the text, the third revising or extending the text, and so on through as many revisions and extensions as there are writers.

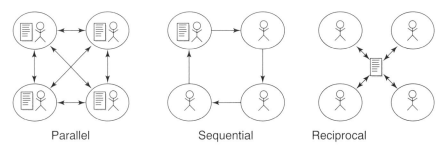

Figure 11.1  Types of teamworking for collaborative writing

*Reciprocal working* is the way a football or basketball team operates. All the partners work together, watching and mutually adjusting their activities to take account of each other's contributions. The technique of brainstorming that I mentioned in Chapter Three is particularly suited to reciprocal working. One person acts as scribe while the others call out suggestions and each person adjusts to and benefits from the contributions of the others in the team. Reciprocal working can equally be used to compose or revise, by the writers composing out loud while one person writes down their contributions, or by having a shared piece of paper or computer file which everyone can write to or amend. There is no limit to the number of writers who can take part in reciprocal working – a text on a computer connected to a network can become a pot of words to be filled, emptied or stirred. Here is a description from a writer who tried this technique with a large group of writers:

> We developed a technique where nobody quite knew who we were writing with because we used to leave things on the machine and people would just add in and take out. Nobody really knew who'd done what.[4]

Each method of collaboration has its advantages and disadvantages. Parallel working has the great benefit that two or more people work at the same time on jobs that are suited to their skills. To do this successfully, however, the writers have to find a way of dividing up the task into independent chunks. If there is too much overlap between the tasks (for instance if the writers are working simultaneously on chapters with similar themes and content) then the writers can get 'out of step': they all have different perceptions of what they should be writing, and what their colleagues are producing, so that when they come to merge their contributions the different pieces of text fail to fit together.

Sequential working has the advantages and failings of the factory production line. Each person in turn can contribute their knowledge to the written product, adding new ideas and text. When one person runs out of time or energy, he or she can pass the draft on to a fresh writer. This method is the easiest to manage; it just needs a means of handing over the text. The difficulty is that words can only capture a small fraction of each writer's ideas and intentions. As the draft is handed on, those intentions are lost and the new writer can only work from the visible text. One way to address this is for each writer to include annotations and notes to guide the next person in the chain. Sequential writing also depends on each person in turn working to schedule. If one person stops work then the entire production line grinds to a halt.

Reciprocal writing can be the most exciting and productive of all the methods. It can give a strong feeling of working together as a team to build a shared product. You have the satisfaction of knowing that when you falter then others will pick up where you have left off. The problems arise from either over- or under-enthusiasm. If the writers are too keen then they may all want to work on the same text at the same time, causing a problem of merging the different versions, or if they 'borrow' a copy of the text and then put the revised version back into the shared pot they may overwrite another person's changes. Alternatively, if the writers lack energy, then the draft can just lie untouched, with each writer hoping the others will find the time or will to contribute.

The three methods of coordination are basic ways in which members of a team can organise themselves. These might change from day to day, or even minute to minute, as the work progresses. They can also be mixed together. For example, the writers might work in parallel but also exchange ideas and notes, or they may pass the draft of an Introduction section in sequence for revision while working in parallel on other sections. From a survey of writers in professional organisations, Ede and Lunsford[5] found that the most frequently used strategies for collaborative writing were:

- One member plans and writes a draft. The group revises it.
- The group creates a plan and outline. One person writes the entire draft.
- The group creates a plan and outline. Each member drafts a part. The group compiles the parts and revises the whole.

All of these strategies move from one method of coordination to another, to make good use of the writers' time and experience. Co-authorship can save time, by having two or more people at work simultaneously, and a team of writers can produce more, and more varied, ideas than a single mind.

---

One way to understand the complex mental and social processes of co-authorship is to look on the writing group as a kind of organism – a many-headed beast formed out of individual writers that exists for the purpose of creating co-authored text. We can then ask the questions that a scientist might ask of a human being. What is it made of? How does it develop and change? How does it function? Let us call this beast the 'group-writer'.

The group-writer exists to write. If the group comes together for a single writing task and its members never work as a group again (for example members of a jury who write down their joint conclusions) then the lifetime of the group-writer is that one task. Normally, though, members of a writing group work together on a series of tasks, often with one merging into the next as the writers put the finishing touches to one document at the same time as starting to plan the next. So a group-writer never dies, it mutates as people join and leave the group and as they move from one writing task to the next.

Even during a writing task, the group-writer may change its appearance. A survey of 23 academics who were asked about their most recent experience of collaborative writing showed that a third of their groups had changed in membership during the task.[6] In two cases the number of co-authors fell (from nine to one and from ten to three) and in four cases it increased (in one case from four to ten).

The success of the group-writer depends on its members working productively together, each member supporting the other writers and promoting the well-being of the group as a whole. In the ideal situation each member would be able to take the place of another, so that if one leaves and another joins, the group-writer would be able to carry on as before. In practice this can never happen, because people differ in their background knowledge, interests, skills and general abilities. Although the members may all be working towards the same goal of completing the writing task, they may also be competing with one another, for example to establish leadership of the group or to claim credit for any success. The group-writer is an unwieldy beast, stumbling in the direction of the finished task, but with limbs flailing and heads knocking.

There are various ways to ensure that the writers work together productively. The most important is that they all appreciate the different ways of writing and that although another person may take a very different approach, it can be equally productive. The writers then need to find ways of reconciling the different approaches and using them productively, so that, for example, a writer with a Planner approach can be given the job of setting down an outline for the entire document while a Discovery writer might produce the first draft of one section.

From this it follows that the writers need to know how they fit into the overall task, what is expected of them and how one person's work meshes with the others. This means deciding at the start how the work will be divided up and coordinated – through parallel, sequential or reciprocal working – with each member taking on tasks according to ability, time and interest.

---

The group also needs to decide how to deal with conflict. Conflict in collaborative writing, as in any teamwork, is not necessarily bad. It can lead to creativity, as the group members spark off opposing ideas and struggle to resolve their differences. The book *Six Studies in Quarrelling*[7] records some delicious, and highly creative, feuds conducted by letter among George Bernard Shaw, H.G. Wells, Hilaire Belloc and others. But conflict within the group-writer needs to be handled to avoid it degenerating into a hostile silence or the break-up of the group.

Disagreement may lie within the group for a considerable time before it is revealed as an argument or a wounded silence. Managing conflict involves realising that the conflict is present, identifying its source (an argument about some trivial aspect of the task may indicate deeper differences of personality or approach) and working to resolve it. Common sources of conflict among writers include having differing perceptions of the audience for the document or different views as to its rhetorical purpose (is it intended to persuade, or to inform?).

Conflict may be implicit in the emerging text itself (for example in alternative drafts written by different people, or in inconsistencies between the sections), sometimes hidden within a single word or phrase. In Chapter Five I introduced the notion of 'semantic potential', how a single phrase or sketch can be subject to many different interpretations. Writers can use this productively, by capturing some troublesome idea in the form of a phrase that marks their confusion and allows them to carry on with the writing. Later, when they come back to the phrase they may find that they bring new understanding, or that by continuing to write they have resolved the problem.

More often, though, the writers do not realise the existence of different interpretations. Each understands a key phrase from one point of view and fails to see the other possible meanings. The phrase lies buried within the text while the writers accumulate other differences in understanding until these explode into mutual incomprehension and conflict. Abstract words with social and political overtones, such as 'democracy', 'freedom', 'oppression', are prime sources of conflict, as are words that can be interpreted in very different ways according to context, such as 'drugs', 'family' and 'technology'. These are words to watch in collaborative writing. Seemingly innocuous words (such as 'creative' or 'mind') can also detonate conflict. Consider how many interpretations there are, for example, of the word 'write'.

What most distinguishes the group-writer from a single writer working alone is talk. The lone writer is mostly silent. The group-writer, when its members meet together, is in continual conversation. As we saw in the previous chapter, the act of writing generates many dialogues – between conceptual spaces, between the writer and the text, with the imagined reader and with the writer's culture – but for a lone writer these are internal, either below consciousness in the continual interplay between conceptual spaces, or as inner language and mental imagery. Only occasionally do they intrude on the outside world with a mutter, grunt or sigh.

In collaborative writing the dialogue is between more than one mind and so the writers must use some external form of communication, which usually means either text or talk. There are many ways to communicate via text: by sending a letter, by electronic mail, by annotating a draft of the document and passing it down the line of writers or back to its author. All of these have the advantage that the writers do not need to be together in one place, the communication can be copied and sent any distance, it can be placed alongside the draft as a margin note and it can be stored as a permanent record of the writers' discussions.

Against these benefits is the problem that communication by text is slow and laborious. It may fit the leisurely labour of a nineteenth-century scholar, but not the frantic pace of work in an inter-connected world. So collaborating writers talk, by telephone and face to face. For a researcher, collaborative writing is fascinating, because the talk between writers brings the writing process out into the open. The conversations reveal how they think and write.

Plowman has studied the interaction between talk and text in collaborative writing.[8] In one case study she observed five postgraduate students working together in one room to write a group essay as revision for an examination. Although the session was held in a room with computers, the students only turned to a computer to type in the final text. The rest of the time they made use of chalkboard and paper and over a period of two hours they selected a question from a previous examination, decided on their writing strategy and wrote out an essay in answer to the exam question.

The first part of the task was to choose a suitable question to answer. This took less than five minutes of discussion and at the end they wrote the question up on the chalkboard for everyone to see. For the remainder of the first session until a coffee break (44 minutes into the task) they generated ideas, took notes and made some plans. For most of the second session they drafted the text on paper and typed it into the computer.

The students chose to operate as a single group rather than dividing up the task and the way they worked is a prime example of reciprocal teamwork. Although they all worked together, they quickly took on individual rôles. Three out of the five students took notes for the first few minutes. From then on, all the notes and the draft were written by one person, Pam. After the break, the students held a short discussion on how to turn the notes into a finished essay. They decided on two stages: first they would write out the notes as a longhand draft, then they would type this into the computer. One person objected that this was inefficient, but they decided that it was the best approach in the circumstances. Typing the notes straight into the computer would mean someone acting as both writer and typist, and that would put too great a strain on one person. Figure 11.2 shows how they resolved the issue, with Pam volunteering to write down the draft ([ ] indicates a part of the conversation that was indistinct.)

This short extract has many layers. At one level, the students are discussing strategies for writing and coordination: how the task will be partitioned and who will do the work. All five students participate (though Mo only contributes one word). Pam raises the problem of turning the notes into a draft. They explore the process involved in typing the notes straight into the computer and the problem of imposing that on one person. They decide to split the task into two separate sub-tasks: write first and then type. At another level they are assigning rôles to individuals: Pam volunteers to write out the draft. At yet another level they are resolving a conflict and, perhaps, taking sides. Mo and Pam agree with Bob that the

| 45.00 | Pam | Yeah. How are we going to work this out? We've got all the notes here but they've got to be put into |
| | Bob | The order in which we put it down isn't it? |
| | Mo/Pam | Yeah |
| | Pam | I mean, I've got rather |
| | Bob | So it's just a matter of clarifying exactly the point we want to make and then [leave it] down to whoever's typing and put it in [like] they would express it. And then they can just <the discussion continues> |
| 46.00 | Val | That means we've got to divide the writing from the typing otherwise the person who's typing will be doing all the writing as well. |
| | Tom | Yeah, I agree but there's no |
| | Pam | OK |
| | Val | So to do – I think we've got a choice between doing it on paper and doing it on [file] and talking and then saying what |
| | Pam | I think we should – I mean I'm prepared to write down OK everything we – we'll write it down on paper first |

Figure 11.2 Extract from the students' conversation on how to transform the notes into a draft[9]

notes have to be put into order. Tom, who had earlier said that writing longhand then typing it up was 'inefficient', tries to argue ('I agree but there's no . . . ') but is cut short by Pam and Val.

Talk between the writers exposes some of the inner dialogue of writing, the mental struggles to explore ideas, organise the work and resolve conflicts. Talk also has value in itself, by mediating between the writers and their text. As an example, Figure11.3 is a section of talk where the students are generating written notes for a section of the essay about how to design a computer-based teaching system.

In this extract all five students contributed. Pam was taking notes and she has a crucial rôle, that of 'gatekeeper' to the conversation: deciding which words to set down as written notes (those shown in italics in the transcript) and asking for clarification. The notes of the conversation become resources for writing the first draft. They also provide material for further talk, as the students later read over them and discuss how to expand the phrases into a complete text. The talk helps the students to generate the text and the text, in turn, prompts talk in a cycle that is very similar to the interaction of engagement and reflection from Chapter One (see Figure 1.1).

| 21.00 | Pam | . . . on to Chris's *theory of explanation* saying that *SOPHIE was good but it did it in a different way to human* and |
| | Bob | [ ] *a good way should be able to do it more than one different way if it's possible to do it in more than one way.* |
| | Mo | Because you will feel suppose that [ ] going to be individualized tuition which should be *adaptable* to the student way of doing the thing. |
| 21.30 | Pam | So it's *adaptability and flexibility* of the system? |
| | Val | And being more sensitive as well. |
| | Tom | There seem to be two points lurking in that as far as I can see. *One is you should be able to do it in different ways.* And there's a thing on top of that which it should be able to |
| 22.00 | | *understand and or comment on the way the student did it.* Which is not quite the same because you can have several different strategies which you can make up as you go along [ ] to be able to take an explanation from a student and see if it's a good one. |
| | Pam | OK. Would it need to be able to carry out the skill in order to be able to do that, say? |
| | Tom | That's the other . . . *whether you can have explanation without domain knowledge.* I happen to think so but can't prove it at all. |
| 22.30 | Val | You can have *fixed explanations in any domain* [ ] interesting. It's going to have to be flexible because possibly things that a student could put down [ ] analyse it. |

Figure 11.3 The students talking while generating notes. Words in italics are also found in the students' written notes.

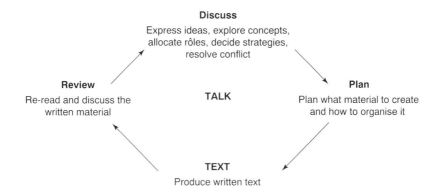

Figure 11.4 The interaction between talk and text in collaborative writing

It is no coincidence that the two cycles should be similar. The group-writer needs to go through the process of planning, composing and revising text. The members carry out this process as individuals if they have been assigned particular sections to write. But the group as a whole also needs to generate and share ideas and to produce a plan, as well as agreeing revisions to each person's contribution so that the text can look as if it has been written by a single mind (or at least by a coherent set of minds). In addition, the group-writer needs to perform functions that are not needed for a single writer, such as dividing up the task, choosing rôles and allocating jobs. The best medium for these activities is talk.

Conversation is easy if the members of the group are together in one room (though there is the real problem of the noise and presence of other people interrupting trains of thought). If the group-writer is distributed around a building, or in some cases across continents, then talk is expensive and has to be rationed. Can writers work together without meeting face to face? When is it more productive to work alone, and when are meetings essential?

There are certainly examples (increasing in number) of people writing together without meeting in person. I have co-written a journal article with a colleague in the United States without either of us crossing the Atlantic, journalists regularly write articles that merge contributions from a foreign correspondent and an editor or specialist writer back at base, and employees of multinational companies produce combined reports from their different sites.

So it is possible to write together without meeting, but the writers generally either know each other well and can anticipate each other's way of working, or are producing a text that is only loosely collaborative (such as a series of individual statements, or a collection of reports). Writers who have tried to work without coming face to face often end up arranging crisis meetings, or sorting out their differences over the telephone. Meeting and talking extend the inner dialogues of writing into shared activities that both communicate meaning from amongst the group and generate new ideas from the interplay of thought, talk and text.

To study the detail of how people write together, the Collaborative Writing Research Group at the University of Sussex decided to observe itself at work. The group (consisting of seven people: two teaching staff, two research fellows, two postgraduate students and an undergraduate; a third research fellow contributed to early drafts) wrote together a book chapter on computer support for collaborative writing.[10]

We employed only tools for writing and communication that are in regular use by many academics – a variety of word processors, electronic mail and the telephone – and we held meetings of the whole group and of smaller working groups. We kept copies of all our notes, plans, drafts and written communication. Each meeting was audio-recorded and we made notes of the activities and discussion of the smaller meetings. The group worked to an external deadline and the whole episode lasted

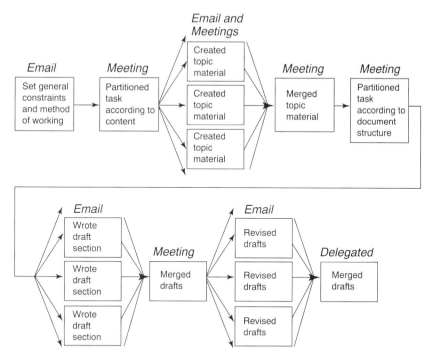

Figure 11.5  How we wrote one collaborative paper

two and a half months. During this time the members of the group also carried on with all their normal academic work of teaching, research and administration: the writing was very much a part-time activity.

Figure 11.5 shows how we organised and divided the complete episode (leaving out many sub-tasks and smaller meetings). The way of writing was not set in advance, but unfolded to meet the needs of the group.

We began with an email message from myself to the other members of the group suggesting that we 'put our ideas about collaboration into practice by working together on a first position paper'. The email message set out some general constraints including the proposed audience, deadline, general style and length, and some possible topics. It also suggested 'ground rules' for collaboration:

- Anyone in the research group could join the team of collaborating authors or not. Anyone who decided to join would be a named author of the paper. Anyone not joining would be welcome to add material, use any of the data and observe the sessions (in the event everyone joined in the writing).
- As initiator of the project, I would act as 'host' for the paper, undertaking to coordinate the discussion and the writing, and to take final responsibility for pulling it all together.
- The main negotiation and exchange of drafts would be over email.

- If the group judged the paper to be acceptable it would be submitted to a conference on computer-supported collaborative writing, with the proceedings published as a book.

At the first meeting the group brainstormed ideas onto a flip chart. A week later we met again and wrote each idea on a separate card, spread out the cards on a large pinboard and grouped them into clusters of topics. Each of the ten clusters was assigned to a sub-group of between one and three people.

The sub-groups met occasionally over the next six weeks to discuss the topics and to share the source material that we had gathered from our research into collaborative writing. During this time the topics altered and some were merged or dropped. Then, at a meeting two months into the project, the group met and discussed notes for six of the topics.

At this meeting the group decided to reorganise the material into eight sections that would correspond to an outline of the paper. Five of the sections were allocated to individuals (in one case a pair of people) to produce first drafts. The group met again a week later to discuss the drafts, to delegate people to produce the unwritten sections, and to re-allocate the sections that had been written to different people for a second draft.

I then collected together all the first or second draft sections and turned them into a full draft paper. Two days before the deadline the group met to discuss this complete draft of the paper. We parcelled out tasks such as making final revisions, writing references, correcting typos and formatting the diagrams. The next day, one of the group members took a copy of the finished draft and produced a neatly formatted version. In the final hours before the deadline the entire group clustered round a computer screen offering last-minute corrections and amendments.

Although I have written this as a relatively systematic and efficient process, it did not feel so at the time. We argued about the structure and content of the paper and only through a frantic burst of activity in the final week did we manage to finish the paper on time. The paper was eventually published and, equally importantly, we all learned a great deal about how to, and how not to, write together. I have drawn our experiences into a set of guidelines for any other group that decides to embark on collaborative writing.

- *Appoint a 'host' for the writing task.* A good host can coordinate the activity, arbitrate in discussions and take on responsibility for pulling the paper through the final stages of revision.
- *Set clear constraints on content, style and structure.* The constraints should guide but not impede the writing and they should be open for revision throughout the task. It may seem unnecessary to add that all the participants should be aware of the constraints and follow them, but in our writing project I wrote the initial list of constraints at the end of a long email message and one group member did not read them until after we had completed the paper!

- *If possible hold a meeting to resolve any major issue needing negotiation.* Although we had intended to use email for negotiation, we needed to make quick decisions to solve problems and reschedule the work. Face-to-face meetings, with everyone present, were often the only convenient way to uncover disagreements and misunderstandings. In general, meetings are good for generating ideas before drafting and for discussing how the drafts should be merged.
- *Plan a writing sequence but be prepared to modify it.* We set out an initial plan of work, but when people were unable to meet deadlines, or discovered new topics to pursue, we altered the schedule to fit their needs. If the work is too rigidly partitioned and allocated to people working in parallel, then each sub-task becomes a critical path. When one person fails to deliver, or moves outside the constraints, then the group needs to spend extra effort on chasing the laggard or repairing the damage.
- *Suit the medium to the activity.* The different parts of the collaborative writing process are suited to different media. *Planning* and *topic organising* is suited to face-to-face meetings, where everyone can exchange ideas and develop a collective understanding of the topic and task. *Brainstorming* and *idea generating* can be done in small groups, or at a distance using fax to exchange mind maps or notes networks, and telephone for negotiation. *Drafting* is best carried out alone or in small groups since it is difficult to write and to hold a noisy debate simultaneously. Email, fax or post may be needed to exchange drafts. *Merging* of drafts is likely to require meetings, unless one person or a sub-group is given sole responsibility for resolving mismatches of style and content. *Revising* can either be delegated to one person or to a group or (as in our case study) carried out in parallel, in which case the group may need to go through a further stage of merging.
- *Keep a clear record of versions and alterations.* Especially in parallel working it is very easy to lose track of the revisions and for the partners to be working with different drafts. If possible, the sessions of parallel working should all end at one time and the results be merged into a new version of the draft.
- *Distinguish the document text from the intentions, ideas and constraints.* The group needs to decide on clear conventions for separating the drafts from notes, plans and annotations, particularly if they are using email where all text looks the same.
- *Annotate the drafts with comments and intentions.* This is particularly important when writing in sequence, because the words on the page are a pale shadow of each writer's ideas and intentions. Comments could include aims, background ideas, sources from which the text was drawn, the status of the text ('good draft', 'needs more work' etc.) and suggestions for further work.
- *Structure the communication to indicate its purpose, intended action and deadline.* In the pressure of writing to deadlines it is easy to forget a request or to miss a deadline, especially if it is left implicit or buried in a lengthy memo or

email message. Put the purpose (e.g. 'help!'), action (e.g. 'can anyone lend me this book . . . ') and deadline (e.g. '. . . by tomorrow') at the top of the message.

- *Be prepared for rapid shifts in individual and collective mood.* The experience of our case study, and anecdotes from other collaborative writing sessions, is that there are occasions when the group experiences collective shifts of mood. These can be sudden and may not be articulated, but if one occurs near an important deadline then it can cause havoc. In our case, disillusion set in when the parts of the second partial draft had been collected together, but had not been merged and turned into a complete paper. Three of the partners kept personal diaries and at that time their entries included: 'I am worried about the work still needing to be done', 'lot of hostility to section 3', and 'I lost hope almost entirely'. Four days later the same people were commenting 'mighty relieved' and 'paper coming together quite nicely'. If the group can recognise that there are likely to be collective shifts of mood and can anticipate the most likely times for problems then they can take steps to relieve the pressure (for example, by planning to assemble the parts into a complete draft at an earlier stage) or to ride out the anxiety.
- *Leave formatting till late.* If the partners are using a variety of word processors then it is wise to exchange the drafts in simple text form so that they can easily be annotated and merged with other material.

Co-authorship is not as hard as it sounds. Writers who regularly work together build up ways of adjusting to each other so that they function as a shared, distributed mind, anticipating problems and accommodating different ways of working. It can even be enjoyable to discover that someone else has taken your half-baked ideas and turned them into gourmet prose. And a novice writer can gain the valuable apprenticeship of working alongside a more experienced mentor.

---

Our group of seven seemed at times to be unwieldy and fractious, yet it was small compared with some of the teams that work on writing and designing documents for industry or on developing course materials for distance learning. Can the techniques and guidelines be scaled up to teams of 10 or more?

The basic approaches and advice are quite general, they can apply to a group of two or of 20. However, when writing becomes an industrial process new factors become important. The more people there are working together, the more possibilities there are for communication and for misunderstanding. These do not grow gradually. Simple mathematics shows that two people have only one line to connect them. Three people can be connected in three ways. Four people can interact in six ways. Five people in ten ways. A team of 10 people have 45 different lines of communication. And that is only for one-to-one contact. If the individuals form into small groups then there are very many ways of combining, and conversely of excluding, people. When complex tasks are shared among many people, the extra burden of communicating and coordinating the work can often counteract the gains that come from division of labour.[11]

The benefits of working in a large team come from being part of an industrial process. If one person is sick, the others can substitute. The writers can call on a wide range of resources, such as picture libraries and graphic designers. The work can be made more routine and less demanding by providing the writers with house styles and guidelines.

Thus, large-scale collaborative writing tends to be highly structured, with the writers working to strict style guidelines and timetables. These need not stifle creativity. As we have seen, constraints provide a framework for writing. Within it, a writer may be able to exercise great resourcefulness and imagination, for example in finding ways to communicate with the reader in clear and unambiguous prose. A large team may have the opportunity to carry out market research, to talk with potential readers and discover their needs. It can lead to concern with aspects of writing that an individual writer may overlook, such as choosing the right tone for people with different needs and cultures.

The Benefits Agency is a UK Government body that administers claims for social security. Their documents may be read by claimants who have just lost their job, or whose close relative has recently died. The readers may be in debt and feel hopeless and desperate. Many have eyesight problems, disabilities or learning difficulties. The Style Guide for the Agency stresses the importance of choosing the right tone.

> Choosing the right tone for our documents is not always easy. We do not want to sound too official, threatening or patronising, but on the other hand we do not want to sound too casual when we are dealing with issues that affect people's lives. In some circumstances, for example letters which deal with the possibility of criminal proceedings and in some warnings that we use on claim forms, we have to adopt a more official approach. We aim to achieve the required formality without intimidation. Similarly, when dealing with bereavement, we have to express sympathy.
>
> To help us find out how our customers respond to the tone of our documents we carry out extensive testing and research on our main documents during their development stages. For example, research on Disability Living Allowance found that some customers thought the phrase *See if you can fill in this form* sounded patronising. We changed it to *Please fill in this form.*[12]

As well as being more structured, large-scale collaborative writing is often more closely and formally linked to other research and design activities, such as market research, graphic design, packaging design and design of instructional and audio-visual materials. If the document is a user guide or handbook for a product, then the text and product may be developed in tandem with, for example, the product designer producing labels or (for computer software) screen information to match the printed guide.

Figure 11.6 shows a flowchart to guide the production of course materials at the UK Open University (UKOU),[13] an institution that teaches students at a distance by

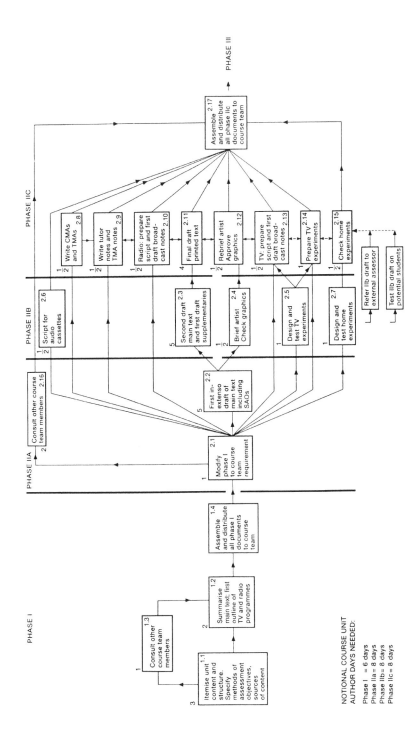

Figure 11.6 Flowchart for the production of course materials at the UK Open University

Source: Kaye, 1973

means of print, television, radio, home experiments and other media. A course booklet can include Self Assessment Questions (SAQs), Tutor Marked Assignments (TMAs) and Computer Marked Assignments (CMAs) alongside instructional text. As the diagram shows, the production process is complex, moving from reciprocal work ('consult other course team members') to a combination of parallel and sequential coordination. The chart is a simplification of the guidelines developed by the UKOU. The complete network, itemising the activities which need to be fulfilled during each phase by the various course team members, specifies over 130 discrete activities.

With such a tight schedule, with so many inter-dependencies, it would not be surprising if the writing occasionally did not go to plan. Writing is a creative activity and creative people can find it hard to work on production lines.

Tony Kaye, a course designer at the Open University, offers a revealing insight into what it is *really* like to work on a large-scale writing project.[14] Writing distance teaching material is not just complex, it is an individual and emotional process. Many of the authors produce three drafts of their material, aimed at different audiences. The first draft is for themselves, to organise their initial ideas. The second drafts may be aimed more at their colleagues in the course team, while the third draft is written more with the student reader in mind. The sense of audience may be complicated by the fact that some UKOU materials are published and read by colleagues at other universities, so they must be seen to be scholarly and authoritative as well as appealing to students.

Receiving comments from colleagues on the course team can, at times, be a traumatic experience and authors use different tactics to cope with their anxieties. Some try and defuse the criticism in advance. Others court sympathy. Some make bargains with their colleagues to leave each other's drafts alone. Others simply become defensive.

At its worst, the course team process can turn into a forum for lengthy academic discussions about the content and structure of the material, until a deadline looms and panic ensues. In extreme cases, the pressure of work can lead to pathological behaviour such as handing in one's work so late that there is no time for anyone else to comment on it, bullying colleagues into accepting sub-standard work, shifting blame onto scapegoats, dropping out of the team and leaving others to cope with the extra workload or even falling physically ill. With so many interacting components and workers, the team manager may simply lose track of the project, in a fog of misleading information and fudged deadlines.

Tony Kaye ends his somewhat depressing account on a more positive note. The conflicts within a team of writers can encourage creativity and healthy debate. When it works well, team writing can produce materials of a high academic standard, well designed and attractive to the student. The UK Open University has a reputation for producing teaching material of the highest quality. The course books suit the needs of a wide range of students and they are paragons of instructional and visual design. For all its occasional pain, large-scale collaborative writing can be successful if it promotes creativity and good design within the economies of scale.

Until recently, collaborative writing remained a curiosity, the practice of a few *avant garde* authors, cerebral scientists and technical authors. In the past few years though, co-authorship has become commonplace. These writing groups often consist of people who rarely meet face to face and who may come from widely differing cultures and organisations. They belong to multinational companies, news teams, project groups and academic teams. Often they are expected to collaborate closely, and to tight schedules. For example, to gain research funds from the European Union, a consortium must consist of partners in three or more different countries and be able to make revisions and write technical addenda to a proposal within days. A grant proposal, running to around 100 pages, must be jointly written and agreed by all the partners. There is no time for leisurely discussions or the painstaking work of scientific cooperation. The tools for this new high-speed semi-formal collaborative writing are the telephone, the fax and the computer.

Chapter 12

# Media slip, dynatext, hypermedia and the docuverse

New technology is changing not only the way we write but the very nature of writing. The computer animates and connects texts into a global web of interactive discourse. A computer can simulate all previous writing tools, from pen and scrolling papyrus to typewriter, transforming and extending these into a new writing environment. Figure 12.1 shows the dates of some of the most important inventions for writing and their consequences. The period between innovations has decreased. From the invention of papyrus in Egypt to the adoption of the paged (codex) book in the second century AD was around 3000 years. The gap from the typewriter to the word processor was about 60 years, and to the World Wide Web a further 30 years. At this rate of change, the inventions are arriving faster than people can adapt to them. Most people in the world are not yet able nor empowered to type, never mind create multimedia Web pages.

Faced with this rapid technological change researchers have tended to be either cautious or intemperate, to carry out meticulous studies of the effects of word processing on the writing process, or to make sweeping pronouncements about the imminent death of the book. Many of the detailed studies are equivalent to researchers in the 1950s analysing the effects of television on learning, or studies in the 1960s into how computers will affect the workplace. They are analysing the new in terms of the old.

When we first invent a technology we tend to use it in ways that feel familiar, that imitate earlier devices. Television in the 1950s imitated theatre, with families

Figure 12.1  Approximate dates of the invention of major writing technologies

gathering round a set in the living room to watch a scheduled programme. The computer in the 1960s was a glorified calculating machine with a trained operator feeding it data and recording the results. Nobody then predicted that television would provide 200 or more channels and that children would zap through programmes in 30-second bursts. Nobody foresaw that personal computers would be in millions of homes, and that children would use them as games consoles and cyberpets.

The computer as a tool for writing is just beginning to move out of its period of imitation. A word processor is still a museum of technology. It has a keyboard that was invented in the nineteenth century and a display that mimics paper in a manual typewriter. Studying how people use word processors will tell us how they have adapted to the change from a typewriter, or how they make use of the additional features of a computer such as the ability to revise on the screen. What the studies will not do is reveal the profound effects that new technology will have on writing in the classroom and the workplace.

Despite the rapid changes wrought by the computer there is no evidence that books will disappear and that writing will become redundant. The invention of photography changed the way we view and value paintings, but cameras did not replace artists. Cinema has not replaced theatre, nor has television replaced cinema. Instead, each invention has influenced the previous technology (for example, cinema has become more of a spectacle to entice people away from television) and has also developed its own genres and variations (television has given birth to the chat show and the soap). People will continue to buy books, but books and bookshops are changing in response to the Internet and the laser printer. Writing will still be valued in the new millennium, but we may come to write in very different ways.

Rather than trying to predict an uncertain future, a safer bet is to describe the important properties of the new technologies and then consider how these might alter the writing process. In Chapter Four I discussed writing media and their

*Table 12.1* Properties of writing technologies

| Manuscript book | Static | Non-linear | Single copy | Pen and paper |
|---|---|---|---|---|
| Print | Static | Linear | One text, many copies | Typewriter and printing press |
| Computer and Internet | Dynamic | Hypertext | Many texts, many copies | Keyboard and printer, speech |
| Future technology | Dynamic | Hypermedia | Docuverse | Media slip |

properties. We can now take the more important of these properties and consider how they might lead to new ways of writing. The properties are shown in Table 12.1.

Text written in pen on paper is static. The only way a medieval manuscript book could be revised was by cutting out and replacing complete pages. The inventions of the printing press and the typewriter did not alter that immovable page. Just ten years ago I edited a magazine that was printed from a typewritten manuscript. I sent the content to a professional typist who typed the text onto a sheets of layout paper, divided by guidelines into columns, headers and footers. She then sent the typed pages back to me and if my proofreading revealed a missing sentence then she would retype the entire page.

The computer has taken away that laborious process by separating the text from the page. Text being typed onto a computer is held as patterns of electrons in a memory chip and whenever these patterns are altered they leave no trace of their past. Writing on computer has become a seamless combination of adding and deleting.

This ability to revise as part of composing has had a greater effect on how we write than any of the previous technologies. No longer does a writer need to make a judgement about whether to embark on another draft. Having written on a computer for over 20 years, I find it hard now to recall the painful decisions I once had to make of whether to type out another complete draft, to send a page to a teacher or supervisor with crossings-out and insertions, or just to submit a poor draft as finished work.

Pennington has studied the effects of children using word processors and has captured their development as four stages, as shown in Figure 12.2: writing easier, writing more, writing different and writing better.[1] The initial effect of using a word processor (once they have learned its basic operations and some basic keyboard skills) is that children find it easier to write. They no longer need to worry about making mistakes because the computer will cover their tracks. The product is usually more fluid than a handwritten text, but rambling and ungrammatical.

After 'writing easier' comes 'writing more'. Because the writing is easier on computer, children spend more time on composing and create longer pieces of work.

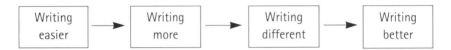

Figure 12.2 Stages of development in expertise with word processing
Source: Pennington, 1996

The next stage shows a qualitative change, to 'writing different'. Children move away from first making a plan and then composing the text from start to finish towards more of a Discovery approach. They begin to evolve the text, inserting words or sentences into the middle of a draft.

Then, as they learn how to revise on the screen, they reach the fourth stage of 'writing better'. Children develop their work over a number of sessions and they begin to adopt a mature cycle of composing, reflecting and revising.

I am suspicious of attempts to portray the muddled process of human development in terms of neat, discrete stages. Children rarely progress smoothly from one stage to another, and by the time they leave school they may not have reached the goal of 'writing better' with a computer. But Pennington's study does reveal the virtues of writing on a computer. Using a word processor makes revising easier, which encourages to children spending more time on revision, which may then lead them to read over their text and to develop a more reflective approach to writing.

The ease of making revisions is only one aspect of the computer as a dynamic medium. Most recent word processors are able to revise text automatically as you write, correcting errors and expanding contractions. When I type the word 'role', for example, my word processor adds the circumflex (to make 'rôle'). If I omit a capital letter at the start of a sentence, the computer adds it for me. As I type 'ys' the computer expands it to 'Yours sincerely,' (in fact, I found it hard to stop it doing so for this example).

Stopping the word processor from always expanding 'ys' is an example of a fundamental problem with computers as tools for writing. The problem is as simple to state as it is difficult to rectify: current programs have no deep knowledge of language. They treat text simply as a string of words.[2]

For example, current spell checkers cannot detect wrongly-used homonyms such as 'their' and 'there', 'here' and 'hear'. Grammar checkers can do this to a limited extent but they often give misleading or unnecessary advice. For a sentence I used earlier in this chapter – 'When we first invent a technology we tend to use it in ways that feel familiar, that imitate earlier devices' – my grammar checker instructs me to 'consider *firsts* instead of *first*' and advises that '*invent* may be confused with *discover*'.

A program that understands language would be able to recognise the grammatical structure of a sentence. For example, it would register the sentence 'Its difficult to understand it's structure' as incorrect English by interpreting the words in their grammatical context. It would recognise 'CDROM' and 'CD-ROM' as equivalent words (and if they both appeared in the same text it might warn the writer of the inconsistency). Such a program lies at the limits of current research in computing.[3] Even then it would be fallible. To realise that I deliberately wrote the words 'CDROM' and 'CD-ROM' in different forms in this paragraph would be beyond the most sophisticated computer style checker.

This needs to be kept in mind when I describe some more advanced computer systems. The computer can take over some aspects of the writing process, such as checking spelling and grammar, and can assist with other aspects like style and layout, but it is no substitute for a trained and creative human mind. The challenge for teachers, managers and writers is to understand the limitations of current software and to learn how to detect when the computer is likely to make a mistake. More generally, we need to find new ways of working that take advantage of the different abilities of humans and computers.

In *The Trouble with Computers* Thomas Landauer refers to a study that compared how office professionals write letters the traditional way (hand-writing a draft and passing it to a secretary to type) and with a word processor. The study found that producing a letter by the traditional method took, on average, 37.8 minutes compared with 22.8 minutes by computer. That looks like a substantial benefit of new technology. But the cost of a secretary's time is about half that of a middle manager. Taking this into account, the total cost of producing a letter was 26 per cent less using the computer. Landauer comments that this is an 'encouraging but not impressive difference, especially if the additional labour costs for learning and maintaining the technology are taken into account'.[4]

That is true, but it somewhat misses the point. A manager who regularly types a letter on a computer has a very different relationship with technology and with secretaries compared to the traditional manager. The computer is on the manager's desktop, not in some remote data-processing department, and the manager has first-hand experience of the benefits and problems of new technology. The manager's act of typing a letter also changes the dynamics of the office. The computer is acting, in part, as an office assistant. The manager no longer has need for one aspect of a secretary's skill. In some companies the consequence of this has been that junior staff are now expected to work without secretaries. In others, the skills of secretaries have grown to include page layout and text design as they become part of a collaborative writing team.

We need not be slaves to the machine. Individually and collectively we can choose to fritter away time on 'updating' the computer with the latest bug-ridden software or to work productively. We can choose to buy programs that are just shopping lists of irrelevant features or ones designed to support the process of writing.[5] And we can choose between viewing the computer as a threat to writing or as the begetter of a new interactive literacy.

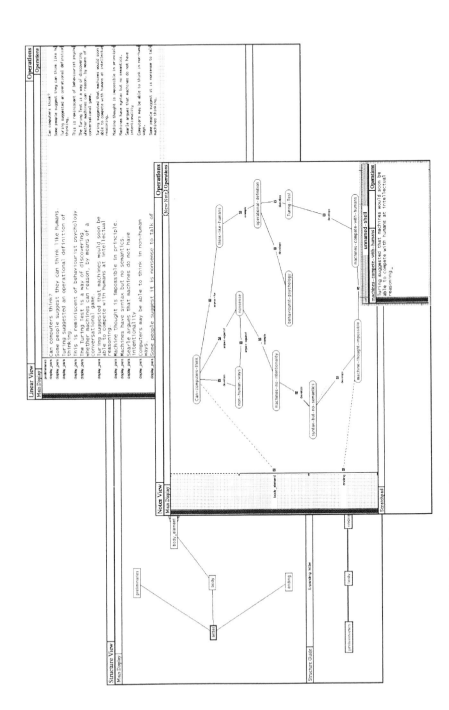

Figure 12.3 The Writer's Assistant, showing its Notes, Structure and Linear views of a document

Over the horizon are programs that can act as active guides and assistants, helping writers to brainstorm ideas, organise the ideas into outlines, write to a given style, and proof-check the text. Figure 12.3 shows screens from the Writer's Assistant, a prototype for the next generation of writing software, developed at the University of Sussex. A writer can create and organise a Notes Network on the screen. The writer then chooses a type of document (such as 'research report') and the program automatically turns the network into a linear draft text and inserts it into an outline for the document. The writer can move between working with ideas, revising the draft, or altering the document structure. The computer monitors the changes and guides the writer.

For all its advanced features, the Writer's Assistant is a conventional writing tool in that it helps a writer to create a linear printed document. For centuries, writers have tried to break away from the linear flow of words. Medieval writers annotated their pages with marginalia and footnotes. Then came the index and list of contents. An index makes links between words. From a key word we can look up in the index and find where else in the book that word occurs. Taking this idea a step further, we can make the links explicit, so that from any word we can jump to related ones, not just within a book but also in other books or documents.

In the early 1970s Ted Nelson coined the word 'hypertext' to describe documents linked together by active webs of association. He realised that the computer can make hypertext possible by setting up links from one word or phrase to another. By selecting a piece of text (with a computer mouse or electronic pen) you can jump within or between documents to another series of words on the same topic. Nelson was far-sighted enough to take this to the extreme: he proposed adding images, sounds and animation to the texts, and then linking together all the documents in the world. He invented the central idea of the World Wide Web, but was unable to implement it with the technology of the time.

We are only beginning to realise the effects of the Internet and the World Wide Web on writing. From any computer connected to the Web, one can access many millions of pages of text. What makes this so different from a library or bookshop is that the pages are all interlinked, into one enormous hyper-document. Navigating the Internet is a voyage of serendipitous discovery. With single clicks of a button I can move from, say, the home page of the Writing and Computers Association to the home page of the Library of Congress. From that there is a link to Today in History, which connects to a page on Benedict Arnold, which contains a high quality facsimile copy of a letter from Arnold in which he pleads for money for his wife. A different set of keypresses from the Writing and Computers page takes me to the home page of Writing Coach Software, and from there to a worksheet on 'How to Write a Thank-you Letter'.

There is no overall plan for the organisation of the Internet; it is a self-organising system in which each link relates two similar pages but with no overall coherence or linear narrative. Some writers have taken that web of association as a model and have created hypertext fiction, where the reader explores a network of inter-connected episodes. After reading each chunk of text (typically a paragraph or a screenful) the reader can select alternative paths to follow. In some hypertexts the paths are shown by buttons at the foot of the screen, in others by highlighted words in the text that link to other episodes.

An early work of hypertext fiction is *Afternoon*. It is a Joycean story[6] in which the reader is taken on a journey around its main characters: Peter, a poet and a technical writer in a software company, his employer Wert and Wert's wife Lolly, and an employee of the software company with the name of Nausicaa.

The story is told through Peter, but the reader may also follow paths from the perspective of the two women. Much of the narrative development in the story revolves around Peter's lunch with his employer. The lunch is at the crossroads of many paths. It may lead to Paul's reflection on his affair with Nausicaa, or to a crazy computer project in which he is engaged. The lunch episode alters in significance depending on where the reader goes next.

The screens of *Afternoon* do not show visible links. Instead, certain words in each page of text will 'yield' to the reader's probing. By clicking on a word the reader is taken to another episode. Most words do not yield, but there is a default path so a click always leads onwards. The reader never knows whether, by clicking on a word, the story follows that particular word's association or the default one. Sometimes the story asks the reader to contribute an answer to a question. After some time exploring the text, the reader may be led back to a page that has already been shown, but the text might be subtly different, or the possible paths changed. There is no central narrative and the reader never knows when the story has ended – there may always be more paths to explore.

To create a story such as *Afternoon* involves a mixture of fiction writing, computer programming and visual design. *Afternoon* contains over 500 episodes and over 900 connections. Standard word processors now allow a writer to create hypertext links within a document or to other documents on the Internet, so they can be used to create simple hyperfiction. For a more sophisticated work such as *Afternoon*, you also need to visualise the complex web of inter-connections and to be able to monitor the reader's path through the text so that, for example, a story can show different links depending on whether the reader is reading a chunk of text for the first or second time.

Michael Joyce created *Afternoon* with the *StorySpace* software.[7] The writer can create a visual display of the episodes and their connections, similar to the Notes Network view of the Writer's Assistant. Then, instead of turning the network into a linear text, the program hides the visual map and displays the text to a reader, one episode at a time, as a screen of text containing words that yield and take the reader on to another episode.

If we take one further step of interactivity on from hypertext fiction, then we reach text-based computer games. The granddaddy of these was Colossal Adventure, invented in the 1960s as a diversion for programmers on the large mainframe computers of the time. It spawned an industry of computer games where a reader/player takes a journey through a fantasy world of dwarves, goblins and wizards, finding gold and battling with assorted mythical creatures.

Some years ago I designed and developed a creative writing scheme for 11-year-old children (some examples of the children's work are in Chapter Two). For part of the scheme the children worked on a computer, with a set of programs designed to develop their writing abilities. The most successful of these was an Adventure Game designer.

Working in pairs, each group of children first drew a map of a 'haunted house'. They named the rooms and wrote short descriptions of each room, as well as sentences describing the moveable objects (such as a candlestick) and the inhabitants of the house. This activity came towards the end of the writing scheme and their writing was rich and evocative (with phrases such as 'filled with a cold, misty fog' and 'ripped victorian pictures'). The children then typed their descriptions into a word processor.

I then added their texts to a program that converted them into an Adventure Game. When they returned for their next session the children were able to play their texts as interactive games, exploring the houses, meeting the inhabitants and searching for hidden treasure. Figure 12.4 shows a short extract from one of the sessions, with the children exploring the kitchen and lounge. The descriptions are all generated from the text that the children had written the previous week. Words in bold face are those that the children typed to explore and interact with the game.

At the end of the session I talked with the children about their experiences. They were fascinated that their words could be turned into a computer game and they talked lucidly about its design, such as where to hide the treasure from the explorer, and which routes through the house would produce interesting stories.

The computer played an essential part in the children's development of writing abilities. It gave them a dynamic medium for composing and revising. It also acted as a bridge between descriptive and narrative writing, since the game turned their descriptions into the setting for a journey through the house. Through designing the game the children came to see how one set of descriptions can create many narratives: each time they played the game they followed a different path through their house and formed new encounters with the characters and objects.

That software only allowed one person to play the game at a time, human conversing with computer. More modern programs enable many people to interact with the computer and also to write to each other across computer networks. The words from each player appear on the others' screens. With two participants the effect is like a CB radio. The first person types a message which is sent, line by line, to the other person's screen. That person replies and a conversation develops. With

You are in a dull, clammy kitchen with a big black stove on the wall. There is a flaming fire on another wall. There is a pane of glass smashed which was in a big window which is all steamed up. There is a sink which is full of dirty dishes.

a secret passage leads west
a wooden door leads northwest
a wooden door leads north
a wooden door leads northeast

The following are also here:
1 – a dazed kitchen maid

a dazed kitchen maid has just left through a wooden door (northeast)
**objects**

You can see
1 – a dirty dish

**north**

You are in a bright coloured happy atmospheric room in it there are two big lounging chairs bright fabric but damaged, a sofa to match chairs, a coal fire still burning, a glass coffee table smashed to pieces. Keys to the cellar lie beside it. Ripped victorian pictures are hanging on the walls.

Figure 12.4  Short extract from one session with the children's interactive story

three or more participants it can rapidly turn into a textual shouting match. But if the dialogue is structured in advance, then by setting a topic and laying down some rules of etiquette it can become an improvised drama, acted out in text on the screens and with the computer capturing a permanent record of the dialogue.

J. Douglas Miller[8] taught a class in creative writing to deaf high school students at Gallaudet University in Washington, D.C. Part of a summer school, the course had no fixed curriculum and no final examination. He was free to experiment with new methods of helping the students to unleash their imaginations. Miller had previously used a computer to allow students to type messages to each other on various topics, with little success. Often the students refused to take turns in sending the messages and the exchanges regularly degenerated into verbal abuse.

Then he hit on the idea of giving the students a scenario (a dramatic situation, a setting and characters) to act out on their screens. Each student took on a character and engaged the others in a dialogue. They also typed out stage directions for their character (such as 'woodcutter breaks into a run, axe high over his head'). To keep up with the flow, the students had to skim read the text as it formed on the screen and to decide when to pick up a cue. One after another (or sometimes together) they added to the emerging dialogue. If the action sagged then someone had to find a way to revitalise it. Meanwhile, the computer recorded every word, creating an instant playscript which they later discussed and revised.

One production was a reworking of the Little Red Riding Hood story. Miller starts by discussing the traditional story, setting out guidelines and provoking the students to think about their characters:

> Especially try to give your character originality. Here are some of the kinds of questions you might consider:
>
> Wolf – what is he wearing? What is his goal in life? What kind of home does he have? Does he have a wife and hungry children to feed? Does he have friends or is he a 'lone wolf'?[9]

The students embarked on the dialogue, each person sitting at a separate terminal. Miller took the rôle of Author, intervening with comments and encouragement. Figure 12.5 shows part of the dialogue, as written by the students at the time. The extract came after some opening descriptions.

The story continued with the woodcutter chasing after the wolf, Red Riding Hood attempting to protect the animal, the woodcutter turning on her and Granny coming to the rescue. The finished work was no masterpiece, but in creating it the children took on personas, experimented with dialogue and expressed emotions through a spontaneous act of collaborative writing.

The product of combining computer-mediated conversations with interactive games is 'text-based virtual reality'. In the 1980s programmers realised that Adventure games need not to be restricted to sub-Tolkein fantasies and began to create computer environments and simulated meeting places such as community centres, shops and universities. These distant relatives of the original Adventure game (called *MOOs* for reasons known only to the initiates[10]) offer a virtual world of shops, games, seminars and interactive tutorials, as well as meeting rooms where visitors can chat by typing messages to each other.

In accomplished hands, a meeting in cyberspace can become an improvised theatre of the absurd. The participants sit at terminals around the world connected to each other through the Internet. They take on new personas and weave elaborate dialogues, sometimes participating in two or more simultaneous threads of inter-action. Some of the characters are human, others are computer programs (called *software agents*), so you often never quite know whether you are conversing with a human being or an artificial intelligence. Watching these human and computer cyberwriters perform is like looking inside the head of Ionesco or Beckett.

My first encounter with a MOO came when I was researching a lecture on interactive writing. I logged on to Lambda MOO, one of the best-known virtual

*Woodcutter:*  The woodcutter is a very unpleasant man. He is covered with grease and dirt. He smells like the inside of one of those porta-toilets. He has not shaven or taken a shower for months. He is isolated from civilization and is psychotic. No one knows what could happen should he meet anyone in the woods. At the moment he is busy chopping wood in the middle of the forest.

*Author:*  Very good, Woodcutter!!!! (Sits on the edge of his seat, eyes bulging with intense interest.)

*RRHood:*  Goodbye mummy, I will give Grandma you love. BYE!

*Wolf:*  (Wolf meets rr hood and they decide to go to the store and buy some candy together then go to rr hood s granny house) . . .

*Granny:*  Granny is a hip granny. She rides on a motorbike and wears a leather jacket. Yet she is a very sweet, old, petite lady with short greyed hair. She is a very energetic lady for a 80 year old woman. She lives in a cottage in the middle of the woods.

*RRHood:*  (Meanwhile RRHood is walking along the path that will lead her to Granny's house when she meets the wolf) Good day, Wolf. How are you? Do you not agree that this is a lovely day today?

*Wolf:*  yeah gday and sure this is a lovely day today and the weather was perfect!!!

*Woodcutter:*  (Hears voices in the distance, stops chopping for a minute, then continues to chop) . . .

*Rrhood:*  (To Wolf) I cannot stay long, Granny is expecting me. So long!

*Woodcutter:*  (rrhood and wolf walk into view of woodcutter. He stops chopping and stares intently at them as they come closer)

Figure 12.5 Example of interactive storytelling with high school students
Source: Miller, 1993, p. 133

worlds and a labyrinth of rooms and buildings. After making an ignominious arrival into a virtual cupboard I ventured out and found a meeting room where other player-visitors had gathered. Their conversation appeared one line at a time on my screen. In the lower part of the screen I could have typed my own responses, but I was too intimidated to take part (in the jargon of MOOs, I was a 'lurker'). Because it was all conducted through text, I was able to save the session as a file on my computer and it is shown in its entirety in Figure 12.6.

Analysing the conversation is a fascinating exercise in forensic linguistics. For a start, it is not clear which of the participants are human and which are generated by computer. The cockatoo, for example, could be a software agent, programmed to interrupt with random remarks. The writers are composing for a specific and immediate audience, but one whose personas are only revealed through the text

Anasazi (sleeping), Ruddy_Guest, Lecturer (insular), Oddjob, Olive_Guest, Vida_Blue, Puzur (daydreaming), autoXer (distracted), ADs (dissappointed), and buffy are here.

buffy grins at Lecturer.

buffy smiles.

ADs [to Lecturer]: I just found out the other day that Richard Pryor has MS. Did you know that?

buffy waves.

Cockatoo squawks, 'No keep the Faith! Keep the jeans:)'

Puzur teleports out.

buffy pokes at Vida_Blue.

Lecturer [to ADs]: sure..it was all over the internet

Oddjob says, 'Yeah help me spell'

Olive_Guest bravely gags the cockatoo, ignoring nipped fingers and frantic squawking.

Vida_Blue pokes at buffy.

buffy pokes at Vida_Blue.

Oddjob says, 'and singed eyebrows'

Buffy [to Vida_Blue]: how are you, cutie?

Olive_Guest [to Oddjob]: R U japanese?

ADs [to Lecturer]: thought you might try correspondance with him - see if he'll endorse your drug or something.

ADs [to Lecturer]: although I gather from the papers that he's a bit of a wanker.

Oddjob says, 'No, UK/USA'

Lecturer [to ADs]: I'm fine except for the fact that I now have arthritis in my right shoulder as a result of typing so hard for 4 weeks. and no. I don't want him to know about my treatment

ADs tries to comfort Lecturer.

@quit

Figure 12.6 MOO conversation

they contribute in return (most MOO participants do not meet together IRL – in real life). Thus, some MOOers adopt new personalities, new interests or an invented occupation, sometimes a change of gender.

Three conversations are intertwined, between ADs and Lecturer, between buffy and Vida_Blue, and between Olive_Guest and Oddjob. Often in MOOs the streams of dialogue diverge as two people exchange messages and then flow together as one person picks up cues from another discussion. The language is informal and mixes idioms from computing, fantasy games and CB radio. Because the players write with conversational partners who pick up their cues and support their thinking, there is no sign of writer's block or even of hesitancy. The text flows freely.

If writing for a MOO is so easy, then can this fluidity of conversation be captured for other types of writing, either by programming the computer to simulate a conversational partner or converting speech into text?

Bereiter, Scardamalia and colleagues in Ontario have developed a technique they call *procedural facilitation* to assist writers by giving them cues to help them to keep writing and to reflect as they compose. The simplest cue would just be to say 'Try and write some more' whenever they pause. More helpful cues are aimed at fostering the different mental components of composing, such as idea generation or goal setting.

They have tried administering the cues by computer. The child types an essay on the computer, and whenever there is a significant pause the computer responds with a cue. The difficulty comes in programming the computer to make the right response. The general method is for it to pick up on a word or phrase in the most recent sentence. So, if the child types 'Drugs can lead to crime for example', the computer interjects with 'Can you think of another example?' That might have the desired effect, but most sentences do not have such an obvious cue word.

Another approach is for the computer to lead a writer through the process of planning, asking first for the type of essay and then (if, say, the writer selected 'argumentative writing') asking for a main topic, arguments in favour of the topic, arguments against and so on. At the end of the dialogue the computer delivers a summary of the cues and responses.

Procedural facilitation is one of a number of ways that a computer might lessen the burden of composing. Programs have been developed to support brainstorming, invention, idea organising, outlining and free writing. They all have some value in helping a writer to discover new techniques, but they have the problem that, first, the child must learn to type and, second, the computer adds another layer of interaction. Instead of getting down to planning and composing, the child converses with a computer that has no deep knowledge of the essay topic and only a limited (and often distracting) repertoire of tricks to encourage writing.

Rather than adding new layers of interaction a computer can simplify the task of writing more directly by turning speech into text. Computer voice recognition has now progressed to the point where the machine can understand continuous natural speech. You speak the words and they appear on the screen. The software can tell the difference between similar sounding words and phrases – such as 'I can speak to my computer' and 'Icons peak to Mike on pewter' – by analysing the relative frequency of the words and the grammar of the sentence ('Icons' and 'pewter' are unusual words and 'peak' is not often used as a verb, so the program tries other alternatives until it forms a familiar sentence).

John Reece designed an elegant series of experiments to test the effects on writing of dictating to a 'listening word processor' (LWP) equipped with a speech recogniser.[11] Because he ran the experiments before accurate and affordable speech recognition became available, he simulated the computer software by the ingenious method of having a hidden human typist who typed in the words to a computer screen in front of the writer as fast as they were spoken. The effect was the same as computer speech recognition: as the writers dictated, the words appeared on the screen. They could also carry out basic revisions by speaking commands to the 'computer'.

Reece compared the LWP with two other methods, writing by hand and dictating into a tape recorder, for children aged 10 to 12. He found that the children wrote better essays with the LWP. The LWP was particularly successful with poor writers. It appears that it combines the benefits of dictation and handwriting. The children could compose fluently, while the LWP showed a visual record of their text. It allowed the children to devote their attention to composing rather than remembering. Whenever they paused, they could read over their text, make any revisions and continue where they left off.

In a further experiment Reece tested whether pre-planning made any difference to the quality. He set 20 grade five and grade six children the tasks of writing three essays, using handwriting, dictation and the LWP. Ten of the children had been given training in how to plan their essays; the other ten composed without planning. Figure 12.7 shows the essay grades (out of 10) for each of the conditions.

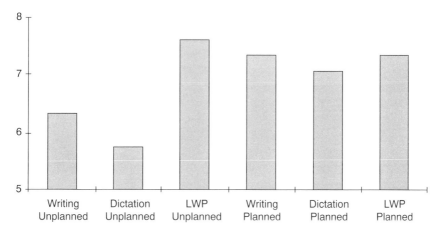

Figure 12.7  Essay grades for handwriting, dictation and Listening Word Processor
Source: based on data from Reece and Cumming, 1996

The children who planned wrote better essays in the handwriting and dictation conditions than those who wrote without planning. But with the Listening Word Processor, planning their essays made no difference. Furthermore, unplanned essays with the LWP were as good as planned writing or planned dictation.

From a detailed study of the results, Reece concluded that the children composed differently with the LWP. They planned as they wrote, using their words as they appeared on the screen as a guide and memory aid. Because the LWP took away the need to concentrate on low-level details such as handwriting and spelling, the children were able to devote their attention to style and organisation. The result was that they wrote better, with less effort.

A listening word processor will not suit every writer. A few chapters back, in the throes of writer's block, I tried composing with a speech-driven word processor (a real one, not a simulation) and I found it hard to maintain the momentum of speaking. The way I write, polishing each sentence, Bricklayer fashion, does not adapt easily to the flow of speaking. Yet if it helps young writers to hand over spelling and transcribing temporarily to a machine then the LWP could be a valuable tool.

Conversion of speech to text is just one way in which writing media are merging. A scanner can turn printed copy into digital characters. The computer can speak digital text. A spreadsheet can be displayed as a graph. Take this one stage further and you have a seamless transition between speech and text, and between paper and computer.

In the near future a writer may work at a digital desk.[12] A display built into the desk shows digital documents as sheets of simulated paper. An overhead camera scans any piece of paper placed on the desk and converts it into computer-readable text. The computer recognises hand gestures, so the writer can move around the simulated sheets, or turn the pages of an electronic book. The desk will also allow a writer to combine informal handwritten notes and sketches with computer-based outlines and plan, and to input new text by speaking, handwriting or typing.

The medieval codex book was a work of individual labour. From many weeks of laborious calligraphy, a scribe could only produce a single copy. Then came printing, which enabled a manuscript to be reproduced many times and opened the door to mass literacy. The source text still existed as a single identifiable entity, written on paper by its author. The new electronic texts exist neither in a visible form nor in a single place. Working at a computer terminal or a digital desk, the writer will be able to merge fragments of text from many sources, retaining links to the original works so that if they are altered the composite document is updated.

The text for this book, for example, is saved on magnetic disks at my home and work, and as printed versions of drafts. Those stored on disk are not quite identical to each other. Some contain earlier versions that I stored on disk for safety and others contain sections that I began and then abandoned. The illustrations are on further files that are linked to the main text. The book consists of many texts and many copies.

Thus, the distinction between source text and copy, and between writer and reader, is breaking down. Writers circulate drafts of their work by electronic mail for comment (one well-known academic author places his work on the Internet each day so that readers can participate in his composing). Instead of waiting for and responding to a finished text, we interact with work in progress. Teachers ask their students to submit drafts for comment and managers demand interim reports. The versions are circulated by email and become sources for further writing. The result is an interconnected 'docuverse'[13] of text under construction.

Continuing this trend, people are now writing directly to the Internet. A tour of 'home pages' on the World Wide Web reveals signs proclaiming 'under construction' or 'work in progress'. As the pages are written and saved to disk they are published, to a potential audience of many millions. Publishing then becomes a process of publicity, of making readers aware of what they already have available on their computer screen. Their text competes with tens of millions of other pages already on the Internet.

The computer may cause the death of writing and of publishing, as people compose by talking, create composite works of voice and image, and publish them piecemeal on the World Wide Web. Or it may enfranchise a new generation of writers, lessening the pain of creativity and encouraging experiment with new forms of composition. More likely will be a combination of these two trends, towards an orchestra of fragmented and multi-modal ways of writing with the computer conductor.

The computer has already begun to absorb the entire writing process, from the gathering of ideas through to the publishing of the finished document. Features such as outliners, spelling checkers and graphic tools have transformed word processors into document processors. Document processors have, in turn, been integrated with other electronic resources such as email and the Internet to produce a complete writing environment.[14]

We can see the first effects of the new writing environment through the changes in working patterns of professional writers. Writers of fiction are now routinely asked to submit their work to the publisher on computer disk and the more commercially successful authors such as Michael Crichton compose with a view to their text being reworked as film scripts and interactive video games.

Many journalists no longer set out on assignments with notepad and pencil, but instead scour the newswires and Internet for stories, conduct interviews by phone or email and file their copy to a central database. Increasingly, journalists must work to a production line of 'rolling news', where they revise their stories as the news unfolds and versions of their text appear in print and in on-line editions of the newspaper.

The veteran journalist Keith Waterhouse laments the move of newspaper offices away from London's Fleet Street, with its social world of pubs and wine bars, into air-conditioned temples of technology.

> Fleet Street was, for better or worse, quite a delicately balanced, intricate, social system . . . a meeting place of minds. . . . What's left? . . . I think a form of journalism where you don't talk about it much but just sit in front of a screen and get on with it may suit a few computer journals and trade papers but it's not good for newspapers – that way blandness lies.[15]

A little further down the road of computer-based writing sits the multimedia author, producing text for interactive presentations. Paul Roberts writes for CD-ROM companies in Seattle. His output consists of short chunks of text, 40 to 200 words in length, that fit onto one screen of a multimedia presentation. Each is a miniature essay on topics that range from classical composers to sports heroes.

> It is, without question, hack writing, the kind of pap work (I used to think) that only the feckless and unprincipled had the nerve or need to take. . . . Today, half the writers I know in this town are either working in electronic publishing or trying to.[16]

Roberts describes, in the tone of a dope addict recalling his first hit, being given his first online assignment.

> He moved deftly from the NDA [non-disclosure agreement] to a terse discussion of production schedules, software requirements, and, finally, the Assignment, handing me a list of 50 subjects, somewhat historical in nature, and a thick stack of reference materials. He wanted 75 words on each by the start of next week. Nothing fancy. Simple declarative sentences. High-school reading level. Tight. No one had ever talked to me about writing like this before . . .

Online writing is short, sharp and segmented. The text generally serves as an extended caption to an image or video. Continuity comes from the flow of interactivity rather than a textual development and each chunk of text must fit a very simple macro-structure, usually of 'topic–elaboration–conclusion'. With no space for narrative progression the writer becomes an anonymous manufacturer of textual parts, welded together by the multimedia producer. Like Keith Waterhouse, Paul Roberts uses the word 'blandness' to describe writing for computer.

> Brevity and blandness: these are the elements of the next literary style. . . . I have participated in, and in some small way precipitated, my own obsoles-cence. For those raised in the tradition of linear print, this may represent the bleakest irony of the digital revolution – that we so willingly took part in our own execution.

These are the anguishings of a profession in change, echoing the forgotten cries of the orator, the scribe and the quill pen maker. Linear narrative writing is in decline. It has been so ever since the invention of the paged book. But the arts of persuasion, of drama and of evocation continue in the new form of multimedia authoring, with written text drawn into a meld of media and interactivity that now includes video, animation, graphic design and music, and may one day embrace dance and sculpture.

Multimedia authoring demands new skills, of media integration, interactivity design and web production. It may be many years before we see a Shakespeare or even a Steven Spielberg of interactive multimedia. Yet so long as we retain our capacity for originality and continue to teach the skills of creative design, adapting them to the affordances and constraints of the new media, then people will continue to create great works of scholarship and imagination.

At the end of the road to automation may lie the intelligent computer, weaver of texts and teller of tales, recounting its Homeric voyages through cyberspace, creating works of wonder that no human writer could match. But that is another story.

# Notes

## Chapter 1 The nature of writing

1   Section 607, 'poetry', *Roget's International Thesaurus* (1962), 3rd edn., London: Collins.

2   W. Strunk and E.B. White (1979) *The Elements of Style*, 3rd edn, London: Macmillan.

3   'Inhibitions, symptoms and anxiety' cited in D. Chandler (1995) *The Act of Writing: A Media Theory Approach*, Aberystwyth: University of Wales, p. 137.

4   The early work of John Hayes and Linda Flower is presented in J.R. Hayes and L.S. Flower (1980) 'Identifying the organization of writing processes', in L.W. Gregg and E.R. Steinberg (eds) *Cognitive Processes in Writing*, Hillsdale, N.J.: Lawrence Erlbaum Associates.

5   F. Smith (1982) *Writing and the Writer*, Hillsdale, N.J.: Lawrence Erlbaum Associates.

6   From J.M. Swales and C.B. Feak (1994) *Academic Writing for Graduate Students*, Ann Arbor: University of Michigan Press.

7   Studies of the lives of composers, painters and writers indicate that almost none wrote major works for the first ten years of their apprenticeship. There was a rapid increase in production of major works between 10 to 20 years after the beginning of practice, followed by a fairly stable level of productivity from 20 to 45 years, with around one major work every three years. See J.R. Hayes (1985) 'Three problems in teaching general skills', in S. Chipman, J. Segal and R. Glaser (eds) *Thinking and Learning Skills*, Hillsdale, N.J.: Lawrence Erlbaum Associates.

## Chapter 2 Becoming a writer

1   G. Kress (1994) *Learning to Write*, 2nd edn, London: Routledge.

2   An excellent and readable account of children's thinking and problem solving is M. Donaldson (1978) *Children's Minds*, London: Fontana.

3   C.L. Kidder (1974) 'Using the computer to measure syntactic density and vocabulary intensity in the writing of elementary school children', PhD Dissertation, Pennsylvania State University.

4   L.R. Gleitman, H. Gleitman and E.F. Shipley (1972) 'The emergence of the child as a grammarian', *Cognition*, 2, 137–63.

5   The samples of children's writing in the remainder of this chapter are from M. Sharples (1985) *Cognition, Computers and Creative Writing*, Chichester: Ellis Horwood.

6   This must be qualified by 'in US and European society'. It may be that children in other cultures reach this point earlier or later, or not at all. The effect of schooling, and the language system, may be substantial.

7   C. Bereiter and M. Scardamalia (1987) *The Psychology of Written Composition*, Hillsdale, N.J.: Lawrence Erlbaum Associates.

8   From I. Broughton (1990) *The Writer's Mind: Interviews with American Authors*, vol. 2, Fayetteville, Ark.: University of Arkansas Press. Cited in D. Chandler (1995) *The Act of Writing*, Aberystwyth: University of Wales.

9   A. Karmiloff-Smith (1992) *Beyond Modularity: A Developmental Perspective on Cognitive Science*, Cambridge, Mass.: MIT Press.

10  The scheme and the results are described in M. Sharples (1985) *Cognition, Computers and Creative Writing*, Chichester: Ellis Horwood.

11  W. Harpin (1976) *The Second 'R'*, London: George Allen & Unwin.

12  They were self-selecting. A larger group of students were questioned about their writing abilities (whether they wrote regularly, whether they had their works published etc.), and the best and worst were chosen.

13  D.H. Graves (1983) *Writing: Teachers and Children at Work*, London: Heinemann Educational Books.

## Chapter 3 Constraint and creativity

1   P.W.K. Stone (1967) *The Art of Poetry 1750–1820: Theories of Poetic Composition and Style in the Late Neo-Classic and Early Romantic Periods*, London: Routledge & Kegan Paul, p. 128, cited in D. Chandler (1995) *The Act of Writing: A Media Theory Approach*, Aberystwyth: University of Wales.

2   This account of Einstein's influences is drawn from A.I. Miller (1989) 'Imagery and intuition in creative scientific thinking: Albert Einstein's invention of the Special Theory of Relativity', in D.B. Wallace and H.E. Gruber (eds) *Creative People at Work*, New York: Oxford University Press.

3   L. Pemberton (1987) 'A story grammar for the Old French epic', Unpublished MSc Dissertation, School of Cognitive and Computing Sciences, University of Sussex.

4   For a readable, though controversial, account of how we acquire language, see S. Pinker (1994) *The Language Instinct*, London: Penguin.

5   I would not for a moment suggest that tabloid journalists make up their stories to fit headlines, but if they did then the set of rules could be a productive tool. Even more useful would be to write a computer program that generates text from a given set of rules. A number of researchers (myself included) have attempted to write programs that generate stories or poems. They work reasonably well for constrained texts such as headlines, but for stories the results are usually bizarre or boring. For an overview, see M. Sharples (1997) 'Storytelling by computer', *Digital Creativity*, 8, 1, 20–9.

6   Psychologists typically describe concepts in long-term memory (LTM) as forming a network of associated meanings. Thus, the word 'cat' is related by meaning to 'dog', 'pet', 'milk' and 'mat' (by rhyme). How these associations are physically embodied in the brain is still unclear – the best evidence is that concepts are both localised and distributed across areas of the brain – but experiments (such as giving a subject a

priming word and then testing whether the person unconsciously activates related words) point to the associative nature of memory.

7   The diagram can be found in almost this form in M. Torrance, G.V. Thomas and E.J. Robinson (1996) 'Finding something to write about: strategic and automatic processes in idea generation', in C.M. Levy and S. Ransdell (eds) *The Science of Writing: Theories, Methods, Individual Difference and Applications*, Mahwah, N.J.: Lawrence Erlbaum Associates.

8   M. A. Boden (1990) *The Creative Mind: Myths and Mechanisms*, London: Weidenfield & Nicolson.

9   C. Bereiter and M. Scardamalia (1987), *The Psychology of Written Composition*, Hillsdale, N.J.: Lawrence Erlbaum Associates.

10   A. Rothenberg (1976) 'The process of Janusian thinking in creativity', in A. Rothenberg and C.R. Hausman (eds) *The Creativity Question*, Durham, N.C.: Duke University Press, pp. 311–27.

11   The distinction between high focus and low focus thinking is taken from D. Gelernter (1994) *The Muse in the Machine: Computers and Creative Thought*, London: Fourth Estate.

12   W. Owen and J. Smyser (1974) *The Prose Works of William Wordsworth*, vol. 1, Oxford: Clarendon Press, p. 148.

13   Cited in L.R. Jeffrey (1989) 'Writing and rewriting poetry: William Wordsworth' in D.B. Wallace and H.E. Gruber (eds) *Creative People at Work*, New York: Oxford University Press.

14   For a more detailed discussion of idea flowing see R.T. Kellogg (1994) *The Psychology of Writing*, New York: Oxford University Press.

15   P. Elbow (1981) *Writing with Power: Techniques for Mastering the Writing Process*, New York: Oxford University Press.

16   In E.P. Vernon (ed.) (1973) *Creativity: Selected Readings*, Harmondsworth: Penguin Books.

17   Cited in A. Koestler (1975) *The Act of Creation*, London: Pan Books.

18   M. A. Boden (1990) *op. cit.*, p. 250.

19   ibid., p. 244.

## Chapter 4  Writing as design

1   D. Chandler (1995) *The Act of Writing: A Media Theory Approach*, Aberystwyth: University of Wales.

2   The studies are reported in J.E. Reece and G. Cumming (1996) 'Evaluating speech-based composition methods: planning, dictation and the Listening Word Processor', in C.M. Levy and S. Ransdell (eds) *The Science of Writing: Theories, Methods, Individual Differences, and Applications*, Mahwah, N.J.: Lawrence Erlbaum Associates.

3   D. McCutchen (1987) 'Children's discourse skill: form and modality requirements of schooled writing', *Discourse Processes*, 10, 267–324.

4   Cited in D. Chandler (1995) *op. cit.*, p. 136.

5   R. Harding (1942) *The Anatomy of Inspiration*, 2nd edn, Cambridge: Heffer, cited in D. Chandler (1995) *op. cit.*, p. 136.

6   M. McLuhan (1969) *Counterblast*, London: Rapp & Whiting, cited in D. Chandler (1995) *op. cit.*, p. 149.

7   For a discussion of the limitations of the computer screen, see K.S. Eklundh (1992) 'Problems in achieving a global perspective of the text in computer-based writing', in M. Sharples (ed.) *Computers and Writing: Issues and Implementations*, Dordrecht: Kluwer, pp. 73–84.

8   B. Lawson (1990) *How Designers Think*, 2nd edn, Oxford: Butterworth Architecture.

9   James Edie, cited in D. Chandler (1995) *op. cit.*, p. 41.

10  B. Lawson (1990) *op. cit.*, p. 91.

11  L.S. Flower and J.R. Hayes (1980) 'The dynamics of composing: making plans and juggling constraints', in L.W. Gregg and E.R. Steinberg (eds) *Cognitive Processes in Writing*, Hillsdale, N.J.: Lawrence Erlbaum Associates, p. 31.

12  This is the weakest of Lawson's 'essential qualities of design'. Design both prescribes and describes as does scientific discovery. Both demand ethical scrutiny.

13  J. Darke (1978) 'The primary generator and the design process', in W.E. Rogers and W.H. Ittelson (eds) *New Directions in Environmental Design Research*, Proceedings of EDRA, 9, Washington: EDRA, pp. 325–37.

14  In G. Plimpton (1958) *Writers at Work: The Paris Review Interviews* (First Series), London: Secker & Warburg, p.121.

15  Gabriel García Márquez, cited in G. Plimpton (1985) *Writers at Work: The Paris Review Interviews* (Sixth Series), London: Secker & Warburg.

16  This notion of effective learning being bounded by what the learner already knows and what can be learned with the assistance of a teacher is what Vygotsky called the Zone of Proximal Development. For more on this, see L.S. Vygotsky (1978) *Mind in Society*, Cambridge, Mass.: Harvard University Press.

17  This discussion of design languages is based on J. Rheinfrank and S. Evenson (1996) 'Design languages', in T. Winograd (ed.) *Bringing Design to Software*, New York: Addison Wesley, pp. 63–80.

18  Apple Computer Inc. (1997) Power Macintosh User's Manual. Cupertino, CA: Apple Computer Inc.

19  Cited in B. Vickers (1988) *In Defence of Rhetoric*, Oxford: Oxford University Press, p. 67.

20  V. Shklovsky (1998) 'Art as technique', in D. Lodge (ed.) *Modern Criticism and Theory: A Reader*, London: Longman.

21  I have taken this example from L. Peach and A. Burton (1995) *English as a Creative Art: Literary Concepts Linked to Creative Writing*, London: David Fulton Publishers. This book gives a highly readable summary of modern literary theory for the benefit of creative writers.

22  Hayes has subsequently revised this model (J.R. Hayes (1996) 'A new framework for understanding cognition and affect in writing', in C.M. Levy and S. Ransdell (eds) *op. cit.*, pp. 1–27). To fit with current usage, he now names the component processes *planning*, *text generation* and *revision*.

23  L.S. Flower and J.R. Hayes (1980) *op. cit.*, p. 40.

## Chapter 5 Planning

1   C.C. Wood (1992) 'A study of the graphical mediating representations used by collaborating authors', *Intelligent Tutoring Media*, 3, 2/3, pp. 75–83.

2   For a detailed account of how to create and use mind maps, see T. Buzan and B. Buzan (1993) *The Mind Map Book*, London: BBC Books.

3   For a discussion of notes networks, and algorithms for automatically turning a notes network into a linear draft see M. Sharples, A. Clutterbuck and J. Goodlet (1994) 'A comparison of algorithms for hypertext notes network linearization', *International Journal of Human–Computer Studies*, 40, 727–52.

4   R.T. Kellogg (1993) 'Observations on the psychology of thinking and writing', *Composition Studies*, 21, 3–41.

5   If mind mapping or network planning does provide the spur to creativity suggested by Buzan, but just takes time to learn, then the computer may offer a solution. New software can offer on-line tools for mind mapping and for producing notes networks. Our team at the University of Sussex demonstrated a program (part of a prototype Writer's Assistant) that can automatically turn a notes network into a linear text.

6   J.R. Hayes and J.G. Nash (1996) 'On the nature of planning in writing', in C.M. Levy and S. Ransdall (eds) *The Science of Writing: Theories, Methods, Individual Differences, and Applications*, Mahwah, N.J.: Lawrence Erlbaum Associates.

## Chapter 6 Composing

1   For a full account of composing at sentence level see G. Jeffery (1996) 'Combining ideas in written text: cognitive aspects of a writing process'. PhD thesis, University of Nottingham.

2   A.Q. Morton (1978) *Literary Detection: How to Prove Authorship and Fraud in Literature and Documents*, Bath: Bowker, cited in A. Glover and G. Hirst (1996) 'Detecting stylistic inconsistencies in collaborative writing', in M. Sharples and T. van der Geest (eds) T*he New Writing Environment: Writers at Work in a World of Technology*, London: Springer Verlag. For anyone hoping to cash in by 'discovering' a lost classic, don't bother; new computer techniques of stylistic analysis can compare so many minute aspects of style – such as the ratio of *with* to *without* – that it is probably impossible to produce a convincing forgery.

3   J.M. Swales and C.B. Feak (1994) *Academic Writing for Graduate Students*, Ann Arbor: University of Michigan Press.

4   M. Sharples and L. Pemberton (1992) 'Representing writing: external representations and the writing process', in P.O.B. Holt and N. Williams (eds), *Computers and Writing: State of the Art*, Oxford: Intellect.

5   S. French and N. Gerrard (1997) 'How to sell your first novel for a quarter of a million and be even more happily married than before', *The Tiddler: The* Observer's *Little Bit Extra*, No. 18.

6   R. Stannard (1989) *The Time and Space of Uncle Albert*, London: Faber & Faber. J. Gaardner (1991) *Sophie's World*, London: Phoenix House. The books also organise the text at a higher level so as to engage the young reader. For example, they both present a series of problems to be solved by the central character.

7   G. Polti (1997) *The Thirty-six Dramatic Situations*, Boston: The Writer, Inc.

8   Note the similarity between this and the one in Figure 5.2 sketched by the two writers to show the shape of their text.

9   U. Eco (1982) 'The narrative structure in Fleming', in B. Waites, T. Bennett, and G. Martin (eds), *Popular Culture: Past and Present*, London: Croom Helm, pp. 245–62.

10   U. Eco (1982), *op. cit.*, p. 259.


## Chapter 7 Revising

1   L. Faigley and S. Witte (1981) 'Analyzing revision', *College Composition and Communication*, 23, 400–14.

2   G.V. Thomas, M. Torrance and E.J. Robinson (1993) 'The effects on text quality of rough drafting and outlining strategies for writing essays', paper presented at *Canadian Society for Brain, Behaviour and Cognitive Science* joint meeting with the Experimental Psychology Society (UK), University of Toronto, 15–17 July, 1993.

3   S. Parrish (ed.) (1977) *The Prelude 1798–1799 by William Wordsworth*, Ithaca, N.Y.: Cornell University Press.

4   L.R. Jeffery (1989) 'Writing and rewriting poetry: William Wordsworth', in D.B. Wallace and H.E. Gruber (eds) *Creative People at Work*, New York: Oxford University Press.


## Chapter 8 Being a writer

1   Quoted in B. Ghiselin (1952) *The Creative Process*, Berkeley: University of California Press.

2   L. Bridwell-Bowles, P. Johnson and S. Brehe (1987) 'Composing and computers: case studies of experienced writers', in A. Matsuhashi (ed.) *Writing in Real Time: Modelling Production Processes* Norwood, N.J.: Ablex, pp. 81–107.

3   L. van Waes (1992) 'The influence of the computer on writing profiles', in H.P. Maat and M. Steehouder (eds) *Studies of Functional Text Quality*, Amsterdam: Editions Rodopi, pp. 173–86.

4   A. Wyllie (1993) 'On the road to discovery: a study of the composing strategies of academic writers using the word processor', MA Thesis, University of Lancaster.

5   A. Gibbs (1995) *Writers on Writing*, London: Robert Hale, pp. 50–1.

6   Ibid., p. 66.

7   Ibid., p. 34.

8   B. Strickland (ed.) (1989) *On Being a Writer*, Cincinnati, OH: Writer's Digest, p. 54, cited in D. Chandler (1995) *The Act of Writing: A Media Theory Approach*, Aberystwyth: University of Wales, p. 234.

9   R.T. Kellogg (1986) 'Writing method and productivity of science and engineering faculty', *Research in Higher Education*, 25, 147–63.

10   A. Gibbs (1995), *op. cit.*

11   These and other accounts of writing rituals are described in R.T. Kellogg (1994) *The Psychology of Writing*, Oxford: Oxford University Press, and A. Gibbs (1995) *op. cit.*

12    J. Hartley and A. Branthwaite (1989) 'The psychologist as wordsmith: a questionnaire study of the writing strategies of productive British psychologists', *Higher Education*, 18, 423–52.

13    R. Boice and K. Johnson (1984) 'Perception and practice of writing for publication by faculty at a doctoral-granting university', *Research in Higher Education*, 21, 33–43.

14    S.W. Freedman (1983) 'Student characteristics and essay test writing performance', *Research in the Teaching of English*, 17, 313–25.

15    D. Lowenthal and P.C. Wason (1977) 'Academics and their writing', *Times Literary Supplement*, 24 June, p. 282, cited in R.T. Kellogg (1994), op. cit.

16    A. Gibbs (1995), *op. cit.*, pp. 50–1.

17    R. Madigan, P. Linton and S. Johnson (1996) 'The paradox of writing apprehension', in C.M. Levy and S. Ransdell (eds) *The Science of Writing: Theories, Methods, Individual Differences and Applications*, Mahwah, N.J.: Lawrence Erlbaum Associates.

18    The topics were 'What governmental agency do you have the strongest feelings about – either positive or negative? Analyze the source of those feelings.' And 'Analyze the most important skills for a new college instructor.' Each student was given two essays so that the experimenters could test another factor: the influence of distraction on performance.

19    P. Salovey and M.D. Haar (1990) 'The efficacy of cognitive-behavior therapy and writing process training for alleviating writing anxiety', *Cognitive Therapy and Research*, 14, 515–28.

20    A. Gibbs (1995), *op. cit.*, pp. 50–1.

21    My accounts of mania and depression and their relationship to creativity are drawn from D.J. Hershman and J. Lieb, M.D. (1988) *The Key to Genius*, Buffalo, N.Y.: Prometheus Books.

22    N.C. Andreason (1987) 'Creativity and mental illness: prevalence rates in writers and their first degree relatives', *American Journal of Psychiatry*, 144, 1288–92.

23    Flow states have been studied in detail by psychologists. A good summary is in M. Csikszentmihalyi (1990) *Flow: The Psychology of Optimal Experience*, New York: Harper & Row. For a discussion of flow in writing, see R.T. Kellogg (1994), op. cit., pp. 117–19.

24    I. Broughton (1990) *The Writer's Mind: Interviews with American Authors*, vol. 2, Fayetteville: University of Arkansas Press.

## Chapter 9 Writing images

1    U. Eco (1984) *The Name of the Rose*, London: Pan Books, pp. 72–3.

2    For a fascinating and learned discussion of writing media and text design, past, present and future, see J.D. Bolter (1991) *Writing Space*, Hillsdale, N.J.: Lawrence Erlbaum Associates.

3    G. Kress, G. and T. van Leeuwen (1996) *Reading Images: The Grammar of Visual Design*, London: Routledge.

4    See Kress and van Leeuwen (1996) *op. cit.*, pp. 9–11, for a discussion of motivated sign-making.

5   Of course, in this context I have yet another motive: to illustrate the semiotics of the underline.

6   G.V. Thomas, M. Torrance and E.J. Robinson (1993) 'The effects on text quality of rough drafting and outlining strategies for writing essays', paper presented at *Canadian Society for Brain, Behaviour and Cognitive Science* joint meeting with the Experimental Psychology Society (UK), University of Toronto, 15–17 July, 1993.

7   For an enlightening account of how figures and diagrams can inform and mislead, see D. Huff (1991) *How to Lie with Statistics*, London: Penguin.

8   For a thorough discussion of typefaces and of layout in general, see J. Hartley (1994) *Designing Instructional Text*, 3rd edn, London: Kogan Page.

9   Sassoon is a registered trademark of Sassoon and Williams. For an account of its design and other articles on computers and typography see R. Sassoon (ed.) (1993) *Computers and Typography*, Exeter: Intellect.

10   Hartley (1994), *op. cit.*

11   J. Hartley and M. Sydes (1995) 'Structured abstracts in the social sciences: presentation, readability, search and recall', *European Science Editing*, October 1995, no. 56, pp. 6–7.

12   J. Hartley and M. Sydes (1996) 'Which layout do you prefer? An analysis of readers' preferences for different typographic layouts of structured abstracts', *Journal of Information Science*, 22, 1, 27–37. The abstract also neatly illustrates the duality of text: the visual design of the abstract acts as a self-illustration of its content.

13   P.J. Brody (1982) 'Affecting instructional textbooks through pictures', in D.H. Jonassen (ed.) *The Technology of Text: Principles for Structuring, Designing and Displaying Text*, Englewood Cliffs, N.J.: Educational Technology Publications.

14   H. Golding (ed.) *The Wonder Book of Do You Know?*, London: Ward Lock & Co. Ltd.

15   G. Waters (1985) *The Usborne First Book of Science*, London: Usborne Publishing Ltd.

16   A. Wainwright (1966) *Fellwanderer: The Story Behind the Guidebooks*, Kendal: Westmorland Gazette.

17   K. Garland (1993) 'Lead kindly light: a user's view of the design and production of illustrated walkers' guides', *Information Design Journal*, 7, 1, 47–66.

18   A. Wainwright (1992) *A Pictorial Guide to the Lakeland Fells: The Northern Fells*, London: Michael Joseph.

## Chapter 10 Messages in bottles and cultures

1   According to NASA, Pioneer 10, now over 6,000,000,000 miles from Earth and still transmitting radio signals, carries a six by nine-inch gold anodised plaque with a picture of a man and woman standing before the outline of a spacecraft. The man's hand is raised in a gesture of goodwill. The physical makeup of the man and woman were determined from results of a computerised analysis of the average person in our civilization.

2   A.H. Clough (1849) *The Bothie of Toper-na-fuosich: A Long-vacation Pastoral*, Cambridge: John Bartlett.

3   J. Ruskin (1903–12) *Works*, vol. 3. For an engaging and influential discussion of the new literary criticism, see Catherine Belsey (1980) *Critical Practice*, London: Methuen. This book has introduced structuralist criticism to a generation of students.

4  V.N. Voloshinov (1986) *Marxism and the Philosophy of Language*, trans. L.M. Matejka and I.R. Titunik, Cambridge, Mass.: Harvard University Press, cited in T. Weiss (1991) 'Bruffee, the Bakhtin Circle, and the concept of collaboration', in M.M. Lay and W.M. Karis (eds) *Collaborative Writing in Industry: Investigations in Theory and Practice*, Amityville, N.Y.: Baywood Publishing Company.

5  Toshiba Corporation (1995) Tecra 710CDT/720CDT Personal Computer User's Manual.

6  M.M. Bakhtin (1984) *Problems of Dostoevsky's Poetics*, ed. and trans. C. Emerson, Minneapolis: University of Minnesota Press, p. 287.

7  L. Flower (1996) 'Negotiating the meaning of difference', *Written Communication*, 13, 1, 44–92.

8  The poem, 'Speak Gently' by D. Bates, is reprinted in M. Gardner (1970) *The Annotated Alice*, Harmondsworth: Penguin, p. 85.

9  Post-structuralism does not end at the covers of a book. Society as a whole can be constituted in a way that meets expectations. They way in which the United Kingdom (and many other Western European countries) is packaged for the tourist industry, through the misty romanticism of grand buildings, unproblematic heroes, and the decent poor, is a deliberately 'easy' portrayal of history.

10  Scott tried to do the same for the American South, and was roundly attacked by Mark Twain in his autobiography *Life on the Mississippi* for 'silliness and emptinesses, sham grandeurs, sham gauds and sham chivalries'. These, Twain wrote, did measureless harm by creating a myth of the Southern gentleman that helped to precipitate the Civil War.

11  R.J. Evans (1997) 'Truth lost in vain views', *Times Higher Education Supplement*, 12 September 1997. His argument against relativism in history is elaborated in *In Defence of History*, London: Granta Books, 1997.

## Chapter 11 Writing together

1  M. Shelley (1985) *Frankenstein, or the Modern Prometheus*, Harmondsworth: Penguin, pp. 52–6.

2  A. Bendixen (1986) 'It was a mess! How Henry James and others actually wrote a novel', *New York Times Book Review*, 27 April, p. 28.

3  T. Pratchett (1992) *The Carpet People*, London: Doubleday. Interestingly, the copyright for the revised book is assigned to Terry and Lyn Pratchett, though the author makes no reference to Lyn Pratchett beyond a cryptic dedication: 'To Lyn, for then and now'.

4  R. Rimmershaw (1992) 'Technologies of collaboration', in M. Sharples (ed.) *Computers and Writing: Issues and Implementations*, Dordrecht: Kluwer, p. 27.

5  L. Ede and A. Lunsford (1990) *Singular Texts/Plural Authors: Perspectives on Collaborative Writing*, Carbondale, Ill.: Southern Illinois University Press. The book is itself an interesting exercise in collaborative writing. The authors take pains not to designate either Lunsford or Ede as first author so, for example, the book jacket repeats their names across the entire page. The book mixes together an empirical survey, a theoretical account and implications for teaching into a somewhat contrived dialogue that nevertheless draws attention to the problems of merging multiple voices.

6  E.E. Beck (1993) 'A survey of experiences of collaborative writing', in M. Sharples (ed.) *Computer Supported Collaborative Writing*, London: Springer-Verlag.

7   F. Brome (1958) *Six Studies in Quarrelling*, London: Cresset Press.

8   L. Plowman (1995) 'The interfunctionality of talk and text', *Computer Supported Cooperative Work*, 3, 3–4, pp. 229–46.

9   L. Plowman (1995) *op. cit.*, p. 245.

10  The book chapter is published as M. Sharples, J.S. Goodlet, E.E. Beck, C.C. Wood, S.M. Easterbrook and L. Plowman (1993) 'Research issues in the study of computer supported collaborative writing', in M. Sharples (1993), *op. cit.*, pp. 9–28.

11  For a very readable and insightful analysis of the problems of working in teams, see F. Brooks (1982) *The Mythical Man-Month: Essays in Software Engineering*, Reading, Mass.: Addison-Wesley.

12  *Benefits Agency Document Design Style Guide*, p.3.

13  A.R. Kaye (1973) 'The design and evaluation of science courses at the Open University', *Instructional Science*, 2, pp. 119–91.

14  A.R. Kaye (1993) 'Computer networking for development of distance education courses', in M. Sharples (1993), *op. cit.*, pp. 41–67.

## Chapter 12 Media slip, dynatext, hypermedia and the docuverse

1   M.C. Pennington (1996) 'Writing the natural way: on computer', *Computer Assisted Language Learning*, 9, 125–42.

2   In common with many word processor users, I now rarely use the grammar checker.

3   For a discussion of the next generation of style checkers, see R. Dale and S. Douglas (1996) 'Two investigations into intelligent text processing', in M. Sharples and T. van der Geest (eds) *The New Writing Environment: Writers at Work in a World of Technology*, London: Springer-Verlag. Robert Dale works for Microsoft, so there is a good chance that this software will soon become part of most word processors.

4   T.K. Landauer (1995) *The Trouble with Computers: Usefulness, Usability, and Productivity*, Cambridge, Mass.: MIT Press.

5   Landauer's book offers a good introduction to user-centred software design.

6   Joycean in two senses: it plays elaborate literary games and its author is Michael Joyce. M. Joyce (1987) *Afternoon: a Story*, Cambridge, Mass.: Eastgate Press. For a description of *Afternoon*, see J.B. Bolter (1991) *Writing Space: The Computer, Hypertext and the History of Writing*, Hillsdale, N.J.: Lawrence Erlbaum Associates.

7   StorySpace is a trademark of rivverun Ltd.

8   J.D. Miller (1993) 'Script writing on a computer network: Quenching the flames or feeding the fire?', in B. Bruce, J.K. Peyton and T. Batson (eds) *Network-based Classrooms*, Cambridge: Cambridge University Press.

9   J.D. Miller (1993) *op. cit.*, p. 133.

10  A successor to the original Adventure was a game called Dungeons & Dragons. Programs that enabled more two or more people to play Dungeons & Dragons were named MUDs, for 'Multi-User Dungeons & Dragons'. Then software was developed that allowed non-programmers to design their own MUDs, by creating and linking together descriptions

of rooms, objects and characters. These programs became known as MOOs, standing for 'MUD Object Oriented'.

11   J. Reece and G. Cumming (1996) 'Evaluating speech-based composition methods: planning, dictation and the Listening Word Processor', in C. M. Levy and S. Ransdell (eds) *The Science of Writing: Theories, Methods, Individual Differences and Applications*, Mahwah, N.J.: Lawrence Erlbaum Associates.

12   Researchers at Xerox have developed a prototype digital desk. W.M. Newman and P. Wellner (1992) 'A desk supporting computer-based interaction with paper documents', *Technical Report EPC-91-131*, Cambridge: Rank Xerox EuroPARC.

13   Ted Nelson, the inventor of the term 'hypertext', also coined the word 'docuverse' to describe this global inter-connectivity of text.

14   For views of the new writing environment see M. Sharples and T. van der Geest (1996), *op. cit.*

15   K. Waterhouse (1992) 'Through a glass mistily', *Guardian*, 30 March.

16   P. Roberts (1996) 'The future of writing', *Independent on Sunday*, 24 September.

# Index